THE FIFTIES

The Fifties

BY PETER LEWIS

J. B. LIPPINCOTT COMPANY

NEW YORK

Designed and produced by
The Cupid Press
2 Quay Street, Woodbridge
Suffolk

Picture Research: Anne-Marie Ehrlich
Index: Ellen Crampton

Printed in the United States of America

The front endpaper reproduces a scene from Elvis Presley's film, JAIL-
HOUSE ROCK. The illustration on the half-title page is of the Festival of
Britain Fun Fair in Battersea Park. The frontispiece is a photograph of an
American atomic test explosion in the Nevada Desert in 1953. The back
endpaper is a photograph of Ascot fashions, 1956.

U.S. Library of Congress Cataloging in Publication Data

Lewis, Peter.
  The fifties.

  Includes index.
  1. Civilization, Modern—1950-   I. Title.
CB425.L38   1978   909.82′5   78-32176
ISBN-0-397-01355-8

Contents

Acknowledgements are made to the following sources of illustrations (the numbers refer to page numbers in the book): Aberdeen Art Gallery, 195; B.B.C. Pictorial Publicity, 209, 213, 224; Camera Press, 57, 76, 167, 174, 201; Central Press, 35; Tony Crawley, 56; E.M.I. Film Distributors, 15; the John French Photo Library, 48; Richard Hamilton and the Kunsthalle, Tubingen, West Germany, 206; John Hillelson, 110, 150, 155; Tom Hustler, 185; Keystone Press Agency, 67, 101, 133; Kobal Collection, front endpaper, 121, 205; Mount Everest Expedition, 240; Pictorial Press, 51, 52; Popperfoto, 1, 13, 16, 28, 55, 180, 190, 202, 238, 239; Press Association, 93; Radio Times Hulton Picture Library, 6, 10, 12, 59, 119, 162, 221, back endpaper; Rex Features, 128, 138, 176, 223; John Sadovy, 109; Syndication International, 68; John Topham Picture Library, 24, 25, 94, 193, 196; United Press International, 71, 80, 89, 114, 122, 124, 235.

Growing up in Birmingham in 1954 in the war-torn landscape of 1944 –
photograph by Bert Hardy

Preface

Dividing history into decades is, of course, an arbitrary practice. Yet certain decades, by general consent, exhibit an identifiable character. The Naughty Nineties, the Roaring Twenties, the Swinging Sixties . . . these are shorthand labels which had enough of the gum of truth to stick. Sometimes the very change of that digit in the date seems to spur people to find a new attitude to life and new fashions of living it. No such ready-made label attaches to the Fifties. Until recently it would probably have been dismissed as a dreary decade, dominated by dull people – the Fearful Fifties, perhaps, or the Conforming Fifties, so much less inventive and reckless than the Sixties which followed. Now that the wave of seemingly boundless prosperity which buoyed up the Sixties and their non-conformity has receded, the Fifties look more sympathetic. Not an occasion for nostalgia – although the hunger for instant replay has already caused much revival of their styles in clothes and music – but a time which feels akin to our present discontents. No period that paid extravagant attention to both Marilyn Monroe and John Foster Dulles, to Billy Graham and James Dean, can be called simple or consistent. It was a time when life was real, life was earnest, for most people (it normally is). But it was a time when hope outweighed despair or cynicism. It was a time when it was pleasant to be young enough to feel concerned, mildly rebellious and naively optimistic that solutions could be found.

One may wonder why there was no mass orgy of hedonism after World War II as there was after the first. The Fifties were nothing like the Twenties – unless the first outburst of Rock n' Roll culture can be counted as a small orgy rather late in the day. The reason surely was that with the explosion of the hydrogen bomb the world suddenly grew old, too old for parties. Indeed it is possible to see the Fifties as a major psychological watershed in history – not the beginning of a new half-century but of a new planet. In the sense that the nineteenth century did not really end until 1914, so the twentieth century did not truly begin until at the earliest 1945, and possibly not until the bigger explosion of 1950 changed the facts of life for all to see. In between had been a No Man's Land and a No Man's Time of warfare and truce conducted according to left-over beliefs in competitive nationalism, in patriotism and in victory in just causes. All these suddenly became untenable, dissolving in the mushroom cloud.

Momentous changes in human affairs take time to sink in. In the Fifties the sinking-in caused confusion of all kinds. The young made attempts to realign their goals to fit the new facts; the old mostly clung on to what they had believed to be the eternal goals listed above. They still sought to save their countries' souls from the sins of rival ideologies. The facts of life have hardly changed since. The problems discovered then are recalcitrantly still with us. What has changed is what people believe. This book charts the tremors of the psychological shock which began in that decade.

★   ★   ★

In my research into the period of the Fifties I owe particular thanks to the following, who kindly spent time with me recalling what they did and thought and felt then, and what they feel about it now:

Larry Adler, Kingsley Amis, John Braine, Sir Hugh Casson, Canon L. John Collins, Alistair Cooke, Diana Dors, Professor J. K. Galbraith, Joseph Heller, Janey Ironside, Tom Lehrer, George Melly, Arthur Miller, Jonathan Miller, Malcolm Muggeridge, J. B. Priestley, Richard Rovere, Arthur Schlesinger Jnr, Kenneth Tynan, Roger Vadim, Gore Vidal, Kurt Vonnegut Jnr, Colin Wilson, Dan Wolf, Tom Wolfe.

They are not, of course, responsible for the context in which their quoted opinions appear or for the view of the period expressed in the book.

I am also indebted to those who have read parts of the manuscript and made valuable suggestions: Larry Adler, Betty Allsop, Peter Black, Oliver Campion, Christopher Dobson, Georgina Dowse, Barbara Goalen, Margaret Hinxman, Vivien Hislop, Angus Macpherson, David Ogilvy, Ronald Payne, Mary Stott, John Foster White and Lord Zuckerman; and to John Hadfield for being my inspirer and scrupulous editor.

CHAPTER ONE

From Austerity to Affluence

Four related words acquired special significance in the Fifties: Austerity and Affluence, Status and Image. Austerity was Britain's peculiar reward for surviving World War II unbeaten at the cost of selling her foreign assets and taking on a crippling load of debt to the United States. Germany's peculiar reward for being beaten was an economic miracle financed mainly by American aid and nursed by armies of occupation. Affluence was the song the sirens sang in the United States, from which war and its economic expansion had finally banished the Depression. The roaring of the American boom rang round the Western world where everyone in every hard-pressed country saw the new world as an Aladdin's cave of American goods, American entertainment and the American style of living.

But the vision was a long way off from Britain, for which the first two years of the Fifties were a continuation of wartime in civilian clothes. Rationing, which still applied to meat, bacon, butter, cheese, tea, sugar and sweets, actually became more austere than it had been in 1945. The meat ration, one shilling and sixpence in 1945, was reduced to eight-pence worth (old style – less than four pence new style) in 1951 as a result of a dispute with the Argentine. It was easier to exhort the country to further sacrifice if, like the Chancellor, Sir Stafford Cripps, you were a vegetarian. This Christian Socialist, dedicated to equal shares and to soaking the rich (who included his own family), was accepted and frostily admired as an incorruptible thorn in the nation's conscience, forever reminding them that there was no jam today and they could only expect some tomorrow if they had earned it. 'A strange monastic-looking man,' said Harold Macmillan, 'emaciated and said to live off watercress grown off the blotting paper on his desk.' In fact he used to be seen lunching austerely in his favourite vegetarian restaurant on the corner of Leicester Square, where the permitted maximum of five shillings for the price of a meal could only be spent by earnest application.

'Our only safety for the future lies in the positive and conscious exertion of spiritual control over material actions,' Cripps said in a speech to the American Bar Association. 'The world crisis is thus in my view basically a moral rather than a political or economic crisis.' It was typical of him to see politics in ethical terms. Stern appeals to principle might in time have closed the dollar gap in Britain's trade with the United States had not cancer removed this economic dictator-by-consent, greatly weakening the Labour government's authority in 1951. Cripps gave his name to an era of austerity, queues, shortages and high income tax (9s. 6d. in the pound again in 1951, almost as high as in wartime), flattening the peaks of the income range and lopping off any surviving Matterhorns. A £15,000-a-year man kept only £5,000 after tax. Only seventy people were known to the Inland Revenue to keep more than £6,000 net. Shortages made life difficult, to the point of exasperation. A coal shortage cut the train services (nowadays it would be staff shortage). Steel shortage closed the car factories (nowadays it would be a demarcation dispute). Even Virginia tobacco was so short that favourite brands were kept out of sight under the counter, reserved for favourite customers. The worst shortage was of housing. Substantial numbers of families lived in 'pre-fabs', flat-roofed boxes made of asbestos sheeting, while rosebay willowherb flowered in purple patches across the untouched bomb sites.

It was in this drab landscape that one of the largest bombed and derelict sites in the centre of London, the South Bank of the Thames was filled by a deliberate gesture of faith in a brighter future, the Festival of Britain. Officially a commemoration of the Great Exhibition of 1851, to demonstrate British achievement in arts, sciences and design, its chief impact was one of surprise that in these depressing times the government should be capable of sponsoring such a fling. Herbert Morrison, the minister in charge, announced it as 'the people giving themselves a pat on the back'. The organizer, Gerald Barry, promised 'fun, fantasy and colour' as 'a tonic to the nation'. But plenty of people thought it the height of irresponsibility to allocate £11 million to having a fling.

On the riverside rose the shapes of a possible future: a 'Dome of Discovery' with a diameter of 365 feet to keep the rain, which was very plentiful that summer, off the exhibits. And instead of an Eiffel Tower

OPPOSITE *The thorn in Britain's conscience: Sir Stafford Cripps*

Festival of Britain: the Skylon and the Dome of Discovery

such as expressed the surging self-confidence of the late-nineteenth-century Paris exhibition, the symbol of the Festival was the Skylon, a useless but elegant exclamation mark supported in thin air by thin cables – like Britain, somebody said, without any visible means of support.

Much to everyone's surprise, when the exhibition and the Funfair at Battersea opened they were an immense success. Over eight million people came to admire this new concept of an environment where everything was intended to lift the spirits. The design team under Hugh Casson and Misha Black (both later knighted) were right in believing that there was hunger for visual stimulation among the British and they got it in the form of sculpture, murals and mobiles by Moore, Hepworth, Piper, Sutherland, Topolski and Epstein as well as a pedestrian precinct which was all grilles and screens and balls and decks and terraces and fountains and colour. Open-air dancing under the floodlights, often in long mackintoshes and trilby hats, a fountain that fell from bucket to bucket like the omnipresent rain, a bewhiskered Emett railway, a tree-walk alongside a forty-foot Chinese dragon – people queued patiently to enjoy such simple pleasures whose lack of sophistication seemed very exciting to people, most of whom had never had a foreign holiday or

Festival goers on the South Bank gaping at the shape of things to come

seen café tables with coloured umbrellas or indeed any fresh paint for as long as they could remember. Up and down the country mini-celebrations occurred in what the official guide called in that unmistakeable paternalistic tone of the period, 'spontaneous expressions of citizenship'. In practice this meant medieval mystery plays at York, madrigals on the river at Cambridge, and the Edinburgh Festival.

And yet the Festival proved not to be the beginning of the new civically planned and visually gayer Britain of which it held out a promise, but the swan-song of the era in which it was patriotic to put the community first and all pull together, as directed. In Sir Hugh Casson's words, 'It made people want things to be better and to believe they could be.' But the Labour Government which had intended the Festival as a celebration of welfare-minded, egalitarian, planner's Britain – a Britain where identity cards were still not abolished – was, by the time it opened, hanging on by a slender majority of six and, by the time it ended, on the point of being ejected. All the public-spirited, though rather dull, values the Festival stood for were going to be swamped in a growing tide of individualism and self-enrichment that gathered to its crescendo in the Macmillan years.

In 1951 the words 'I'm all right, Jack' still meant, as they meant in the cruder wartime version, a totally reprehensible attitude towards Jack, whom you were supposed to care about. By 1959 they were a joke and the title of a film which simply stated a philosophy that was taken for granted. The Conservative victory under the slogan 'Set The People Free' that October looked rather hollow when you examined the figures and discovered that more people had actually voted Labour than Conservative. But it was enough to drive Labour out of power for what they were to call, in their turn, 'Thirteen Wasted Years'. Setting the people free took longer than anticipated, but the first casualties were those identity cards and the Festival site, in 1952. It was two more years before ration books could finally be burned or torn up by a thankful population – meat, bacon and butter were the last things to be freed. Only two of the industries nationalized by Labour were set free – road haulage and (temporarily as it turned out) steel. But at least the South Bank was freed. The Skylon was made into ashtrays. The other structures were dispersed to linger only in the imagination of designers; in its place Conservative freedom provided London with the first of the giant company headquarters built in the style of Orwell's Ministry of Truth – the Shell building (1958). It was a monument to the newly discovered Parkinson's Law. This concept, brilliantly and amusingly elucidated in a book of that name published the previous year by Professor C. North-cote Parkinson, stated: 'Work expands to fill the time available for its completion.' The Shell complex was proof that it also expands to fill the space available for its proliferation.

To cross the Atlantic in the early Fifties from the modest hopes of Britain to the United, Euphoric, You-name-it-they-had-it States was to court vertigo. The years of abundance in America began in 1950 with the defence expenditure triggered off by the Korean War, and the boom continued with only a hiccup or two of recession in 1954 and 1958. Focussing on one tiny segment of the statistics of abundance, let us examine corporation presidents and millionaires. In 1952 the president of General Motors drew a salary of $201,000 with another $380,000 in bonuses. The salary and bonuses of the president of Du Pont totalled $503,000. Quarter-million-dollar incomes (not including bonuses) were drawn by the top oil company bosses. By comparison the top directors of Shell and Imperial Chemical Industries in Britain were still drawing about £50,000 ($140,000) at the end of the decade. The Prime Minister's salary was still £10,000 ($28,000). Only the Queen, with a total annual income from the state of £475,000, came out at better than American rates – $1,330,000 – but two-thirds of that sum was specifically for

I'M ALL RIGHT, JACK: *Peter Sellers as the shop-steward in the famous film that summed up the philosophy of the late Fifties – the Age of Affluence*

maintaining her enormous household. Ten years later there would be four hundred Americans with an annual income like hers, of over a million dollars. The number of resident American millionaires was estimated in 1953 at 27,000. In the following ten years it rose to 80,000.

In 1957 *Fortune* magazine published a list of America's richest men, putting at the top the shy, reclusive, almost unknown J. Paul Getty, who turned out to be living in a modest room at the Ritz Hotel, London, conducting his world-wide oil business through the hotel switchboard with the minimum secretarial help. *Fortune* put his personal assets at approximately $1,000 million. Second and third places also went to American oilmen, H. L. Hunt and S. Richardson. The British were squeezed by the tax-man until the pips squeaked – Aneurin Bevan's phrase. Fifty-two of those earning $500,000 in the United States were paying no federal tax at all.

Richesse oblige. With the spotlight on him, Mr Getty could no longer keep his bolt-hole in the Ritz private and was shortly settling into Sutton Place, the Duke of Sutherland's Tudor manor house in Surrey, with seventy-two rooms and 750 acres. Characteristically, he later insisted it was a bargain at $500,000. For this the Getty Oil Company, which paid the bill, got a headquarters and a great deal of publicity, on the whole favourable, since Mr Getty was bowing to the style which England expects. A long-winded man for such a recluse, he devised an 800-word standard apology for not being able to help out the writers of the 3,000 begging letters he received monthly. Another curious contradiction in his character led to his installation of a notorious coin-box and enamelled sign, 'Public Telephone', for the use of his guests. Anecdotes of his parsimony abounded. He admitted he had waited ten minutes to enter an exhibition to take advantage of the cheaper rates after 5.30 p.m. The only respect in which he was obviously not thrifty was wives – he had already discarded five. It seemed a very old-fashioned and Victorian success story. Getty believed in self-help, the philosophy of Samuel Smiles, though smiles were the last thing he could manage in public. Owner of a fabled art collection in California, which he was too busy ever to visit, his soon familiar face, like a bloodhound lugubriously scenting wasted pennies, was one symbol of the times: if you, too, struck oil you could be as rich and careworn as Getty and have as little time and capacity to enjoy it.

OPPOSITE *Poor Little Rich Man – J. Paul Getty among the art treasures in his Tudor manor house, Sutton Place*

Getty still embodied the old-fashioned American ethic of thrift. But in the ever-expanding American economy whose production doubled in the decade, it was almost a patriotic duty to consume as conspicuously as possible. Could consumption be doubled to keep pace? Well, advertising could be, and was, persuading Americans to throw thrift to the winds with awe-inspiring contortions of logic. Take an advertisement for Chevrolet (1956) endorsing the case for the two-car family. Its true reasoning was that doubled car consumption would be good for General Motors and what was good for General Motors, as its president, Charles E. Wilson, memorably announced as his political philosophy, was good for the country. But how to allay old-style qualms about waste and self-indulgence? The answer was in the picture – a family happily grilling hamburgers in front of their two cars in their double carport, a sort of burnt offering before the altar of mobility. 'Going Our Separate Ways We've Never Been So Close' said the caption boldly. And beneath, the copy-writers had reared a paradox that would have delighted Lewis Carroll: 'The family with two cars gets twice as many chores completed, so there's more leisure to enjoy *together!*' Having it both ways, it was clearly aimed to assuage the consumer's guilt. A picture of the American family began to be glimpsed as a super-mobile group that could get together to grill a hamburger only if it drove to the appointment. But as the decade advanced, guilt noticeably wore off. The number of two-car families doubled in the Fifties to reach fifteen per cent of American households (and would double again in the next ten years).

The essential discovery, now that everyone had heard of Freud, was that guilt could be harnessed to salesmanship. It was used aggressively as a selling aid for Gleem toothpaste – 'For Those Who Cannot Brush After Every Meal' (who can?). It could be assuaged to lower sales resistance – 'To make that job easier, you *deserve* M and M candy' (after which, naturally, you need Gleem all the more). One of the psychologists, who moved into the salesman's world like witch doctors and made a killing, was Dr Ernest Dichter from Freud's own city of Vienna, the 'father' of Motivational Research, whose institute could be hired to help sell anything for $500 a day. He was prone to Delphic (and cloudy) utterances such as: 'To women, don't sell shoes, sell lovely feet.' Psychologically illiterate sales directors were putty in the hands of such experts in the unconscious mind, with their battery of mumbo-jumbo such as word-association lists, ink-blot tests, lie detectors and eye-blink counters, hypnosis and 'depth' interviewing of housewives.

Say the word 'soup', Dichter's institute would report, and 80 per cent of subjects tested would reply 'Mother'. The merest simpleton could draw the conclusion. Sell your brand as Mother's soup. Of course there was nothing to guarantee that the soup you were canning would measure up to the quality or taste of Mother's, nor that other soup canners would not make the same sales appeal. In fact there was precious little to rely on in the unconscious unless the product was good enough to sell itself to the conscious senses, in which case the unconscious appeal was superfluous. But this did not prevent claims being made for motivational research and the like as extravagant as those made for corn cures and patent all-purpose medicines by the pedlars and mountebanks of time immemorial. When baking a cake, manufacturers of cake-mixes were told, women were acting out symbolically the birth of a child (not for nothing was the vulgar phrase for pregnancy a 'bun in the oven'). Simply to add water to a dry powder was not enough to satisfy this ritual urge. Allow them to add an egg to the mixture and the symbolism (of conception presumably) would be fulfilled. Whether the satisfaction occurred, and whether it outweighed the inconvenience of having to have an egg handy, was as hard to substantiate as most other claims for the wonders of depth psychology.

Deep down in those subconscious depths was the suggestion that you could make people believe anything you wanted them to believe, if only you knew how to pronounce the magic formula that brought the genie from the bottle. Naturally the next field in which to try out this half-truth was politics, where people have been trying since the time of Demosthenes to fool all of the people all of the time. The presidential election of 1952 saw the first large-scale hiring of skilled advertising men to do the politicians' persuading for them. The Republicans put their trust in the advertising experts of Batten, Barden, Durstine and Osborn. The Democrats had trouble placing their $8 million account. They finally chose the agency that dreamed up a well-known series of ads that appealed to a deeply buried vein of female exhibitionism: 'I dreamed I stopped the traffic in my Maidenform Bra' (she wore nothing else). Unfortunately for Adlai Stevenson, it proved harder to stop the traffic in his egghead's bow tie.

Another shaft of light into the murky depths of the human psyche was alleged to be cast by the discovery of the 'brand image'. This was largely the doing of an Englishman, David Ogilvy, who reached Madison Avenue via Oxford and a post in the British Embassy in Washington. Looking like a scholarly Foreign Office man he took the hard-selling American advertising world of those days aback by the very stealth of his

approach. He dramatized the product, by imagining and scripting two
human brand images of conspicuously unAmerican snob appeal: Commander Whitehead of Schweppes and 'The Man In The Hathaway
Shirt'. Commander Whitehead, a jovial, dashing, red-bearded figure
with a Homburg and a briefcase, cheerfully splashing tonic water about
on convivial occasions, looked too good to be true. The surprise was that
he really was a former naval commander and actual president of
Schweppes' American subsidiary. His value was partly to bewilder
those Americans who felt that to dilute hard liquor with tonic water or
soda was in some way unmanly. Commanders, R.N., are a notoriously
hard-drinking breed, which scotched that suspicion. On top of that he
was pictured in such chic situations as the bar of the Metropolitan
Opera House confiding such pearls of worldly wisdom as 'A punctilious
barman (or butler) will always serve you Schweppes Club Soda for
highballs'. The parenthesis 'or butler' was sheer image building. So
was the use of a word like 'punctilious'. Ogilvy was addicted to words
that the straight-talking huckster-style admen of the day would blink at.
He called a shirt 'ineffable' on one occasion. It was his inspiration to
claim that 'At 60 miles an hour the loudest noise in this new Rolls Royce
comes from the electric clock.'

With 'The Man In the Hathaway Shirt' Ogilvy possibly over-stepped
into self-parody. With a black eyepatch, pencil moustache and
Viennese or Hungarian look of disdain he was pure Ruritanian musical
comedy. The roles he played in the glossy pages of *The New Yorker*,
for instance, were almost parodies of gracious living and social superiority. The pith helmet with an attentive elephant in waiting. The
conductor's baton with attendant symphony orchestra. The book-lined
study with a telescope at the open window. Beside it our hero would be
making notes – a gentleman astronomer like that gentleman chemist,
Sherlock Holmes. But it worked. Eyepatches became the rage at fancy-
dress parties. And Hathaway, 'a small company of dedicated craftsmen
in the little town of Waterville, Maine,' said their advertisements, 'who
have been at it, man and boy, for 114 years', sold out their stock of shirts
within a week of the first eyepatch appearing in *The New Yorker*. In fact
the anonymous man in the shirt was a male model but he was also, so it
happened, a baron, the son of a Tsarist diplomat, by name George
Wrangel. With curious fitness, fate had it in store for him to marry an
heiress and settle down in a castle in Spain – he who had conjured up so
many of them in the imagination of junior executives.

'Images' were a sort of charade, amateur theatricals to grace the

A Hathaway shirt advertisement in THE NEW YORKER. *The copy is headed with the line 'Urbane, yet light-bodied: Hathaway's Batiste Oxford '56'*

hard face of commerce, and they became popular for their own sake. Before long workaday products were seeking brand images. In 1956 the Marlboro cigarette, formerly considered rather a ladylike thing to smoke, acquired its cowboy, with a tattoo on the back of his hand and the message: 'A man's cigarette that women like too'. Brands of petrol, it was claimed, had distinctive images and even more so did the brands of automobiles they fuelled. 'It makes you feel like the man you are' claimed an ad for Buicks. But what sort of man was that? Research (depth research naturally) among some Chicago car owners came up with the following automobile 'personalities': Cadillac – flashy; Ford – young and speedy; DeSoto – conservative and responsible; Pontiac – stable and conventional; Mercury – assertive and modern. The amazing Dr Dichter made one of his most celebrated discoveries for the automobile industry: that a man is seduced into the showrooms by a 'mistress' (a convertible) but comes out having settled for a 'wife' (a saloon or sedan). The hard-top – wife and mistress combined in one body – was claimed to be the most successful innovation the industry had made in years.

Once more politics was tempted by the song the sirens sang. If cars could have images, so could political candidates. The reason the Republicans won an election was 'Ike's father image'. The reason the Democrats lost was that Stevenson lacked 'the presidential image' – which sounds suspiciously like saying he didn't become president because he didn't become president. Certainly his 'egghead' image fitted awkwardly into a Maidenform-Bra-moulded mind. Stevenson himself was one of the few to speak out strenuously against the newly received wisdom – 'the idea that you can merchandize candidates like breakfast cereal'. The truth may be that in the long run, as Lincoln thought, people are not fooled. But in the short run the new game of image-building spread, even to conservative England, even to the most patriarchal conservative, Harold Macmillan, who by the late Fifties was being promoted with his enthusiastic cooperation as 'Supermac' and sold on the hoardings by Messrs Colman, Prentice and Varley, the advertising agents.

A good deal of credulity and nonsense was indulged in in the name of psychology but there was no nonsense about the concept of 'psychological obsolescence', the new technique for making people dissatisfied with what they had bought more quickly than ever before. Could people be made to change their durable possessions as if by the whims of fashion? Again it was the auto industry that led the way in the early Fifties after suffering two costly setbacks. The Ford 'Edsel', unveiled as the car that had everything in the way of advanced engineering, flopped like a dead duck with the public which presumably was little interested in engineering. Then Chrysler announced in 1953 a slimmer, shorter, more compact and parkable car to meet modern conditions. This eminently reasonable development cut their sales by half. Detroit took the hint. What the public wanted was not economy, practicality, money-saving and engineering quality but extravagance and swagger. In a word, styling.

For the rest of the decade automotive stylists were gods in the plants of the Big Three: Chrysler, Ford and General Motors. Chrysler's next Plymouth, the 1955 model, was sixteen inches longer and three inches lower than its predecessor, the longest and lowest car for the money. Sales lifted immediately and the trend ahead was clear. Everyone's new model was longer and lower and fancier, as if squeezed underfoot.

The more they were squeezed the more chrome was exuded, as if from a tube, at each end. Ford's chief designer, George W. Walker (whose salary of ˢ200,000 was perhaps the explanation why General Motors paid its president the curious figure of ˢ201,000), was dubbed 'the Benvenuto Cellini of Chrome'. The chief stylist at General Motors, Harvey Earl, paid a visit to an air force base where, seeing the new twin-tailed fighters, he was inspired to 'intuit' the automobile shape of the future – twin tail fins. The Cadillac 'La Espada' exhibited at Earls Court in 1955 had tail fins moulded out of its flanks while the exhaust pipes were carried in rocket motor nozzles. But what was this in front on either side of the radiator, carrying the bumpers like gulls' wings? Two enlarged bomb-shaped protruberances of pure dazzling chrome – or were they bombs after all? On closer inspection they were equipped with central nipples of white rubber. Perhaps Dr Dichter had something after all. Tail fins grew longer and flashier from 1956 until 1960 when at the limit of evolution they dropped off. But whatever the possibilities of female protruberances up front, what actually developed were lamps. Lamps of every size sprouted in pairs where no one had seen the need for lamps before, until there were as many as four pairs on the front of a Cadillac, and there were models which carried fourteen lamps as if they were Mississippi riverboats.

The automobile industry had become as fashion-conscious as the rag trade, and it had discovered how to make people discontented with even last year's model. By 1960 the average trade-in period of American cars was just over two years while in the London *Times* you could read an essay on the heartbreak of selling your loved and familiar car. This attitude was no longer conceivable to an American mind where the basic body silhouette was changing every second year. The redesigning and retooling involved added ˢ200 to the cost per car, with a further ˢ100 for 'brightwork' or 'Borax', as functionless chrome was called in the trade. The heavier load of accessories and metal trim drove up petrol consumption: from twenty miles per gallon the average dropped to fifteen and below. But who was counting? The formula was to 'sell more car per car'. Everything about the industry glorified waste. There was a half-hearted and unconvincing attempt to justify fins. They were claimed to have stabilizing qualities in a cross-wind. But their true justification was symbolic. They symbolized all the money that was around, the flamboyance expected of the richest nation on earth. The front of a 1956 Cadillac looked like a chrome version of an oriental shrine, which is what it was: the object of ritualized washing and polish-

The two-door, hard-top version of the 1959 Buick

ing on Sunday morning, an observance as solemn as church-going, a service of Holy Carmunion.

By 1959 the car body could be streamlined no further. The Pontiac crouched a whole foot lower than it did before, and General Motors shareholders were beginning to complain at annual meetings of bumping their heads or not being able to wear a hat in a Buick. So the designers turned in a new direction, the second-car market. Detroit-made compacts began to challenge the cheap Volkswagens and foreign imports: only, being produced under the Detroit philosophy of more car per car, they were soon so accessorized, automated and air-conditioned that they were no longer cheap. The advertising for them talked scathingly of 'one-car captivity'. And in the richer suburbs there was an intense social pressure – that of the young. No girl, reported David Riesman, the sociologist, would go to a dance unless she was picked up in a car belonging to or driven by her escort, which was likely to be 'the second car'. To be driven to a dance by taxi or one's father would be social death. It did not take long to see the extension of the concept. The two-car family led to the two-refrigerator, two-washing-machine, two-bathroom family, along with that favourite Fifties fad, 'His' and 'Hers' towels, toilet articles, perfumes and accessories. But the basic discovery of the Detroit mentality was that a design did not have to be better

lectra, which measured only 54 inches in height

engineered, more functional or more beautiful than what what was already on the market in order to outsell it; it just had to be newer.

The easiest thing to change was the colour. Household utensils, vacuum cleaners, telephones, typewriters, baths, wash basins, refrigerators and cookers blushed pink and then into other pastel colours every year or two. Refrigerators could hardly grow tail fins but they acquired streamlining, a sort of bulbous teardrop shape as if poised for take-off from the kitchen floor. After modulating through the pastel palette, kitchen equipment came back to its original key – exciting, brilliant white – with a square, boxy outline. And just as cars acquired more and more lamps, cookers acquired dials. Control panels bristled with up to thirty-five switches and buttons as if the housewife-technologist required the skills of an airline pilot. On close examination by the American Consumers' Union, some of these switches were found to be connected to no vital function of the machine whatever. They were pure 'gimmick' – a much-used Fifties word which had not yet become a term of abuse.

Who dared abuse gimmicks or any device to keep production and consumption in pace with one another, both bounding inexorably upwards? The alternative was believed to be another Great Crash. The maxim 'Waste not, want not,' became obsolete too; 'waste not, work not' was the new fear. Many people expressed it. *Retailing Daily*, for instance, declared: 'We are obligated to work on obsolescence as our contribution to a healthy, growing society.' You can't do much more violence to sense and language in one sentence than that. A spokesman for Cornell Business School put it more succinctly: 'Marketing men have to face the fact that America's capacity to produce may have outstripped its capacity to consume.' It cost money to grow obsolete ever faster. The more the styles changed, as the Consumers' Union director, Dexter Masters, pointed out, the greater the disguised price increase to the consumer in shorter-lived products and heavier repair bills. Things were not being made to last. It was like riding in an aircraft which had no stable cruising speed. It had to keep accelerating or it would drop out of the sky.

It was easier to see what was happening if you were a visitor from a less frantically prospering land. J. B. Priestley, affronted by the impact of Texas on his English prejudices in 1954, described the ugly results with pungency in *Journey Down A Rainbow*. He summed up the system of increasing productivity plus high-pressure advertising and salesmanship, plus mass communications, in the word Admass – 'the creation of the mass mind, the mass man.' One of the characteristics of Admass was the uniformity of the food on offer. 'If a good Admass man does not order a steak, either he is not hungry or he can't afford the price.' Between Fort Worth and Dallas he found the nomads wandering from motel to motel, 'the tuneless gipsies of the machine age', along roads lined with trailer courts, gas stations, second-hand car dealers, supermarkets, drive-in banks, movie theatres and restaurants, all serving the same food, movies, television, songs and cigarettes. 'It offers movement without any essential change,' he wrote, 'It is a street three thousand miles long. You burn 150 gallons of gasoline to arrive nowhere.' This pattern of life was being copied in Britain and all over the motorized world with greater or less fidelity.

Priestley's warning was that it was essentially a cheat. It did not offer more choice but less than there was before. The freedom to wander at will is illusory if all the destinations are indistinguishable. 'The people who live there are dissatisfied, restless and bitter,' he warned, 'Especially the women – still girls in a mining camp.' It may be unfair to picture the horrors of Texas as if they are worse than the horrors of industrial Britain. The motel-supermarket-hamburger civilization has now been superimposed on what was left of nineteenth-century towns, and has further worn down the differences between one region and the next, but it is doubtful whether the mass mind or the mass man has yet come to pass, except to the extent that people always conform to a prevailing style while it lasts. It can be argued that mass communications have simply speeded up the whole process of change enormously, rather than imposed a massive and rigid uniformity. 'I think my pessimism was justified,' said Priestley looking back on it, 'I think the odds are very heavy against getting a square deal from anybody about anything.'

It is doubtful whether many of the denizens of Admass society saw themselves as victims in the way Priestley did. For a time it seemed as though the white working class had vanished. Tom Wolfe recalls:

> It became impossible at that time to use words like 'proletarian', 'working class' or 'Blue Col'. They had too much money. They were no longer wearing string vests, they were wearing Lacoste polo shirts with an alligator emblem on the pocket or 'Cisco Kid' shirts with diagonal zippers. You began to see them in the expensive cars. It was the working class who wanted to use their money for flamboyant display. The reason American tourists became a byword for vulgarity in Europe was that suddenly they were working-class Americans going abroad. There had never been such a period before, of such security and stability. The United States seemed to be in great shape. We were the most powerful country in the world and the overwhelming fact was that astonishing amounts of money had come into ordinary people's homes. Hence the cars, the holiday trips, the barbecues, the pets – I remember in 1959 being amazed to discover how many people in the suburbs of Washington were keeping pet *chimpanzees*!

People with new money spread out into the newly-built suburbs where the houses, like the cars, had got longer and lower and were dignified with the name 'ranch-style' as though there were unspoilt acres in which to roam outside, rather than the swallowing of land in highways, parkways, expressways and cloverleaf intersections to enable suburban man to reach what was once a rural neighbourhood. The newest style was 'split-level' – a living room with a picture window and an adjoining dining area, a kitchen and, up a few stairs above the double garage, three bedrooms and two bathrooms. The price would be about $25,000 in a place like Park Forest, outside Chicago. The suburb was home for thirty million Americans. Of course, the price and income range varied, and so with it did the 'life-style' – a term for which the Fifties were still groping.

One of these styles was invented on the eve of the Fifties by Abraham Levitt, who was already seventy years old, on a potato patch on Long Island. He began building extremely cheap mass housing for war

An aerial view of the original Levittown on Long Island

veterans, who camped out for nights to secure a house on no deposit whatever. He called it Levittown. By the Fifties his ranch model homes, built in about five varieties of finish and colour scheme, were selling for $9,000. Leaving behind him a suburban town of 100,000 people on the potato patch, Levitt went on to build bigger Levittowns in Pennsylvania and New Jersey. By the mid-Seventies the $9,000 ranch model was worth $30,000 and more, and the policemen and firemen who originally lived there had been replaced by the middle class. Community life had faded away. The object of suburban man was to move onward and upward to a better suburb. Suburbs dedicated ostensibly to the cult of the the family, centred on children and leisure in a calming, country atmosphere, were striving places. Sloan Wilson captured the values of 'Westport', Connecticut, in a famous book: 'On Greentree Avenue finances were an open book. Budgets were frankly discussed and the public celebration of increases in salary was common. The biggest parties were moving-out parties given by people who were finally able to afford a bigger house.' That was in *The Man In The Gray Flannel Suit*, whose title became a kind of cat-call at the conforming commuter who sacrificed his integrity for a safe income and suburban comfort. Sloan Wilson did not sneer at it that way in his autobiography, *What Shall We Wear To This Party?*:

The war left them (veterans) with a lust for security and permanence, even luxury and prestige. If big companies of that day insisted on a kind of uniform of the day, be it gray flannel or pinstripe, the eager veterans donned it cheerfully. The structure of large corporations, with chains of command, was not unlike the armed forces.

In the novel, Tom Rath, a veteran paratrooper, and his wife Betsy are continually complaining at suburban life or feeling guilty about corporation values. The big company is referred to as 'the mink-lined rat-trap' and, after a good talking-to from Betsy, Tom spurns it in favour of old-fashioned American self-reliance. They resolve to get up early, have a proper breakfast, walk to the station, give away the TV set, and go to church every Sunday instead of lounging about drinking Martinis. It is almost too virtuous and optimistic to believe, but the Fifties readers seized on it as a model. Probably Tom's fellow commuters sincerely enjoyed their Sunday morning Martinis, just as they enjoyed shining the tail-fins and chrome of the Plymouth and cutting their grass with power mowers (power mower sales quadrupled). Betsy's neighbours, the wives, probably enjoyed lives centred on the rearing of so many extra children (the child population under fourteen increased by 50 per cent). The social round consisted overwhelmingly of scouts and brownies and camp and parent-teacher associations and dancing classes and backyard barbecues and coffee 'klatches' and cocktails and canapés . . . gin imports trebled and vodka sales were multiplied by ten. If it sounds boring, and it does, well, it also endures. Indeed, despite the Sixties' experiments with alternative life-styles, the despised suburban style looks like seeing the century through, for all its drawbacks of loneliness, boredom and exasperation, which made the man in the New Yorker cartoon say plaintively at the cocktail party: 'I want to talk about something else besides kids and illness!'

Sneer though they might, a series of interviews with graduates of the Class of '55 at Ivy League colleges conducted by Time magazine showed the strong streak of conformity of the Fifties. The overwhelming majority of these, the best qualified young people in the country, said they wanted a protected life in a big corporation, a home in the suburbs and a family of five or six children. They were, in the title of another influential book, examples of The Organization Man. William H. Whyte pointed out in his study that the American Dream had changed. Instead of being a dream of individual salvation through competition, hard work and thrift, it had been perverted by the 'tyranny of the majority' into putting loyalty to the organization first. The corporations

increasingly used 'personality testing' in selecting their executives.
Whyte even gave tips on how to answer the questions correctly – that is,
in the way the corporation would like you to: 'Repeat to yourself – I like
things pretty well the way they are. I love my wife and children but I
don't let them get in the way of company work.' Herd life extended
beyond the office out to the organization man's natural habitat, the suburban community, where he found even watching television was a
group activity. In Chicago's Park Forest, where the modest houses cost
$17,000 and the gray-flannel, or rather charcoal-suited, inhabitants were
typically earning $6,000–$7,000 and were aged between twenty-five and
thirty-five, the house agent's advertisements stressed the feeling of
'belonging':

> A cup of coffee – symbol of PARK FOREST!
> Coffee pots bubble all day long in Park Forest.
> This sign of friendliness tells you how much neighbours enjoy each
> other's company.

Dr Dichter would have been proud of that piece of depth thinking.
Don't sell the house, sell the bubble of the coffee pot.

Soon it was not enough to demonstrate your success in life by the
acquisition of material goods. A refrigerator? – 87 per cent of households
had one. A washing machine? – 75 per cent owned one too. Vacuum
cleaners, pop-up toasters, food mixers – by 1960 they were common to
70 per cent of American families. Britain could not match these percen-
tages but it was catching up, 'keeping up with the Joneses'. In 1958,
when hire purchase restrictions were finally abolished, the throttle was
opened. You could become the owner of a Ford Popular for a down pay-
ment of £4. 8s. 5d. or of a refrigerator for £3. 3s. 3d., with years to pay.
By the end of the decade, four British families out of five were the hire-
purchasers of £1,000 million-worth of goods. Foreign holidays were
booming in the first years of package tours: 3.5 million Britons went
abroad by 1960. Like the Americans, many of them had never crossed
the Channel for pleasure before. They found that £15 or £20 a week
went as far in an erstwhile fishing village on Spain's Costa Brava as it did
at an English seaside hotel or holiday camp, with cheap wine and
reliable sunshine thrown in. The Spanish were soon obliging enough to
provide tea and chips as well.

One of the by-products of contact with Europe was a boom in wine
sales, which nearly doubled at home, and a long-overdue improvement
in restaurant standards. British restaurant cooking had been despaired of

after fifteen years of siege conditions until the counter-attack of *The Good Food Guide*, founded in 1951 by Raymond Postgate, a pioneering *bon vivant*, and compiled by himself, his friends and any members of the public who could be bothered to write in with their recommendations (one who did was a lion tamer). Slowly an underground resistance movement grew, catering for discriminating customers. The war-time legacy of the five-shilling legal maximum on restaurant bills was an open cheque for profiteers to pose as restaurateurs. Gradually the prevailing barbarism was tempered. This central registry with its annual guide set standards of value for money ('ample helpings' was a common form of praise in the early, newly-derationed days) and a little more sophistication of taste than that for which British boarding schools and service canteens had trained the middle classes. Government-approved 'mousetrap' had for so long banished regional English cheeses, for instance, that they were given up for dead. But with a little encouragement Wensleydale and Caerphilly, Double Gloucester and proper Stilton from Melton Mowbray began to flower again. British and Australian substitutes for burgundy began to give place to the real thing. In the early Fifties Oxford and Cambridge parties were launched on a tide of sharp South African sherry, and Commemoration or May balls were danced on cheap, acrid champagne. It was not the taste buds but the purchasing power of Academe that needed nursing. Once even one good restaurant in a county, such as The Bell at Aston Clinton, Buckinghamshire, started raising standards the word passed along the grapevine and the effect was cumulative. It is hard to convey to those who do not remember the abysmal depths of post-war British catering what a heady sensation it was to be invited to strike a blow for improvement – or to strike a restaurant off for bad cooking, uncleanliness or lack of attention. It is America's misfortune that it has encouraged standardized mass catering to swamp the country, coast to coast, with the Admass steak and chicken and seafood.

But it was from America that British consumers took the idea of the founding of the Consumers' Association and its magazine *Which?* in 1957, which was soon selling 300,000 copies – almost as many as *The Times*. About £7 million was being spent annually on pushing the claims of washing powders such as Tide, Daz, Omo and Persil, compared with £1.7 million on pushing the performances of music, opera, ballet, theatre and visual arts. Now, for the price of its modest subscription, *Which?* and its laboratories revealed that the cleaning power of these rivals was practically identical. Though they fell far short of the giant-killing exploits of Citizen Ralph Nader in the decade to come, the consumers' organizations provided a rallying point and the hard evidence to contest the claims of £450 million–worth of advertising a year, roughly the same as was spent on schools. In other respects American firms brought American techniques to bear in the opposite direction. The advertising was American, led by such firms as J. Walter Thompson and applied to the products of eight hundred American firms dominating the British consumer – Thomas Hedley (Tide and Daz), Hoover, Singer, Heinz, Kellogg, Kraft, Gillette, Kodak, Woolworth, Colgate-Palmolive, Esso and Ford to name only the top twelve. In the event it was Alaska which became the 49th State of the Union (in 1959) but it could easily have been Coca-Colonial Britain. When Prime Minister Macmillan uttered the famous slogan 'Some of our people have never had it so good', he had even borrowed the phrase from America. Two years earlier, George Meany, chairman of the combined American unions, the AFL-CIO, proclaimed that American labour had 'never had it so good' – which was true. Macmillan had the grace to add the question: 'It it too good to last?'

In Britain it was too good to last, but the slogan led to a disastrous period of false optimism. Macmillan, one of the wiliest politicians of his time, also said, with typical understatement, as the Fifties drew to an end: 'We have not done badly. But we have not done quite well enough.' That blandly papered over the facts that Britain's share of world trade had steadily declined, its prices had risen more and its exports less than those of its ex-enemies, the Germans and the Italians. Despite what seemed to be a nice little boom, British productivity had grown more slowly than that of any comparable European country: 40 per cent compared with Germany's and Italy's 150 per cent, not to consider Japan's 400 per cent. Exports had risen by 150 per cent from Germany and 180 per cent from Italy but only 28 per cent from Britain. The only thing in which Britain held a clear lead was price increases – 10 per cent compared with 2 per cent in Germany. Alongside the German economic miracle and the U.S. trading surplus with the world, it began to look as if Britain was the new Sick Man of Europe. Over the next fifteen years of constantly recurring crises it was going to get much worse. But the original damage was done in the Fifties and it was the product of ignorance and laziness and bloody-mindedness. *The Economist* had declared in 1954: 'The miracle has happened! Full employment without inflation.' It was wrong. The average wage in 1950 (£6. 8s. 0d.) had almost doubled by 1959 (£11. 2s. 6d.) but by then the pound had lost a third of its value. This was only a modest puff of inflation by subsequent standards: by 1974 the 1950 pound would have been worth only one-third of a pound. It was a foretaste of the wages-prices spiral and the increasingly futile chase after higher incomes.

To sum up: in a time of unprecedented expansion of world trade Britain, the nation of shopkeepers, paid itself higher wages for producing very little more, while putting up its prices much faster than its competitors. Ignoring the foundation of the European Economic Community until it was too late to join on favourable terms, Britain lost its position as a first-class trading power without even noticing.

Instead, inspired by Mr Macmillan as Chancellor, the State instituted a national lottery – the Premium Bonds – in 1956. Instead of putting their money into business, people lent it to the government in the hope that ERNIE (the nickname of the Electronic Random Number Indicator) would select their number for the top prize (then) of a modest £1,000. The chance was not high, though that never deterred a gambler, and the real winner was always the government which thus borrowed the punters' money interest-free. The chance of winning £75,000, then the top prize on the football pools, was too small to be visible but in the Fifties this slender possibility mesmerized the nation. Winners of the Treble Chance swooned at the sight of the cheque and were generally paraded to the Press and public as examples of how, at any minute, any humble citizen who had never had more than a day out at Blackpool could strike gold. A follow-up study showed that very few of them ever had any higher ambition for using the money than buying a house or two for the family and perhaps a shop or pub. They declared almost unanimously that it would not change their way of life, which makes one wonder what was so attractive about that way of life (in fact, nearly all pools winners were forced to move, through the envy of neighbours). But the dream, 'When I come up on the Pools' became the Fifties equivalent of breaking the bank at Monte Carlo for the Edwardians.

In the United States it was not the £75,000 cheque but the \$64,000 Question, the top prize in a double-your-money television quiz, that dominated people's fantasies. When the first contestant to go for the top prize, Marine Captain Richard MacCutchin who, oddly, specialized in *haute cuisine*, pulled it off by describing the ingredients of a royal banquet given by George VI to the President of France, three-quarters of American television sets were tuned in to watch him wrestle for the answers. Perhaps it was this climate of hysteria and sanctified greed that broke the moral fibre of a mild-mannered English instructor at

Columbia University called Charles Van Doren. He attained the status of a baseball hero by surviving round after round of the quiz 'Twenty-One' until the pay-off reached $129,000 and the audience a breathless 25 million viewers. But, it later came out, he and other contestants were being primed with the answers beforehand. All their brow-knotting agonies were carefully rehearsed. Van Doren's excuse to the investigating congressional committee was the most interesting part of the unedifying episode: 'I was almost able to convince myself that it did not matter what I was doing because it was having such a good effect on the national attitude to teachers, education and the intellectual life.'

In Britain one of the quintessentially Fifties symbols of the search for El Dorado (or the golden calf) was a gold-plated Daimler which belonged to a curious pair of headline-hunters, Sir Bernard and Lady Docker. To be more accurate, while Norah Docker sought the cameramen Sir Bernard hung about like a good-natured but rather dim St Bernard dog providing the money for her extravagance. The Edwardian Gaiety girls would have recognized Norah. Once a café dancer, she, too, showed a talent for marrying rich men – Sir Bernard was the third – and it was she who decided that the Docker Daimler should be gold-plated and that the seats should be upholstered in zebra skin. 'Mink,' she explained in a line worthy of Anita Loos, 'is too hot to sit on.' Hither and thither rolled the famous car, disgorging Lady D, followed by Sir Bernard, like minor royalty to perform no very clear function other than to open things or attend functions and be recognized. Norah, for instance, would arrive at a Yorkshire pit village one Sunday morning to be shown round the mine in a white helmet. Her escort of miners went pink with pleasure at calling her 'My lady' in speeches at the pit canteen. In return she showed them the Daimler and invited forty of them to visit her on the Dockers' yacht, *Shemara*, where pink champagne was served amid costly fitments which were often detailed in the newspapers.

Norah was a card. She made the headlines by having a glass of wine thrown over her at the plushy Caprice restaurant in London. She caused an international fuss and was banned from Monte Carlo by Prince Rainier for tearing up a tiny paper flag of Monaco in pique at a banquet. But she knew her public. They liked watching her play out a Cinderella fantasy, wearing gold *lamé* and riding in a gold-plated carriage to a ball from which she did not return until well after midnight. Nobody questioned her right to flaunt her way of life. She was a professional celebrity – one of the last to flourish without benefit of television.

Sir Bernard and Lady Docker with the gold-plated Daimler

Then the Birmingham Small Arms Company revealed after many a summer that the car she sat in like a burnished throne, and even some of the furs she wore, were not provided by her Prince Charming, Sir Bernard, but by them, the nuts and bolts firm of which he was chairman, as a business expense which they were no longer happy to provide. That took the gilt off the gingerbread and the Daimler bumpers. Sir Bernard was ousted as chairman. Norah complained bitterly that her style had brought the company free publicity worth far more than it cost. But the curious pair who for a time were so well-known simply for being rich vanished from the public eye – towards a tax haven in Jersey.

There was a fascination with Britain's self-made millionaires, like the former roller-skating rink proprietor, Charles Clore, whose empire included shoe shops and shipyards and even the shores of Loch Ness. There was the estate agent's clerk, Jack Cotton, whose property devel-

opments in Birmingham made him big enough, in partnership with
Clore, to take over the Ritz and Selfridges, to put up the $100 million
Pan-Am office building in New York and to threaten to present Piccadilly Circus with a hideous skyscraper of advertising signs, while he
contemplated his Rembrandt at the Dorchester. Isaac Wolfson, son of a
Russian refugee in the furniture business in Glasgow, became lord of
chain store after chain store in the Fifties. Vast benefactions brought
these men knighthoods or baronetcies or honorary degrees from universities they had endowed but not had the chance to attend. Meanwhile
Roy Thomson, once a Scots Canadian radio salesman, bought his way
via *The Scotsman* newspaper and Scottish Television to the proprietorial
chair of the *Sunday Times* and the ailing newspaper empire of Lord
Kemsley, *en route* to *The Times* itself.

There was one constant factor in the careers of these rich men. Priding
themselves on their hard-headedness, they were eventually prepared to
take on a poor commercial risk, or found a college as a pure give-away
gesture, in order to win a richer prize – prestige. Thomson said later of
The Times, which would cost him millions, 'It is an honour to under-
write a national institution.' Harrods was in low water financially when
Hugh Fraser, a Scottish draper, made his take-over. Claridges and the
Savoy had to fight off take-over bids with borrowed money. And the
brashly commercial Lord Wolfson (as he became), who went to a State
elementary school, was perhaps thinking of his equally unacademic
predecessor, Lord Nuffield, when he too, with his endowments, had an
Oxford college named after him.

If the millionaires sought their status symbols, so did the world in
general. The term status was popularized in 1958 in an influential book,
The Status Seekers by Vance Packard, whose sensitive antennae picked
up many new social currents of the time. He even told his readers how to
pronounce it – 'stay-tus' or 'stat-us' was permissible. It was not a new
idea, especially to the British who had long known the social significance
of the right address or style of house. Packard's discovery that one
particular square mile of high status addresses in New York ran east of
Central Park, from 65th to 78th Street, came as no surprise to Londoners
who knew the precise social shading between neighbouring postal
districts. After all, the postal map of London s.w.1 had been drawn
with a special excrescence to enable Harrods to be included in it and thus
avoid the ignominy of falling within the outer darkness of s.w.3 or 7.
So it was no surprise to learn that the inhabitants of an area next to
low-status Levittown sued the U.S. Post Office to change their address

to 'North Wantagh'. American house advertisements lapsed into French when they wanted to indicate high status: 'Une Maison Ranch très originale' or 'Une maison contemporaine'. Less coyly they would talk about 'a supreme achievement in luxurious, suburban living.'

Tests in the plusher environs of Philadelphia showed a distinction between chic and unchic speech which in the case of 'toilet' (chic) and 'lavatory' (unchic) was the precise opposite of Nancy Mitford's rules for U and Non-U in England. But the real dynamite in Packard's book was his Status Table of jobs, compiled in a University of Chicago study, in which people were asked how they rated the social standing of one profession compared with another. In the first grade they put architects, Federal judges, legal partners, medical consultants, bishops and stockbrokers – ahead of such second-rung occupations as newspaper editor, engineer, general practitioner, college professor or county judge. The distinctions near the bottom were equally interesting: barbers, bartenders and truck drivers, for instance, rated better than waiters, taxi drivers and night-watchmen, who in turn could look down slightly on gardeners, miners and dustmen. No comparable list existed for England, where it is doubtful if architects and stockbrokers would have rated quite so high or gardeners and miners so low. But the British professional classes had been examined by the academic team of Lewis and Maude in 1952, who found cause for concern that taxation had reduced the differentials between the professions to such an extent that they feared their quality might not be maintained. Very few professional men then could expect a net income of £2,000 a year by the age of forty. Those few were likely to be surgeons, dentists, accountants and solicitors in private practice, certainly not schoolmasters, university lecturers, architects in public service (most of them) or vets. Yet the income of college-educated Americans of about that time was over $7,000 – considerably more than £2,000 ($5,600).

Meanwhile there was the consolation of rubber plants, wall-to-wall carpeting, panelled executive dining rooms, directors' bathroom suites and, of course, hierarchies of secretaries and secretaries' secretaries to emphasize status in the office. It was at the end of the Fifties that the joke became popular about one high-powered executive calling another on his car telephone only to be told: 'He's on the other line'. The entire cycle of wealth and waste, consumption and status buying, accompanied by the deep roar of the capitalist engine turning over ever faster, needed a name by which to handle its concepts and in 1957 it got one. An unconventional Canadian professor of economics at Harvard, John

Kenneth Galbraith, crystallized all these phenomena in a book whose title, *The Affluent Society*, meant many things to many people. For some it was a reassuring catch-phrase like 'You Never Had It So Good'. For others it implied that the centuries-old problems of poverty and inequality had been swept away in the tide of prosperity. The irony of this was that Galbraith's working title for the book was *Why People Are Poor*. 'As I dealt with the conditions and consequences of affluence,' he explained, 'under which the existence of the poor had been buried, the poverty I had set out to write about got pushed further and further towards the back of the book. A lot of people never read that far.' Those who did read from end to end discovered that, far from giving its blessing to ever-expanding production and consumption, it pointed out its futility. Galbraith challenged the conventional wisdom that everything would be all right if only the Gross National Product were big enough. By now, sheer production was a self-defeating process. After a certain point the wants which it is intended to satisfy have to be artificially created in the first place by advertising and salesmanship. Worse than this, the consuming public was required to incur enormous hire-purchase debts which stimulated chronic inflation, while very low priority was given to 'unprofitable' public services such as education, housing and preserving the environment. The comment, 'Vacuum cleaners are praiseworthy, street cleaners are an unfortunate expense,' was a typical piece of Galbraithian 'Canada Dry'. It was the picture of public squalor which accompanied private affluence that made the most immediate impact on the thinking of the time. The most-quoted passage described the affluent American family taking a weekend outing in its mauve and cerise, air-conditioned, power-steered automobile passing through cities made tawdry by litter, blighted buildings and broken pavements, into the bill-boarded countryside where they picnic on packaged food by a polluted stream and camp out on a filthy parking lot.

> Just before dozing off on an air mattress beneath a nylon tent amid the stench of decaying refuse they may reflect vaguely on the curious unevenness of their blessings. Is this, indeed, the American genius?

With an astringent readability and clarity rare among economists, Galbraith's book had a tremendous reception, partly, he believes, because of the Soviet Sputnik which went up into space just before it was published. It caused anguished soul-searching in the United States. 'Anything that seemed to offer an explanation of why a vastly less productive society had brought off this breathtaking achievement was not dismissed but welcomed.' Looking back, Galbraith now sees the book as having had three forms of influence.

> First, it drew attention to the need for a balance between public and private spending. Secondly, nobody could any longer advance the belief that sheer production – the worship of the Gross National Product – was the final test of a society's economic vigour and success. Thirdly, it made people aware of the effect affluence was having on their environment.

But he is far from optimistic about how effective these arguments have been in altering policies.

> It helped the decision, alas more rhetorical than real, to mount a direct attack on American poverty in the Sixties. But the basic situation has not changed very much in twenty years. It's very hard not to contrast the squalor of the public services of the city of New York with the luxury of Park Avenue. You cannot doubt it would be a better city with more public and less private investment. Perhaps the book helped to prevent things from getting even worse. But when I wrote it, nobody had realized anywhere in the world how unbelievably expensive it is to make an agreeable modern city, from managing traffic and removing rubbish to providing better education, housing and transport. This is still not understood. We may reach a point where the public costs of city life have to be greater than the private. Britain has gone farther than any country in the West towards getting a balance between private affluence and public consumption. It is a costly and difficult thing to aim at but I still think it is right.

Did the experience of plenty bring about a fundamental change in the American or British character? It is tempting to believe so. The Fifties began in both countries with a general respect for self-denial, saving and security. By the time the decade ended self-indulgence was almost the orthodoxy; the fulfilment of economic wants without delay was a virtue. 'Why deny yourself?' asked one advertisement (for menswear). 'Pamper yourself' cried another, 'Give yourself this Christmas gift – now!' 'Hark the *Herald Tribune* sings, advertising wondrous things,' sang Tom Lehrer. What had happened to the old thrifty, puritanical streak which Middle America had inherited from the pioneers? We have already seen how the creators of wants, the psychology-manipulators in advertising, had set about trying to undermine it. Perhaps they succeeded better than they deserved.

How else can one explain the emergence of the 'throwaway philosophy'? In the Fifties the things you bought to throw away ranged from

Kleenex to baking tins, from razors with only one blade (supplied by vending machine) to watches not worth repairing. New York became conditioned to skyscrapers which were torn down after a few years' life to be replaced by newer skyscrapers. And the ultimate development in disposable packaging was the TV dinner, the domestic version of the airline dinner, bought complete with disposable tray, containers, cups and utensils, all of them made to be thrown away. By 1960 the American family was throwing away an average of 750 cans a year. America, hitherto an exporter of metals, began to import half of those it needed. It was calculated that the United States was using up eighteen tons of raw material per head of population per year, or ten times as much as the average citizen of the rest of the non-Communist world. By 1959, its wants took care of 60 per cent of the world's oil production. Still nobody really worried. Affluence was not a matter of gold-plated bath taps or Daimlers or tooth-brushes or mink-handled beer can openers – though these were available – it was a matter of 531 competing brands of coffee or 249 brands of washing powder on the American market, whose only *raison d'être* was that a change of packaging and advertising (New Wonder Ingredient!) gained them shelf space in the supermarkets until the next brand came along. All this was generally approved of, even though many of the 750 cans (and Coke and Pepsi bottles) thrown away by each family may have cost more to make than the contents. People reacted to the statistics of plenty with a simple Gee Whizzery. Nobody questioned the proposition 'More Is Better'.

In 1954 Fairfield Osborn warned his countrymen: 'We Americans have used more of the world's resources in the past forty years than all the people in the world had used in the four thousand years up to 1914. Man is becoming aware of the limits of the earth.' But was he? There was no discernible attempt to use less oil, to cut down the size of the cars or the extravagance of the packaging industry. Nobody was yet greatly concerned about the poverty of what had just been called the Third World. There was little enough concern with poverty nearer home. Galbraith pointed out that there were, in 1959, thirteen million American households which were poor in the sense that their family income was below $3,000. In another influential book Michael Harrington calculated there were between forty and fifty million American poor, the 'invisible' third of the nation which existed below the subsistence line in urban ghettos and pockets of rural misery, which he christened 'The Other America'. Galbraith recalls that he astonished Premier Nehru in the 1950s by telling him that the Punjab was a better place to

live and offered a higher general level of income than rural West
Virginia, Georgia and Mississippi.

Instead of worrying about that, the fashionable thing to worry about
was how people were going to adapt to all the leisure which the automated future would provide. 'The creative use of leisure' sociologists
called it and it worried them badly that fret-work and bird-watching
might be all there was to fulfil people after pressing the buttons at the
fully-automatic, atom-powered, closed-circuit-TV-monitored, computer-
directed plant for a couple of four-hour shifts a week. A false alarm.
'We failed to see there would come a point where additional leisure
would become more stultifying than satisfying and that the mass of men
would be incapable of absorbing any more,' wrote the Harvard sociologist, David Riesman. More spare time, it was discovered, meant more
time spent watching TV, the chief leisure activity for all classes. Findings
from the unions were a surprise to those who had glimpsed Utopia as a
world where work became unnecessary: one American union polled its
members and discovered that though they thought work was boring,
they would rather do that than do nothing. Industrial workers in
general used their shorter working week to do a second job. All this was
to seem academic by the Seventies when the boom finally stopped and
the dream future of abundance and leisure popped like a rosy soap
bubble. Looking back at those debates on how we could fill in the time
on our hands, the novelist Herbert Gold reflected that the Fifties were a
time of 'happy people with happy problems'. It was just that the problems were far bigger than people realized. Instead of automated leisure,
enforced unemployment was on its way back. Instead of how to feed
the pockets of rural poor in the overlooked parishes of the affluent
society, the problem was how to feed the overpopulated two-thirds of
the world. Instead of how to stimulate demand sufficiently to absorb all
that the machines could produce, the problem was what to substitute
for the planet's fast-dimishing raw material and energy resources. But a
taste of plenty was such a heady new experience for those lucky enough
to get it, especially the war-worn British, that that first, childlike squeal
of delight, the deliberate waste, the throwing around of money and
goods, is easy to comprehend. You can forgive people in the Fifties for
their eagerness to believe that the problems of highly industrialized
societies had been solved, that capitalism worked and that the industrial
revolution was at last delivering the goods for everyone . . . that there
were practically no losers. Well, we know better now.

CHAPTER TWO

A Woman's Place

Nothing about the Fifties was more paradoxical than the role women played in it. After sharing the camaraderie of the fighting services or the hardships of civilian bombing on equal terms, surely women would not go meekly back home to wife-and-motherhood? But they did, with a fervour that would have amazed the feminists of their grandmothers' generation. Birth rates soared and career women sank in prestige to the level of drop-outs in the great breeding stakes. But then, having thrown away the chance of greater equality, women gradually proceeded to win it back by devious ways until by 1960 there had been a stealthy but profound erosion of male dominance with hardly a male being yet aware of it. A decade which venerated both Dr Spock and Marilyn Monroe was not a simple one.

In the early years the baby boom carried almost all women before it. Women gave up their jobs in droves and went home to have children in hordes. The United States population increased by twenty-eight million in ten years, at a rate even faster than India's. In Britain the birth rate 'Bulge', which hit its peak in the late Forties, went down more slowly than anyone had expected. The marriage age steadily dropped until half of American brides married by the time they were twenty and three-quarters of English girls were marrying by the age of twenty-five. Why was this? Partly because the Happy Housewife beamed at the world from countless advertisements, looking out of her gadget-lined nest. At her side, in popular myth, was an amiably aproned husband demonstrating 'Togetherness', the new wonder ingredient in marriage. Suddenly the climate was imbued with a new Puritan ethic, not the work ethic but the breeding ethic. The proper function of woman was to raise a brood much larger than women had wanted since before 1914. The vogue for large families – for third, fourth, even fifth and sixth babies – spread, especially among university graduate mothers. The most important task to which a woman's higher education could be put was, by wide agreement, raising the next generation. By the mid-Fifties more than half the girls at American universities were dropping out of college in order to marry and help their husbands to get through.

The Fifties were not a permissive era. The pressure to marry young went along with a renewed convention of pre-marital chastity. Once again the rule was that Nice Girls Didn't – certainly not without the understanding that there was a 'moral' engagement with their partner, even if he had not yet bought the ring or made the announcement. Geoffrey Gorer, investigating English attitudes to sex by questionnaire in 1950, found that 55 per cent of men and 73 per cent of women disapproved of women having sexual experience before marriage. About 50 per cent disapproved of it even for men. 'The high value put on virginity for both sexes is remarkable and, I should suspect, specifically English,' Gorer wrote in *Exploring English Character*.

This may have been due partly to prudence. Contraceptives in Britain were still kept out of sight, even male ones, and had to be purchased rather furtively, like guilty secrets. As a result they were often not employed and, even if they were, there was a widespread superstition that the Catholic church made sure that one in twenty (or was it ten?) was faulty, as a sort of divine vengeance. As for the United States, Betty Friedan testified to 'the awkward indignity of getting a diaphragm in New York if you weren't married – and sometimes even if you were.' It was also due partly to the obstacles of fashion. The would-be seducer of the Fifties had to reckon with an armoury of uncooperative underwear which stood between him and his objective. The nylon stocking was still suspended from a constricting girdle of unyielding firmness, a fortification virtually impossible to bypass without active collusion, and preferably plenty of time. Unpremeditated impulses were often frustrated by such hurdles. The frustrated resorted to petting as a substitute. 'There was necking (acceptable), soul kissing (exciting, dangerous) and petting, which was subdivided into above the waist and below. The last two were beyond the pale. The trick was to stay very, very popular without going 'all the way'. Like most girls of my generation, I managed to graduate from High School with my virginity intact,' wrote Janet Harris looking back on the Fifties in *The Prime of Ms America*. In England a debutante of 1957, Anne Browning, looked back on her season in *Dance Little Lady* in similar terms: 'If there was sex in the bushes, no one knew about it and it certainly wasn't the accepted thing. If you went out to dinner, you didn't think of how to get out of going to bed with him, it was how to get out of the car without kissing him.' The British film *Genevieve* (1953) was unusually piquant for the time because the old car's destination was tacitly acknowledged to be a 'dirty weekend' in Brighton.

It is an extraordinary fact that in 1954 the hero of a bestselling novel like *Lucky Jim* never once gets to the point of making love to any of the

girls he pursues. One expels him from her bedroom when he is drunk
and hopeful with a brisk 'Out you go!' Another, after describing her
loveless relationship with an unsatisfactory husband, is amazed at Jim
Dixon's remark that she would have been better off if she hadn't
married. 'I couldn't do anything else, could I?' 'Why not?' he asks,
reasonably enough. 'Christ, haven't you been listening? I was *in love*.'
It was still taken as self-evident in even the most up-to-date fiction that
being in love normally had only one outcome, marriage. Wedlock was
not only a solution to urgent physical needs, it was a social duty. 'People
got married with the same sense of cultural duty that people today
(often the same people) get divorced,' according to the novelist Malcolm
Bradbury, 'You owed it to yourself and to the times . . . There was a
secret, suspect taste for girls of rather better background than oneself:
hypergamy – marrying upward – a Fifties custom extensively explored in
Osborne's play *Look Back In Anger*.'

Upward sexual-social mobility was a favourite theme of Fifties
writers. It was what got Joe Lampton to the top. It was the usual reason
for the angry young hero's spleen; Jimmy Porter goads the hapless
colonel's daughter, Alison, as immobile and submissive as the very
ironing board at which she uncomplainingly stands, for being middle
class. But he does not complain of her being a placid, ironing housewife.
Jimmy and Alison ended the play as playmates pretending to be squirrels and bears. If that sounds nauseatingly juvenile, it had a certain
aptness in the Fifties when marriage was for many an institution for
recreating one's childhood and centering life once more on the nursery.

'After 1949,' wrote Betty Friedan, 'Career Woman suddenly became
pejorative, denoting a ball-busting, man-eating harpy, a miserable
neurotic witch from whom man and child should flee for very life.' That
may be an exaggeration for polemical purposes, but pressures against
career women were extreme in the Fifties, especially in America. It
would not have been necessary otherwise to insert an advertisement like
this in the *New Yorker*:

> Would You Have Your Baby
> Delivered By A WOMAN DOCTOR?
> An Appeal to women by
> Eleanor Roosevelt
> Women! – Help the institution helping women – The New York Infir-
> mary – 1,145 babies last year – These women doctors have shown their
> skill and knowledge are in every way equal to the best in the medical
> profession!

Betty Friedan, who was to give the whole phenomenon of fulfilment-through-motherhood a name – *The Feminine Mystique* – also made a revealing admission when she came to look back on those unliberated years in a later book (*It Changed My Life*):

> To be honest, those years were not all self-delusion. The babies, the bottles, the cooking, the diapering, the burping, the carriage wheeling, the pressure cooker, the barbecue, the playground and doing-it-yourself was more comfortable, more safe, secure and satisfying than that supposedly glamorous 'career' in which you somehow didn't feel wanted and knew you weren't going to get anywhere.

This, of course, was exactly what the heroines of women's magazine stories felt in those years when they decided to chuck New York and go home to marry Henry. *Look* magazine put out this breath-taking testimonial to the great American mother in 1956:

> The wondrous creature marries younger than ever, bears more babies and looks and acts far more feminine than the 'emancipated' girl of the Twenties or Thirties. If she makes an old-fashioned choice and lovingly tends a garden and a bumper crop of children, she rates louder Hosannas than ever before.

Two doctors who attained the status of gurus to the decade added the awesome sanction of Freudian psychology to the doctrine of putting motherhood first – Doctors Bowlby and Spock. Dr John Bowlby was the author of a bestseller, *Child Care And The Growth Of Love* (1953), which popularized the theory of Maternal Deprivation, the gist of which was – and is – that the first five years of a child's life are crucial. Deprived of its mother's constant care in those years, it will grow up emotionally handicapped, incapable of forming deep relationships and might steal in an attempt to compensate for a lack of mother love. Such a theory might have been tailor-made for the justification of the housebound mother. Both evidence and conclusions were of dubious general application. But nobody then dared question the magical properties of the first five years when Oedipal fantasies were supposed to be raging in the unconscious. Maternal deprivation was made the scapegoat for retarded development, anxiety and guilt feelings, promiscuity, instability and divorce – even for stunted growth. It took the place in mid-twentieth century demonology that masturbation filled for the Victorians.

Bowlby wrote of 'the absolute need of infants and toddlers for the continuous care of their mothers. Some will exclaim "Can I then *never* leave

my child?"' And if some did, the answer was No – or Not for more than
a week. Even then they were warned to expect emotional aloofness on
their return. 'I don't think a week's holiday away from your child is worth
the inevitable upset,' Bowlby declared. Above all, he insisted sternly,
'The mother of young children is not free, or at least should not be free,
to earn.' And that was that. The Fifties graduate mothers were no more
inclined to argue with the infallibility of Freud than monsignori argued
with the infallibility of the Pope.

   You might think there was something wrong with you if you did not
enjoy this form of dedicated slavery but at least a woman had someone to
share it with: her husband – and that third party in almost every educated parental home, Dr Benjamin Spock. It was *McCalls* magazine
which coined the emotive new word 'Togetherness' in 1954. Togetherness meant more than keeping each other company; it meant that a man's
place was also in the home. True, he had to make distracting, bread-
winning forays away from it but then, with glad and hastening steps, he
returned to the true centre of his life, the children whom he helped to
feed and bath and dress and play with, even cook for, in domestic
servantless days like these. Man's role was no longer confined to the
rough work, the barbecueing and the earnest car-washing. In 'the
symmetrical family', as the British sociologist Michael Young christened
it, the demarcation of roles was blurred. 'There is now no sort of work
in the home strictly reserved for the wives,' Young concluded. 'Even
clothes washing and bed making were frequently mentioned by husbands as things they did as well.' Such conscientious couples even tried
to share the child bearing as far as possible. 'Natural' childbirth was their
ideal. A process so hedged about with medical mystery and old wives'
tales that no man was allowed to share in it now became an experience he
must not miss for the world. Fathers-to-be attended the ante-natal
clinics and classes – typically taken by a tough and childless instructress
– in order to be taught breathing exercises and given labour notes for the
day. Erna Wright, one of the chief apostles of Dr Grantly Dick Read in
England, wrote, 'The experience *ought* to be shared as part of Togetherness.' Togetherness and self-help in the birth process, followed as a
matter of course by breast feeding, is now embraced with less evan-
gelical fervour than it was by Fifties pioneer couples.

   Dr Spock's *Baby And Child Care* was published first in the United
States in 1947 and in Britain in 1955 and there were mothers who
boasted they had worn out several copies. Its worldwide sale was to
reach twenty million copies. In fact it is more than one book. The

second edition in the Fifties was much revised, and the third edition, the Sixties version, still more so, each time diluting a little more the original message of permissive parenthood. The 'Permissive Society' could be said to have begun in the cradles of the Spock babies of the Forties and Fifties, who became the student protestors of the Sixties. Spock's basic purpose was to reassure. Parents were encouraged to trust their commonsense and instinct ('You know more than you think you do'). In contrast with the previous orthodoxy of rigid feeding by timetable and letting babies cry rather than 'spoil' them, he advised natural loving care as the guide. He also went along with the Bowlby theory to the extent of discouraging mothers from working: 'the extra money she might earn or the satisfaction she might receive is not so important after all.' Later this was revised to the hedging advice to discuss the matter with a social worker before deciding. But by the third edition Spock had withdrawn a longish way from the doctrine that natural loving care cures all ills. 'Easy-going parents must not be afraid to be firm,' he was suggesting, 'Moderate strictness is not harmful.' By 1974 he was sounding the danger warning with something like panic. He prefaced a book called *Bringing Up Children In A Difficult Time* with a 'Statement of an anti-permissive author': 'How did I ever get the reputation of being an advocate of excessive permissiveness?' he asked plaintively and disingenuously. He should have read his earlier editions.

So it was that a generation of highly educated women occupied their minds with Bowlby and Spock and *The Joy Of Cooking* and little else. Not only did they disclaim any career but motherhood, they even began to question the need for the higher education itself. A *Guardian* article noted: 'A group of Girton, Cambridge, undergraduates in 1959 agreed on television that politics was not a good career for women. It was unfeminine and difficult to combine with marriage. After marriage, only the exceptional woman is now going to go on working outside her home.'

And yet in 1953 another keenly awaited publication lit a fuse which eventually would explode many an illusion of carefully tended domestic bliss. It was the second Kinsey Report, entitled *Sexual Behaviour In The Human Female*. As bombshells went, it outclassed Dr Alfred Kinsey's previous findings about the Human Male. The sexual behaviour referred to turned out to be sexual misbehaviour by the standards of the time and on a widespread scale. Half of the 6,000 women questioned admitted to having intercourse before marriage and a quarter of them to adulterous intercourse after marriage. Pious shock and horror was expressed at this frailty in the face of temptation – far

John French's photograph of Barbara Goalen, in long gloves, of course

more so than at the evidence that men behaved in the same way. But the really challenging upshot of the report was not this predictable hypocrisy. It was the reaction to the evidence that women were the equals, if not more than the equals, of men in sexual responsiveness and capacity. The established, and now publicized, fact that women's sexual capacity increases with age, at least until the late twenties, and stays at this peak for decades, while men's is already declining, came as a shock both to men, who suddenly discovered they were the unlucky sex, and to women who had not realized what they had been missing.

Kinsey and his colleagues had also broken a taboo by openly discussing the female orgasm, a subject still shrouded in misinformation. His finding was that the capacity to experience it was much more highly developed in wives who had indulged in intercourse before marriage than in those who had remained chaste – in short there was much to be said against chastity. The report also found what a lot of sexual incompatibility and discontent existed. Two-thirds of the marriages investigated were in danger at some point because of sexual dissatisfaction.

Kinsey himself refrained from moral judgments. But such findings as these were greeted with dismay and defiant incredulity by professional moralists and church leaders. For the uncommitted public, however, there were two effects of startling importance: sexual frankness took an immense leap forward and the image of women could be said to have been changed for ever. 'Any picture America had of its women being shy, gentle creatures living sheltered lives, untainted by the world, is shattered by the facts in the report,' commented one newspaper typically. Even more than the image was shattered. If women could enjoy sex as much as men, as the report affirmed, then the implication was that they always should and those who realized they were not achieving Kinsey's statistical norm of orgasm soon asked themselves why not ? Those who had accepted the old beliefs about women – her slower sexual arousal, natural chastity and requirement for serious emotional involvement – were bound to ask themselves whether they had been led up the garden path. It can hardly be pure coincidence that within three years of Kinsey's appearance the limits of permissible sexual explicitness in the arts and entertainment had radically changed and with them the public image of the ideal woman as projected in, above all, films.

The Fifties saw two quite different examples of feminity held up for admiration. The model queens of the magazine covers, Suzy Parker in America and Barbara Goalen in England, were ladies who were photo-graphed in long gloves. Miss Parker said she thanked God for high cheek bones every time she looked in a mirror and, on cover after cover, very little beyond her cheek bones was exposed. Barbara Goalen seldom appeared without a liberal helping of diamonds or pearls at throat, wrist and ears. Grace Kelly, every inch a lady on screen, became every inch a princess when she married Prince Rainier in 1956 and became Her Serene Highness of Monaco. Claire Bloom, Chaplin's girl protégé in *Limelight* (1952), had none of the waif-like frailty of Paulette Goddard in *City Lights* (1931) but a look of cool composure and high caste. Nobody could have called Katharine Hepburn, Ingrid Bergman, Deborah Kerr or Vivien Leigh 'sex objects'. They were objects of high style, like Garbo and Dietrich. But their magnetism was beginning to be chal-lenged as early as 1953 by Marilyn Monroe, playing the busty gold-digger, Lorelei Lee, in *Gentlemen Prefer Blondes* alongside Jane Russell, whose bust, supported by a specially cantilevered bra designed by her master Howard Hughes, was the most noticeable asset she had.

The bust, bosom or cleavage was for the Fifties the apotheosis of erogenous zones. The breasts were the apples of all eyes. Never in this

century at least had so much respect been paid to mammary development. The very concentration of attention on female breasts seemed to
swell them with pride to melon-like proportion – or disproportion, for
they would flatten and disappear just as mysteriously ten years later.
And Fifties gentlemen actually *did* prefer blondes. Three out of ten
brunettes dyed their hair blonde to compete. It was as though men,
American men particularly, underwent a wave of nostalgia for maternal
breast memories. Brassieres upholstered with foam rubber were produced as beauty aids even for the well-endowed and even for pre-
pubescent girls. Whole careers were built on breasts. Jayne Mansfield's
were insured for a million dollars. According to her publicists, who had
little else except her lubricious reputation to publicize, they measured
40 inches. She herself, taking a deep breath, once claimed 44.

In the competition for titillation Britain put her best bust forward in
the equally platinum, equally pneumatic person of Diana Dors (37–24–
35, as the newspapers always labelled her). She was a typical Fifties
phenomenon, a celebrity contrived out of sex appeal and publicity
alone, both of them rather naive and innocent by the standards of subsequent hype and hoop-la. The pictures she shot for the cinema were
negligible compared to the pictures she shot for pure publicity. Perhaps
the most notorious was the photograph in a mink bikini with rhinestone
straps paddling a gondola at the Venice film festival of 1955 – a picture
that inspired a musical on the London stage. When she reached her
ambition, Hollywood, over-zealous publicity backfired on her: she was
pushed into her own swimming pool by a sensation-seeking photographer along with her husband, Dennis Hamilton, who had vowed to
make her 'the female Errol Flynn'. The subsequent punch-up led to
such headlines as 'Go Home Mr. Dors And Take Diana With You'.
Hollywood did not welcome British competition at its own game.

Miss Dors, who has since shown herself to be a capable character
actress, remembers her bubble-bathing days as a cushion for male
dreams with amused tolerance:

> In 1951, when I was nineteen, I became the first home-grown sex
> symbol in austerity Britain. It was like being a naughty seaside post-
> card. Men have always been hung up on breasts, especially American
> men, and in those days it was the only part of the body which could
> be shown. The Americans started it with Jane Russell and were also the
> most hypocritical about it. On American television they would insist on
> putting a piece of gauze across my bosom. When I was filmed wearing
> a bikini, it had to have two lower halves. The one for American show-

Jayne Mansfield, Queen of the Erogenous Zones

Diana Dors, 'the first home-grown sex symbol in Austerity Britain'

ing had to cover the navel. When I look back on those days now, I think how perfectly harmless it all was by comparison with today's pornography. We never really showed anything. Under all those carefully arranged bubbles there was a flesh-coloured leotard. It was a gigantic con, really.

But nothing could compare with the two universal sex-symbols of the decade, Marilyn Monroe and Brigitte Bardot. One was the illegitimate child of an insane mother, the product of orphanages and foster homes. The other was the offspring of doting, bourgeois parents, who should have given off the opposite kind of vibrations. Yet both women brought a more intense and child-whorish eroticism to the screen than had been seen before, while retaining a suggestion of innocence at the heart of it. Both appeared as nearly naked as possible after the censor had cut or covered his pound of flesh. And both were obviously walking, wriggling and giggling embodiments of Dr Kinsey's findings. Not only did they enjoy, indeed relish, healthy sexual appetites, they made it obvious that they would satisfy them where and when they felt like it, on their own terms. Both of them gave out pert repartee in the traditional Mae West manner. 'What did you have on?' – 'I had the radio on' said Monroe. 'How do you like Englishmen?' – 'To tell the truth I haven't tried one yet,' replied Bardot. But there the resemblance to the old movie queens stopped. These two treated *men* as playthings. Their deepest emotions were narcissist. Their true love affairs were with the camera and with those flickering images of themselves which turned on the rest of the public as well. Their lack of involvement on any deep level with men was, in its way, a liberation and perhaps explains why so many women, too, admired them, copied their looks and envied their freedom of behaviour.

Monroe's neurotic and unhappy character was not then obvious. Only two or three years before her breakthrough, her anonymous photograph, naked, ripe, glistening and stretched out with parted lips on red velvet, was adorning calendars in half the bars and filling station offices across America. The calendar was 'discovered' to help publicize an early film, *Clash By Night* (1951), and the fuss put her in the headlines and the box office draw category. By 1956 she had become Hollywood's best-known female and had married in succession the sportsmen's baseball hero, Joe Di Maggio, and the intellectuals' Broadway hero, Arthur Miller. She was also the girl most men wanted to go to bed with. Her prestige could be gauged from the quality of her attendants: Miller, Lee Strasberg, her acting coach, guru of the fashionable Actors' Studio, and

Laurence Olivier, her leading man in *The Prince And The Showgirl*, whom she infuriated by her 'unprofessionalism'. She was also a kind of mascot of the liberal intelligentsia – had she not come up the hard way from the very bottom of the heap to stand by Miller's side defying the anti-Communist witch-hunters who wanted to jail him?

On this very honeymoon she arrived in England, an unusually star-struck England, took to bicycling around her home in Windsor Great Park – and hit disaster. The filming was bedevilled by her personal problems, her sleeping problems, her lateness on the set, her acting problems. Her Method acting coach, Mrs Lee Strasberg, was banned from the set after telling Olivier, the world's foremost non-Method actor, that his performance was artificial. Ultimately there had to be added to the list her marital problems. Miller found himself playing the role of her doctor, manager, analyst and trouble-shooter with an increasingly frustrated, impatient and high-handed Olivier, who was having marital problems himself with the mentally troubled Vivien Leigh, who had just announced a miscarriage at the age of forty-one. By the end of the decade Monroe's marriage was only just hanging together. She had needed forty-two takes to get her lines right in one scene of *Some Like It Hot*. In *Let's Make Love* she had a well-publicized affair with her co-star, Yves Montand. The last service Miller could do was to write the script of *The Misfits* for her. She played it opposite Clark Gable just before he died.

She was never more than a light comedy performer who made a virtue of her acting limitations by being amusing as she demonstrated them. But her caressable curves and wondering eyes and hushed baby voice dominated the pleasanter fantasies of people all round the world. She did much to mitigate the charmlessness of the Eisenhower-Dulles-strategic-bomber image of America. It would have been hard for the toughest, most stable and secure character to stand up to being dream symbol to the world. Norma Jean Baker, her name, her face, her life altered by exploitation and cosmetic surgery, stood on too little solid ground to remain certain of her own identity behind the camera's image and two years later, at thirty-six, she was dead.

It was also the camera that created Brigitte Bardot. Her picture on the cover of *Elle* magazine, when she was still a schoolgirl of fifteen from a strict bourgeois family, led her to Roger Vadim, who let her out of her birdcage by marrying her in 1952 despite parental reluctance. In 1953 he unveiled her at the Cannes film festival where she stole the limelight to such an extent that established stars could only get their pictures

The famous nude calendar picture of Marilyn Monroe by Tom Kelley

BB au naturel: the opening shot of ET DIEU CRÉA LA FEMME

taken by posing with her. On the traditional visit to the American aircraft carrier in the harbour, reported *Paris-Match*: 'With a toss of her
head that sent her ponytail flying, the *Midway* was engulfed in a streak of
lightning from thousands of flashbulbs and cries of admiration.' Just as
Monroe represented the acceptable face of the United States, Bardot
symbolized the France which the world liked to imagine. Bardot's
sensuality, too, was not that of a *femme fatale* but an *enfant fatale*. Not
for nothing was she dubbed BB – pronounced Bébé. She was the first of
a line of 'nymphets' who would also include Carroll Baker in *Baby Doll*
and be raised to the permanence of art in Nabokov's *Lolita*.

Her baby chin, her drooping petal of lower lip, her tousled mane of
blonde tresses, her girlish gingham dresses with white *décolletage*, combined to create a look of chaste girlhood with a strong hint that she
would be quite prepared for you to sully it. It was a look copied by
would-be sex kittens from sixteen to twenty-six all over Western
Europe. She made the calendar girls of the Fifties, with their airbrushed
flesh and gleaming swimsuits, look like dinosaurs.

But at first resistance was considerable. Vadim's *Et Dieu Créa La
Femme* (1956) was the watershed film which liberalized the cinema, but
only after it had run into censorship trouble everywhere, especially in
the United States where the Hollywood decency code still insisted on
separate beds for married couples. 'The people of Philadelphia don't
want this type of film,' declared its District Attorney, 'It's dirt for dirt's
sake.' Nevertheless eight million people saw it and, even with the cuts,
they were impressed. What did they see? In fact: a full-length cinemascope colour spread of BB on her stomach at the water's edge displaying

The Sex Kitten as marketed

a bottom 'as bare as a censor's eyeball' said *Time*; BB rescued from the sea in a clinging wet dress; her wedding night concealed behind some strategically tossed bed linen; and her breasts showing in faint outline through the sheet she is holding up for modesty's sake (they were never seen unveiled). But in their mind's eye, audiences were convinced she had been virtually naked throughout. Roger Vadim, a shrewd marketer of his wife's attractions, had calculated this. He had to show the print a second time to censorship boards to convince them they had imagined the nudity. He now explains the phenomenon in this way:

> The reason people thought she was naked all through the film was because she displayed a different attitude to sex from the one that pre-

vailed in films at that time. She was not submissive. Neither was she a whore. She was not like Deborah Kerr, Grace Kelly, Michele Morgan. For the Americans it was the first declaration in a film that love for pleasure is not sin. Even in France, which had been permissive over books and plays, films were treated surprisingly strictly. The difference between the way we saw life as young people – especially the amoral attitude to sex – and the conventional way of portraying it on screen was so great that I knew we were on the verge of a big change. After *Et Dieu Créa La Femme* they accepted the idea that love could be filmed erotically without being pornographic. Today, of course, it is a film for children Though it was far from being a great film it altered the boundaries and opened the way for the New Wave of realism, cinema *vérité*. That was the end of the cinematic euphemisms for making love – the misty dissolve, the rocketing fireworks or rearing waves which had been the director's equivalent of the novelist's three dots . . .

With all eyes – or rather all lenses – on her, Bardot soon put her emancipated amorality into practice. Before filming was finished, she had left Vadim, her director husband, for Jean-Louis Trintignant, her actor husband in the story, a situation which Vadim took with apparent aplomb as he continued to encourage her to strive for even more realism in his rival's arms. Soon the summer revels of BB at the then uncrowded, unchic little port of St Tropez, with a succession of young actors and guitar players (Trintignant soon withdrew to the peace of Army service), were spied on and peeped at by the photographers and published in countless magazines and newspapers. She held her Mediterranean court in consort with Françoise Sagan whose bitter-sweet novelettes, like *Bonjour Tristesse*, also revolved round heroines who chose and discarded their lovers at whim. Mademoiselle Sagan was celebrated for the variety of her partners and for driving fast sports cars in bare feet as an example of the free life. Between them these two young women filled the vacuum of French life in the dying days of the Fourth Republic awaiting De Gaulle's return to power. It was reported that BB was the basis of forty-seven per cent of French conversation – how this was computed is not easy to see but people said such things. Her smuggled photographs were highly prized and highly priced in Moscow. And though the whole cult was largely founded on a pout, a posture, a rear view of ponytail and hindquarters and some carefully arranged shower curtains, sheets and wet clothing, the significance of it was that a young woman created a new lifestyle indisputably of the Fifties in which she took a man's attitude to sex. Or rather, showed that a woman's and a man's attitude to sex could henceforward be one and the same.

Sexual intercourse began
In 1963
Which was rather late for me

lamented Philip Larkin wryly, stating the received opinion about the permissiveness of the Sixties. But the facts strongly suggest that the current of liberation really began to flow in 1953, the year not only of the Kinsey Report but of two significant debuts: those of James Bond and *Playboy*. Ian Fleming's *Casino Royale* (1953) was not a bestseller but it introduced James Bond, the agent with the number 007, a licence to kill and a taste for the best of everything, especially girls. His career of sado-sophistication, or 'snobbery with violence' as it was dubbed, brought his sales up to eighty million copies and does not need chronicling again except to point the contrast between him and his forbears in popular secret agent fiction. John Buchan's heroes and Sapper's Bulldog Drummond were as patriotically gritty as he and deserved as well of their country, but their relations with women, if any, were models

A typical Parisian background for the author of BONJOUR TRISTESSE

of chivalry and restraint. Bond's exotic tastes – the dry Martini shaken, not stirred, and the monogrammed cigarettes, outclassed Captain Hugh Drummond's preference for beer and his cigarette case with 'Turkish this side, Virginian that.' But when it came to women, the Captain was a non-starter. For all his Mayfair address in Half Moon Street, Drummond led an irreproachable married life with Phyllis – that is, when she had not been temporarily kidnapped by a fiend in human shape. Bond treated each assignment on Her Majesty's Secret Service as an invitation to a gastronomic and sexual binge. His licence to seduce was as much his right as his licence to kill. The girls were always willing and always high-caste, even if like the Creole beauty, Solitaire, of *Live And Let Die* (1954) they were also half-caste:

> She took his face between her two hands and held it away, panting. Her eyes were bright and hot. Then she brought his lips against hers again and kissed him long and lasciviously as if she was the man and he the woman . . . "Curse this arm," he said, "I can't hold you properly or make love to you. It hurts too much."

But once our hero was free and the villain disposed of, M always granted him 'passionate leave', thus setting the seal of HMG's approval on well-earned fornication, unthinkable in Colonel Buchan's day. And his effortless success compared very piquantly with Lucky Jim's struggles to rouse the opposite sex to carnal delights in the same year of 1954. Kingsley Amis, who wrote an adventure for Bond as well as creating Jim Dixon, reflects aptly on the reasons for his: 'What happened was that we came in at the tail end of the literary tradition to the effect that no decent girl enjoys sex – only tarts were supposed to do that. Buchan's heroes believed this. Fleming's didn't. I remember thinking, when Bond arrived, this is more like it. Bond enjoyed sex without losing his status as a servant of the Queen'.

The linking of sexual enjoyment with social status also proved a golden formula for Hugh Hefner, who had failed as a cartoonist and copy-writer on *Esquire* in Chicago and was doing none too well as a promoter of a magazine called *Children's Activities*. His next venture, worked out on the kitchen table and launched in November 1953, was called *Playboy* and concerned adults' activities of an uninhibited kind. He announced his credo unashamedly in his first editorial: 'We believe we are filling a publishing need only slightly less important than the one just taken care of by the Kinsey Report.' *Playboy* was described as a pleasure-primer, its symbol was a rabbit and its bait was the Playmate of the month, the girl who was unfolded in the centre wearing a staple through her navel but not much else. In the first issue she was none other than Marilyn Monroe in the notorious nude calendar pose, on which Hefner spent $500, most of the capital he had borrowed to launch the magazine. His priorities proved to have been right. He sold 53,000 copies (now collector's exhibits) and made a profit. Before he marketed *Playboy* – and got fined for sending the Monroe picture through the mails – the only full-page colour nudes outside nudist magazines were the aborigines of the *National Geographic Magazine*. By its fifth birthday *Playboy* was beating Hefner's old employer, *Esquire*, with a circulation of 850,000. In the first year it had been careful to disassociate itself from the truck-driver's pin-up image by boasting of the high social and business standing of its readers . . . 'seven corporation presidents, fourteen vice-presidents, psychiatrists, a mortician and three embalmers' were listed among the first subscribers. The embalmers may well have been attracted by the waxed and polished surface of the monthly Playmates. Miss January and Miss July were posed as carefully to conceal as to reveal. The retoucher's air-brush was much in evidence and towels, tights, flimsy nightdresses and even scanty skirts were tactfully placed, to mitigate the wrath of the Federal post office. What Playmates invariably displayed, giving generous measure, were a collector's pair of breasts. 'If you had to sum up the idea of *Playboy* it is anti-Puritanism,' said Hefner at the time. 'We offered an alternate life-style with more play-and-pleasure orientation.' In spite of the cumbersome public-relations prose, the editorial message came through loud and clear: enjoy yourself. The Puritan ethic was being replaced by the Hedonist ethic, right there in the heartland.

Hefner himself was soon to develop this idea in his so-called 'Playboy Philosophy' at tedious length. As the Fifties ended he was on the point of multiplying millions by opening the first Playboy Club, in Chicago, where the girls, not the customers, were dressed as rabbits. Typical of the ambivalence of the anti-Puritan ethic in Hefner's hands, they were supposed to be untouchable. Their Bunny tails, as Norman Mailer put it, were 'puffs of chastity which bobbled as they walked.' The Lucullan excesses which Hefner promised were all in the mind, at any rate as long as the Fifties lasted. Later he was to acquire his pleasure dome, his fabled mansion, his circular bed, his non-stop room service of food, drink, movies, closed circuit television and girls from the Bunnies' dormitory, the Xanadu of the Middle West over which he presided as Chicago's Kubla Khan. Or so the stories went, and excellent publicity they proved to be. But he grew rich on no more than a promise. He himself was still quietly married to a girl he had been introduced to at high school. He admitted to have been a virgin at twenty-two. His friend, Mort Sahl, wrote: 'It is predictable that a shy man should merchandise anticipation of pleasure – with no delivery date. For the twenty years I knew him he had been close to only three girls, maybe only one.'

It was the fact that people believed sexual liberation was going on – somewhere else – that was influential, even if it was not really happening. The effect on the image of the happy, fecund housewife and mother of the suburbs was puzzling. Women felt they were being asked to fulfil two contradictory roles, that of the homemaker and the seductress, simultaneously. Traditionally these two stereotypes of womanhood had been kept separate. The idealized goddess and the erotic temptress were realized in the persons of different women. When they began to overlap women felt confused and disoriented. Monroe and Bardot could hardly be held up as examples of the joys of fidelity, domesticity and mother-hood which were being hymned in the magazines. Their liberated lives could not be carried on in the child-centred suburbs. Sex-as-procreation was being separated from sex-as-fun. Previous attempts to do this had always foundered on the fact that the fun usually resulted pretty soon in procreation but at this very time field trials of the contra-ceptive pill were taking place which would soon make the division practical and permanent for the first time in history.

'The suburban housewife was the dream image of the young American women and the envy, it was said, of women all over the world . . . She had everything that women ever dreamed of.' So wrote Betty Friedan, who *was* a suburban housewife in the act of writing the book which was to shatter this image. The housewives in question found that they were not especially fulfilled. After all, they were the women who bought and devoured a novel which revealed the unsatisfied desires seething beneath American small-town togetherness – *Peyton Place*, which earned Grace Metalious $56,000 a year in royalties.

They were also the women who went more and more to seek the aid of psychiatrists and marriage counsellors. The Marriage Guidance Council, in its infancy in England as the Fifties began, expanded its clientele by 30 per cent to about 18,000 people, and it was then only prepared to counsel those whose sexual relations took place within marriage. By 1959 a third of those cases were about the way these rela-tions had failed to meet expectations, particularly women's expectations, since twice as many women as men applied to it. The chief casualties of the Kinsey-backed revolution in sexual attitudes were, interestingly enough, husbands. 'Many clients try to overcome their difficulties by recourse to books on sexual technique. This is much commoner among men than among women,' wrote one of the best-known counsellers, J. H. Wallis, in *Marriage Observed*. 'Sometimes, literally, the husband had the book at the bedside . . . It is difficult for a woman to understand a man's sensitivity to any slur on his virility. "Next time it will be better" comforts him as little as "Never mind, we'll open a tin of something" soothes her wounded self-esteem at a spoiled supper.'

Despite marriage guidance, divorces were climbing steadily. In 1950 there were 385,000 divorces in the United States compared with 264,000 in the last pre-war year, 1940. Britain's pre-war rate of divorce had quadrupled from 8,000 to 32,000. The Royal Commission on Marriage and Divorce, appointed in 1951, was greatly alarmed by the trend. When it reported in 1955 it demanded less permissiveness, not more. Its members declared that divorce by consent would lead to social disaster. In a gesture worthy of King Canute they went further: 'It may become necessary to consider whether the community as a whole would not be happier and more stable if it abolished divorce altogether,' they wrote.

Why was 'Togetherness' proving so difficult to achieve, despite the fact that everybody believed in it? During the later Fifties a new cartoonist called Jules Feiffer began to contribute faint pencil drawings to an unorthodox paper, *The Village Voice*. His tortured men, baffled by neurotic women, were the new decade's equivalent of Thurber's mid-Western Valkyries of the war between the sexes, only now both sexes were tied in impotent knots of ill-understood Freudian theory. A typical Feiffer couple, solemnly offering each other elaborate explanations of why they could not hit it off, are asking in their thought balloons why the other partner can't, for Pete's sake, make a straight pass. *Sick Sick Sick* he called his first collection and subtitled it 'A Guide to Non-Confident Living'. 'I'm trying to explain the complete breakdown in communications. People who are on intimate terms are incapable of expressing themselves to each other,' said the thin, melancholy Feiffer. In a revealing article, 'Men Really Don't Like Women' (*Look* magazine) he expressed himself capably, though pessimistically, enough: 'The American woman is a victim. Her trouble is she is doing comparatively well as a victim. Her problem is not taken seriously. Woman is a second-class victim. And what is her problem? We all know it is man . . . Man has always seen woman as his enemy. But he needs her.'

What he wrote was already forming in the minds of married women torn between homes and the lure of careers, between the roles of sex objects or earth mothers. What they had begun to realize was that they were getting a rough deal and that no one else would take any notice. 'Each suburban wife, as she made the beds, shopped for groceries, ate peanut-butter sandwiches with her children, chauffered Cubs and Brownies, lay beside her husband at night, was afraid to ask even of herself the silent question, "Is this all?"' *The Feminine Mystique*, which dared to put the silent question, did not see the light of day until 1963, when it sold three million copies, but it was already being written and its audience was waiting. In Britain in 1957 a third of married women were working again. They were being wooed back, because there was already full employment, as teachers and as nurses. Many of them went only partly for the money. It was often the better-off women who sought jobs. It was to escape boredom and the frustration of having no one to talk to all day but children. In 1958 the Civil Service led the way towards equality by granting equal pay. In the same year the Church of England led the way out of a moral impasse which trapped the Catholic Church by giving birth control its blessing under the name of Family Planning. By now there were fewer paeans of praise to fecundity in the magazines; instead they were asking 'Why Young Mothers Feel Trapped' (*Redbook*) or, with more than a hint of desperation, offering '58 Ways To Make Your Marriage More Exciting' (*Newsweek*). Graduate wives complained bitterly, especially in the *Guardian*, of living like cabbages. Ten years before, in the years of the baby boom, Simone de Beauvoir's *The Second Sex* was met with extreme hostility in France. In America a critic said confidently she did not know what life was all about. Years later the feminists were inspired by her most famous statement, 'One is not born a woman, one becomes one', to conclude that the inferior status of 'the second sex' was not a natural phenomenon but a man-made one. But at the time, characteristically, it was suggested that the book must have been written by Jean-Paul Sartre, the companion whom de Beauvoir was famous for not being married to. Once the contraceptive pill (invented in 1952) had become available and accepted and made any further baby boom unlikely, years of frustrated and dammed-up feminism were ready to burst in the new wave of women's liberation. The Fifties were not ripe for it, but all through their later years the question became more urgent: what is the place of women in the second half of the twentieth century? The Fifties gave two conventional answers – the home and the bed. Both were confidently given and both were found wanting.

CHAPTER THREE

The Cold War

The very words 'Cold War' are now almost as dead and emotionally dust-laden as 'The War of the Spanish Succession' or 'The War of Jenkin's Ear'. It is almost incomprehensible that at the height of Cold War Fever (and temperatures ran very high) people like Mrs Eleanor Roosevelt sincerely believed people would be 'better dead than Red' as the slogan popularly put it. The question of the decade – 'Are you now, or have you ever been, a Communist?' – put to thousands of civil servants, teachers, writers and actors at tribunals and loyalty hearings, was sometimes put in another, more colourful form. 'Are you now, or have you ever been, a member of a godless conspiracy controlled by a foreign power?' Counsel Richard Arens would thunder on behalf of the listening House of Representatives Committee on UnAmerican Activities. It was not hard to guess what was the wrong answer. But it is hard to re-create the atmosphere of fanaticism and fear in which it seemed unsurprising that the gramophone records of Paul Robeson were expunged from the catalogues and the novels of Theodore Dreiser and the detective stories of Dashiell Hammett were purged from public libraries. You would not have supposed it possible to aid the Communist cause by stripping, yet Gypsy Rose Lee was banned because years before she had spoken up for the Hollywood Anti-Nazi League. There was a word for that kind of thing: it branded you as a 'premature anti-Fascist'. So acutely did some people feel menaced by the 'godless conspiracy' that in Brooklyn, when a sewer explosion blew out the man-holes, they panicked and shouted 'The Russians!'; in Boston an antique exhibition barred Russian pieces from being exhibited; in Bournemouth the conductor of the municipal symphony orchestra barred pieces by Shostakovitch from being played. A Hollywood studio decided it was not safe to make a picture about the peacemaker, Hiawatha, because 'It might be regarded as a message for peace and therefore helpful to Communist designs'. In twenty-six states 'Reds' were disqualified from running for office, working as civil servants, and some from holding passports or drawing unemployment money. In Birmingham, Alabama, you could be banished from the city for being seen talking to a Communist, which was held to be committing a public nuisance.

In the Cold War irrational behaviour like this acquired a sort of sacred aura. No anti-Communist action or pronouncement could possibly be ridiculous. Fear infected Americans with a mass hysteria which had not been seen since the Great Crash. Like 1929, 1949 had been a bad year for believing that God was on America's side. It was the year when Mao Tse-Tung took final control of the Chinese mainland, despite the $3 billion of aid which had been lavished on Chiang Kai-Shek. Suddenly the 180 million people loyal to Communism at the end of the war had turned into 800 million. 'The odds were nine to one in our favour in 1944,' said Congressman Richard Nixon grimly, 'Today the odds are five to three against us!' Soon they were longer still. Far sooner than anyone thought possible, the Russians exploded an atomic bomb. In June, 1950, North Korean Communists nearly overran the southern half of the artificially divided country, the half which the U.S. had occupied and paid for since the war. Fortunately for President Truman the American troops dispatched to stop them were officially declared a United Nations army engaged in a 'police action' to restore peace. So, although the North Koreans were soon to be backed by 250,000 Communist Chinese troops, officially there was still no hot war – only a cold one, in two versions, foreign and domestic.

The domestic Cold War began in earnest in Britain with a series of alarming spy cases. The worst came in January 1950, when Dr Klaus Fuchs, head of theoretical physics at the Harwell atomic research establishment of the Atomic Energy Authority, was arrested on information supplied by the FBI. Fuchs had worked on the atom bomb project at Los Alamos. 'When I learned the purpose of my work, I decided to inform Russia . . . I had no hesitation in giving all the information I had,' he said in his confession at the Old Bailey trial. 'All the information he had' was enough to save the Russians ten years' research. The Western sense of security was shattered. His fourteen-year sentence hardly evened the score. Congress demanded that the British be trusted with no more atomic secrets. When interrogated by the FBI in his British jail, Fuchs identified photographs of one of his contacts, Harry Gold, who named a trail of others which led eventually to an obscure machine-shop manager of Russian parentage, Julius Rosenberg, and his wife Ethel. Ethel's brother, David Greenglass, claimed he had passed on to Julius some sketches and notes from Los Alamos about the plutonium bomb dropped on Nagasaki. Sentencing the couple to death a year later the judge said, without any visible justification, 'I believe your conduct has already caused the Communist aggression in Korea, with resulting casualties exceeding 50,000 Americans.' In fact no one then knew what

Ethel and Julius Rosenberg – Spies or scapegoats?

had caused the Communist aggression in Korea. Much later, Khrushchev stated in his Memoirs that it was entirely the idea of the North Korean Leader, Kim Il Sung. 'It is not in my power, Julius and Ethel Rosenberg, to forgive you. Only the Lord can find mercy for what you have done,' said the judge. There were many then and there have been many since who believed the Rosenbergs were victims of an FBI frame-up but the American people were baying for scapegoats, not least for the grave reverses in Korea. Scapegoats were at hand.

Even greater passions were aroused by a spy case of absolutely no strategic significance whatever, the case of Alger Hiss, who was finally jailed in January 1950, after two years of allegation and wild rumour. What made Hiss significant was his impeccable background, his WASP family, his Harvard Law School education, his career on President Roosevelt's wartime staff and then in the State Department Far Eastern section, his acquaintance with Dean Acheson, Adlai Stevenson and John Foster Dulles. He was president of the Carnegie Endowment for International Peace when Whittaker Chambers, a renegade and self-confessed

In the British Embassy in Washington the Minister, Sir John Balfour, listens to the views of the white-suited First Secretary, Donald Maclean.

Communist 'spy' then on the staff of *Time* magazine, accused him of having passed him documents from the State Department during the late 1930s. No more celebrated case was brought before the House UnAmerican Activities Committee, where Representative Richard Nixon made his political reputation with it. If Alger Hiss could betray his country for the sake of Communism – and he is still trying to establish his innocence – where else among the highest in the land might treason be found?

By now it was all adding up to one conclusion. The great reverses in China and Korea, the Russian atom bomb, Hiss, Fuchs and the Rosenbergs . . . the explanation was . . . conspiracy! There must be a vast underground network of spies. In the coming witch-hunt thousands of people were to be deprived of their livelihood and reputation but, as we now know, the most serious spies went undetected. Donald Maclean had in 1950 been made head of the American department of the Foreign Office after dramatic breakdowns and drinking bouts. He had been found asleep on the floor of a taxi outside a night club and claimed he had hired it for the evening as his bedroom. He had lurched about a London drinking club soon after the Hiss case claiming 'I am the English Hiss!' No one thought this, and his habit of assuming a second personality whom he called 'Gordon' after the gin, should cast doubt on his fitness for promotion. He had spent most of the Forties in the Washington embassy, sat on the Anglo-American committee on atomic information and had a permanent and unrestricted pass to the headquarters of the Atomic Energy Commission, which he frequently used late at night. Meanwhile the noisy, more drunken and flagrantly homosexual Guy Burgess arrived to join the Washington embassy with a record of indiscretions which included loudly pointing out the local head of intelligence in a Gibraltar restaurant. He stayed with the first secretary, H. A. R. Philby, who had promised to keep an eye on him. Philby's job was to liaise with the FBI and CIA on intelligence matters. It was thanks to them that he learned that the hunt was on for a leak on the Washington embassy wartime staff which could only have been Maclean. According to Philby later, the FBI were still very much off the scent. 'Characteristically they had put in an immense amount of work resulting in an immense amount of waste paper. It had occurred neither to them nor to the British that a diplomat was involved.' Philby claimed he thoughtfully put them on the right track to divert suspicion from himself. At the same time he arranged for Burgess to be sent home to extricate Maclean before the net closed. Burgess got himself caught for speeding three times in the same day, caused a deliberate rumpus with his inimitable flair for trouble-making, and departed under an engineered cloud. What Philby did not guess was that, having warned Maclean for him, Burgess would join him on the night ferry to St Malo *en route* to Moscow, on 25 May 1951. He and Maclean were next glimpsed by the Western Press in the National Hotel, Moscow, in 1956. 'We are convinced we were right in doing what we did,' they said in a prepared statement. They did not, of course, mention that they fled because they knew the alternative would have been even less attractive, since at that time Philby was still in the West, having been publicly exonerated by Harold Macmillan. The 'English Hiss' would have served as a description of him too. Between the three of them, they shared intimacy with such Establishment groups as pre-war Cambridge, the Foreign Office, *The Times*, the BBC and the Athenaeum. It was not reassuring.

But British concern about a high-placed Communist conspiracy was nothing to American paranoia. Conspiracy was a favourite word of J. Edgar Hoover, the Top Cop of the FBI for twenty-five years, whose informants, telephone tappers, handwriting experts and double *agents provocateurs* had been harassing 'Reds', whether real or imaginary, since the war ended. 'A world-wide conspiracy embracing a third of the world's population' he pronounced the enemy to be, and added that it threatened 'the erasure of freedom, perhaps for ever, from the parchment of time' . . . a windy piece of rhetoric typical of the times if not of J. Edgar, whose taste ran to Tarzan movies where the dialogue is less verbose. However, the more scary his pronouncements, the bigger his budget became. But there was always room for one more in the Conspiracy hunt. 'How about Communists in government?' suggested a friend to Senator Joe McCarthy from Wisconsin, who was looking round for an issue to help get him re-elected. And so, on 9 February, 1950, to a startled audience of women Republicans in Wheeling, West Virginia, McCarthy raised the favourite bogey: 'How can we account for our present situation unless we believe that men high in this government are *concerting* to deliver us to disaster? This must be the product of a great *conspiracy*, on a scale so immense and of an infamy so black as to dwarf any previous such venture in the history of man.' There was the ultimate, definitive statement of the conspiracy theory of human affairs. Then, waving aloft a sheaf of papers, he uttered the famous lie that was to catapult him into the limelight for four years: 'I have here in my hand a list of 205 names that were made known to the Secretary of State as being members of the Communist Party and who nevertheless are still working and shaping policy in the State Department.' The list proved a flexible document in the days to come. Sometimes he said it contained eighty-one Communists, sometimes fifty-seven, sometimes 'a lot'. He never actually produced it or named the State Department Communists on it. His rambling six-hour speech about his 'cases' to the Senate left his fellow Senators confused, bewildered and finally despairing of ever making sense of the list. But he was careful to appeal to the have-nots against the privileged and college-educated 'who have been selling this nation out – the bright young men who are born with silver spoons in their mouths.' Just a month after Alger Hiss's conviction, no one felt like arguing. Even when the Senate's own inquiry reported that his charges were 'a fraud and a hoax' it did not stop his rocket rise to influence. The Republicans, led by Senator Taft, began to sense they had an election winner here. In that year's elections McCarthy went for

Senator Tydings of Maryland, who had pronounced him a fraud, with typical unscrupulousness. A faked picture in the campaign newspaper showed the senator juxtaposed as if in intimate conversation with a former Communist Party leader, Earl Browder. Tydings was unseated.

The other great Communist-hunter in Congress, Richard Nixon, was on the verge of being picked for Vice-President. He got one last bit of mileage out of the Hiss case. When Whittaker Chambers produced his book *Witness*, Mr Nixon turned book reviewer in the *Saturday Review*. He called it 'a great book which sheds a withering light on the nether-world of deceit, subversion and espionage which is the Communist conspiracy.' (What other word, indeed, would meet the case?) For Chambers, his witness of doubtful character, he found this Nixonian

' "*Nixie*" *the kind and the good*'

endorsement: 'Is it not better to tell the whole truth in the end than to refuse, as Hiss did, to tell it at all ?' Chambers, for his part, had given his endorsement in the book: 'During the case Nixon and his family were at our farm, encouraging me and comforting my family. My children have caught him lovingly in a nickname. To them he is always "Nixie", the kind and the good. I have a vivid picture of him standing by the barn and saying in his quietly savage way (he is the kindest of men) – "If the American people understood the real character of Alger Hiss, they would boil him in oil." ' His charm was at its peak. The Republicans, like Chambers, soon decided they wanted to go back to dear old Nixie.

These were the Cold Warriors who set the tone for the Fifties. None of them was more enthusiastic to turn on the heat and get the thing over than General Douglas MacArthur, the 'United Nations' commander in Korea, who was at pains to point out he had 'no direct connection with the United Nations whatsoever'. He, too, had a weakness for hellfire sermonizing – 'There can be no compromise with atheistic Communism, no half way in the preservation of freedom or religion. It must be all or nothing,' he declared, appealing to the American people from Korea over the President's head. After his 'over by Christmas' offensive into North Korea had ended in a rout he began to drop dark hints about Red China's inability to wage 'modern war'. He threatened 'an expansion of our military operations to its interior bases'. He suggested that North Korea should surrender to him personally any time it was ready. The Bomb sounded as good as dropped. When he publicly questioned Truman's decision not to use Chinese Nationalist troops in Korea, Truman decided the pretensions of his Caesar had gone far enough. 'I'm going to fire the son of a bitch right now,' he said. And so, after General Marshall had spent a night in meditation on the consequences, the failed haberdasher from Independence, Missouri, took on the seventy-year-old national warhorse with his belligerent scowl, his dark glasses and his frayed, oak-leaf-encrusted battle cap (he was believed to have a man on his staff who did nothing but fray his caps). 'I never did understand, an old man like that and a five-star general to boot, why he went around dressed up like a nineteen-year-old Second Lieutenant,' said Truman, reminiscing years afterwards to Merle Miller. 'There were times when he wasn't right in the head. And he just wouldn't let anybody near him who wouldn't kiss his ass.' And so the telegram was sent, a come-uppance which deserves quotation as an act that may have saved the world from early extinction by sheer megalomania: 'I deeply regret that it becomes my duty as President and Commander-in-

Chief of the United States military forces to replace you as Supreme Commander, Allied Powers; Commander-in-Chief, United Nations Command; Commander-in-Chief, Far East; and Commanding General, U.S. Army Far East. – Harry S. Truman, Commander-in-Chief.'

MacArthur, living legend and darling of the China Lobby which still hoped to see Chiang Kai-Shek back in China, returned to a public uproar which was definitely in his favour. 'Impeach the Judas in the White House' was typical of 78,000 telegrams and letters which poured into Washington. 'The son of a bitch ought to be impeached,' trumpeted McCarthy. The dismissed general received a bigger ticker-tape reception than Eisenhower's in 1945. He addressed Congress and a vast television audience with a Hollywood tear-jerker speech about his fifty-two years service, now ended. He was fading away 'like the old soldier in the ballad, an old soldier who tried to do his duty as God gave him the light to see that duty.' He may not have meant it, but that was precisely what he was about to do.

It may have disappointed many fearless patriots like John Wayne, who presided over the fragrantly entitled 'Motion Picture Alliance for the Preservation of American Ideals'. Wayne wrote: 'There are now and there were then (in the early Forties) a tight group of Communist conspirators in our midst . . . we didn't make "Hollywood" and "Red" synonymous. The Communists, their fellow-travellers and their dupes did that.' And the Duke made sure that they no longer gave employment in the studios to these conspirators. It may have disappointed the fearless patriot, Mickey Spillane, who wrote these lines for his detective, Mike Hammer, in *One Lonely Night* (1951 – sales three million): 'I killed more people tonight than I have fingers on my hands. I shot them in cold blood and I enjoyed every minute of it . . . They were Commies. They were Red sons of bitches who should have died long ago.' The columnist Westbrook Pegler must have approved that passage, for he wrote: 'The only sensible way to deal with them is to make membership in Communist organizations a capital offence and shoot or otherwise put to death all persons convicted of such.' For a long time it seemed impossible to refer to Communists without using the words 'conspiracy' and 'sons of bitches'.

But the Cold War was fundamentally one of history's wars of religion, and there were those who realized that the struggle to preserve American Ideals from the ideas of Marx and Lenin had to be conducted on a religious or moral plane. Billy Graham blasted Communism on the Deity's behalf: 'A great sinister anti-Christian movement masterminded by Satan has declared war upon the Christian God!' But the man who combined the gifts of preacher and politician, and who felt called, like John the Baptist (or, to be exact, John the Presbyterian), was Foster Dulles, minister's son, Wall Street lawyer and by divine right Secretary of State. He had been advising the State Department for two years under Truman. When Eisenhower made him its head he declared that American policy would be based on 'openness, simplicity and righteousness.' 'There is confusion in men's minds and corrosion in their souls,' he announced, 'The moral force of Christendom can make itself felt in the conduct of nations.' If MacArthur had acted as if he thought he was Napoleon, John Foster Dulles, a bleak, remote and charmless human being, acted as if he was, at least, another St Paul. Dulles' message was exactly what a badly shaken nation wanted to hear – God was, after all, on their side. Not only that, said Dulles; America was the chosen instrument of God's vengeance on the Communists for 'trampling on the moral law. For that violation they can and should be made to pay.'

So the stage was set for the inquisition. Fuelled by fear, soured by defeat and reinforced by Dulles's essential ingredient, self-righteousness, the American inquisitors devoted themselves single-mindedly to unmasking a conspiracy which did not exist. The American Communist Party at its peak in the Thirties might have been 100,000 strong and dominated several labour unions. Any chance it might have seemed to have to influence an election had been disproved by Henry Wallace who, with Communist support, polled only one million Presidential votes in 1948. By 1950 the party was in a state of disintegration and many of its leaders had been locked away. None of this abated Joseph McCarthy's crusading zeal in the Spring of 1950 when he found he suddenly had the ear of the nation. The man he described as 'the top Russian espionage agent in the United States – Alger Hiss's boss' turned out to be a blameless university professor and China expert, Owen Lattimore, but it did not matter. 'I am willing to stand or fall on this one,' he had said – but when he was proved wrong he did not fall, he rose yet higher.

Protected by Senatorial immunity from ordinary fears of libel, he plastered America's public servants with smears like a bill-poster. The repertoire of insult was colourful: 'Left-wing bleeding hearts', 'Parlour Pinks and Parlour Punks', 'Egg-sucking phony liberals' and 'Communists and queers who sold China into atheistic slavery'. He called Truman and his secretary of state, Dean Acheson, 'the Pied Pipers of the Politburo'. He described General George Marshall, the revered Defence secretary, as 'a man steeped in falsehood, always and invariably serving the policy of the Kremlin'. He said Hiss had been a supporter of Stevenson whom he called 'Alger . . . I mean, Adlai Stevenson.' Given his head at the Republican convention of 1952 he accused the Democrats of having been in charge of 'twenty years of treason', a phrase which stuck, much to the Republican advantage. 'I will not get into the gutter with that guy,' said their candidate, Eisenhower, who owed his wartime career to General Marshall's promotion of him. Yet when his campaign train reached McCarthy's state of Wisconsin, where he planned to speak in defence of his old chief, he thought better of it and let that guy from the gutter stay on the train. The press had advance copies of the speech in which he was to defend Marshall, so that his climb-down was plain for all to see when he failed to deliver it.

If the President could not afford to defy McCarthy, it was not surprising that Washington career men toed his line. He boasted of his 'loyal American underground' who informed on their colleagues' ideological impurities of deed or word. Even Dulles found his State Department appointments were being vetted by McCarthy through his henchman, Scott MacLeod. They almost stopped the appointment of the Moscow ambassador, 'Chips' Bohlen, because McCarthy resented the fact it had been made 'over his head'.

'The most gifted demagogue ever bred on these shores', McCarthy's biographer, Richard Rovere, wrote of him. 'For publicity he had a talent unmatched by any other politician of this century. He invented the morning press conference for the purpose of calling an afternoon press conference to say he expected to make a shattering announcement later in the day.' He always carried a briefcase bulging with documents which he said were incriminating and were usually irrelevant to whatever accustations he was making. His talent for imaginative lying helped to elect him to the Senate after the war as 'Tail Gunner Joe'. 'Yes, folks,' ran his campaign leaflet, 'CONGRESS NEEDS A TAIL-GUNNER.' In that case they got the wrong man. He wasn't one. His job was to interview pilots on return from their missions. He invented his military record. He affected a limp because one leg was 'full of shrapnel' (he broke it falling downstairs during a party). He was given the Distinguished Flying Cross, though his service record showed no combat missions, and he waited till 1952 to claim it. As a con man he knew that paradoxically part of his appeal was his unsavouriness, so unlike the smooth Washington types with silver spoons in their mouths. He boasted a permanent five o'clock shadow and lived the part of a hard-drinking, hard-swearing, poker-playing small town boy who belched and spoke his mind.

Senator McCarthy – 'It makes me sick, sick, sick way down inside'

He never caught a single credible Communist. Even this singular lack of results did not undermine him. It was the hunt that counted. Perhaps his most memorable line would come when, having hectored a witness into incoherence, he would say: 'It makes me sick, sick, sick way down inside.' Then he strode away – but only as far as the corner of the hearing room, temporarily out of range of the television cameras. What it was like to be in the hot seat in front of his permanent sub-committee was described by the editor of the *New York Post*, James Wechsler: 'The grand inquisitor was by turns truculent, contemptuous and bland. He acted like the gangster in a B movie rubbing out someone who had got in his way . . . It was not quite possible to communicate the horror of examination by McCarthy. I do not recommend the experience.' Reputable government officials grovelled to assure him of their impeccable record of loyal activities in the YMCA, as a boy scout, a churchgoer, a Sunday School activist. When he attacked the Army, the Secretary, Robert Stevens, offered his services to Tail Gunner Joe 'to assist you in correcting anything that may be wrong' and ended up offering to resign.

It was not, perhaps, as improbable as it sounds that McCarthy should have made a target of the Army. America had been amazed for some months by stories of U.S. prisoners of war in Korea who had 'gone over to Communism'. When the war ended twenty-three of them refused repatriation, later in 1953 changing their minds. They were promptly locked up in military hospitals as mental cases, but not before some of them declared they were *not* victims of brainwashing and mental torture by the enemy, as the Army had claimed. So a belief that there were Communists in the Army could be made to sound almost plausible.

Another epidemic of fear which McCarthy triggered off was book-burning. All over the country, and particularly in American libraries abroad run by the International Information Administration, intelligent men rushed to destroy books by 'suspect' authors, embracing among others Sherwood Anderson, W. H. Auden, Theodore Dreiser and Edmund Wilson. The climax to this ludicrous campaign from the Dark Ages came in 1953 with the tour of Europe by McCarthy's two young assistants, Mr Cohn and Mr Schine, who not only sounded like a bad vaudeville act but performed like one. Roy Cohn, twenty-seven, with a legal background, was the more serious of the two, with an unappealing scowl and an arrogance that would have befitted a crown prince of Prussia. David Schine, twenty-six, and hired by Cohn as his 'consultant', was the heir to a hotel chain, whose proudest achievement was to have made the world's largest collection of specimen cigars.

This pair had already laid waste the 'Voice of America' broadcasting staff. What, Europe wondered, were they looking for on their whirlwind tour which allowed them an average of twenty-eight hours at every city they investigated? In Vienna they discovered the sinister fact that the Soviet Information Centre stocked Mark Twain, hitherto considered reliably American in outlook. At one point they fell out and Schine chased Cohn through a hotel lobby swatting him over the head with a rolled-up magazine, to the delight of the large Press corps, who wrote stories headlined after the dialogue of the famous duo, 'Positively, Mr Cohn!' and 'Absolutely, Mr Schine!' A month later, McCarthy announced that the U.S. Information Service abroad had on its shelves thirty to forty thousand Communist volumes. We shall never know whether he was counting Mark Twain.

It was his pair of puppies who proved to be his downfall. Cohn's attempt to get his friend Schine out of his army service backfired. The Army brought an investigation into McCarthy and the blackmailing pressures he had put on it. The Army's counsel, a correct and old-fashioned Boston gentleman called Joseph Welch, was finally exasperated enough to tell McCarthy what he was: 'Until this moment, Senator, I never really gauged your cruelty or your recklessness. You have done enough. Have you no sense of decency, sir, at long last? Have you left no sense of decency?' The audience cheered in the hearing room and, in their millions watching him on television, took a hard look and saw that Welch was right. McCarthy was dumbfounded at the reaction. 'What did I do?' he asked. No more than usual, was the answer, but at last it was enough to break the spell. The Senate democrats were no longer afraid of him. Within a few months, in late 1954, the Senate censured him and although Nixon, his loyal backer in the past, considerately struck out the word Censure from the resolution, which condemned him for conduct unbecoming to the Senate, he was finished in Washington. He lingered on, drinking more heavily, occasionally interrupting proceedings with a bit of the old invective, but nobody took any notice. His squad of reporters, a dozen strong, who had tailed him for five years, was disbanded. And when he died of drink in 1957 it was to a strangely quiet Press, considering that only just before his fall he was supposed to have the support of fifty per cent of his countrymen, according to the polls, and a power almost greater than the President's.

But the end of McCarthy by no means meant the end of the witch-hunt. The House UnAmerican Activities Committee had been sitting before McCarthy and it went on after him and in the long run it damaged more people. The Fifties were the years of its vendetta with show business, which began in 1947 with the jailing of 'the Hollywood Ten', writers who held that their political opinions were no business of the Committee, relying on the First Amendment to the Constitution which guarantees freedom of thought and belief. This, too, was held to be UnAmerican. They were given a year's jail for contempt. In the Fifties the question was whether you could claim protection under the Fifth Amendment, which grants the right not to incriminate oneself. In practice it made very little difference whether an actor, writer or director accused of being tainted with Communism claimed the right to be silent or not. He would still be out of work. People who kept silent were assumed to have something to hide. They were called 'Fifth Amendment Communists' and they were on the 'Black List' which, officially, never existed. In effect there were several black lists. The House Committee published a cumulative index of names and organizations and there was the Attorney General's list of about two hundred organizations which were considered to have been Communist or Communist Front. These included such 'subversive' bodies as wartime committees for Soviet-American friendship or for Russian War Relief. Two ex-FBI men, Vincent Hartnett and Theodore Kirkpatrick, compiled a handy compendium in book form of members of these dangerous organizations in the communications industry. It was called *Red Channels* and a copy was standard equipment for every Hollywood producer and every radio, television and Madison Avenue advertising executive. To be named in *Red Channels* was to be unemployable . . . unless you cleared yourself by making a voluntary appearance before the House Committee or McCarthy's Sub-Committee as a 'friendly witness' who shopped his former friends to prove the 'sincerity' of his repentance. It was a symbolic act. Most of the names were well-known to the witch-hunters already. Larry Adler was blacklisted as a performer throughout the Fifties. Even as a harmonica player he had to come to England to get work. Adler recalls: 'I was listed in *Red Channels* for being associated with eight organizations. The one that counted against me most was the Anti-Fascist Refugee Committee, which I worked for in the late Thirties. I was offered a deal by Roy Cohn. To clear myself I could appear in secret session before the McCarthy committee so that nobody would know. I needn't even name names. They had the names. All I need do was agree to a list of people who had already been named, so I wouldn't be hurting anyone. I said to Cohn, "If you have the names, why ask me?" I remained on the Black List.'

The tragic testimony of Larry Parks

The Hollywood Ten could not write movies again, except under pseudonyms (some of them had four). One of them, Dalton Trumbo, actually won an Oscar in 1957 for *The Brave One* under a pseudonym, Robert Rich. Naturally he could not collect it. But blacklisted television writers, who had to appear in person at the studios, had to ask a 'clean' writer (or even a non-writer) to 'front' for them.

Television had its own witch-hunting body, AWARE Inc, which put out bulletins accusing radio and TV performers of Communist sympathies. The bulletins were written by Vincent Hartnett, who had been responsible for *Red Channels*, and AWARE was backed by Laurence Johnson, a supermarket owner with influence on the sponsors of radio and TV programmes, since their products were often sold through his chain of stores. If he demanded that an artist was dropped, the artist was dropped, nationwide – until a Texan broadcaster, John Henry Faulk, who was blacklisted by AWARE, brought and won a libel action in which he was awarded the record sum of $3,500,000 after a six-year struggle. 'The terrible thing is,' he wrote in his book on the case, *Fear On Trial*, 'that many of those victimized, and the American people as a whole, accepted this sentence of Guilty. They accepted the right of the vigilantes to bring the charges, to make the decision and to pronounce the sentence. And we all kept quiet. We felt that silence would make us safe.'

'Every intellectual who is called before one of the committees ought to refuse to testify,' wrote Einstein in an open letter to a New York teacher, one of thousands required to take a loyalty oath as a condition of further employment. 'He must be prepared for jail and economic ruin, for the sacrifice of his personal welfare in the interest of the cultural welfare of his country.'

The University of California's loyalty oath caused thirty-seven resignations and two-hundred refusals to sign – but this was an exceptionally high number of protestors. At Penn State, for example, one of the English teachers was Joseph Heller, then at work on a novel to be called *Catch 22*. The loyalty oath duly turned up in the book – Major Major is blacklisted and is thereby debarred from taking the oath. But Heller himself signed, like most people, 'because otherwise I would have lost my job,' he recalls frankly. 'It was an infringement of liberty but it was only a tiny inconvenience compared with having no job. I weighed it by priority.' *Catch 22*, though ostensibly about World War II, was in fact largely concerned with the Korean War and the state of mind prevailing in the Fifties. There is a reference to the Alger Hiss case in which microfilm is discovered hidden in a tomato, instead of the famous pumpkin from which Whittaker Chambers produced some with a flourish. 'I was trying to deal with the climate of the Fifties during which there was great disposition among Americans to trust their government,' says Heller now.

It is only against this background that one can begin now to understand the behaviour of Hollywood and Broadway, of the star names who confessed so eagerly and abjectly to their previous sins and were meat and drink to the H.U.A.C. Like reformed alcoholics, they could not wait to let the world know how misguided they had been and who had led them astray. Larry Parks is remembered for being one of the first to inform on his Communist friends before the committee, better remembered perhaps than he is for impersonating Al Jolson in two films which made him, at that time, a star. But his evidence does not read to his dis-

credit nearly so much as to the discredit of the committee. All day long
he insisted that they already knew who the fellow-Communists of his
branch had been in the Forties and that he did not want to 'crawl
through the mud for no purpose'. In the late afternoon the Committee
pulled its favourite form of persuasion: it went into secret session, with a
direction that if he didn't sing in secret he could expect to be jailed for
contempt of Congress (i.e. the committee).

> PARKS: I do not believe it befits the Committee to force me to do this. I
> don't think that this is fair play. I don't think it is in the spirit of real
> Americanism.
> CHAIRMAN: I direct the witness to answer the question.

When he finally named seven people he was told he should be comforted by the fact that all of them were already under subpoena to
appear. 'It is no comfort whatsoever,' said Parks abjectly. It was also the
end of his screen career.

Elia Kazan, director of Arthur Miller's stage plays and of many films
as memorable as *On The Waterfront*, calculated more shrewdly. He not
only informed on fellow-members of the Communist Party in 1934–6
and requested a public session in which to do so 'because secrecy serves
the Communist cause'; he took a display advertisement in the *New York
Times* to justify himself. 'Liberals must speak out,' he declared and,
having listed the films he had made, added: 'The motion pictures I have
made represent my convictions. I expect to continue to make the same
kind of pictures.' Indeed he did. His statement ended: 'I have placed a
copy of this affidavit with Mr Spyros P. Skouras, president of 20th
Century Fox.' It was Mr Spyros P. Skouras who let it be known that if
Kazan did not testify helpfully, the pictures he had just made might
never appear and he would not be directing any more. It was a common
enough pressure in Hollywood, where all the studios played the committee's game rather than risk loss at the box office. Clifford Odets was
one of those named by Kazan. A week later whom should Odets name
but Kazan? No hard feelings there. Edward G. Robinson, one of those
who had supported the Hollywood Ten, was still trying to clear himself
in 1952. He pleaded, hardly sounding like the tough guy the public
identified him with, 'Surely there must be some way for a person falsely
accused of disloyalty to clear his name once and for all? What more can
I do?' There was, of course, something – name some names of those who
had duped him, and he duly did. So did the choreographer Jerome
Robbins. 'I am going to see *The King And I* tonight,' said one of the

committee to him unctuously, 'and I will appreciate it much more.'

It was in this atmosphere of craven piety that Lillian Hellman, the playwright who had *carte blanche* in Hollywood to write what pictures she liked, administered a cold douche to the nation's conscience by stating unequivocally that she refused to inform on anybody else but herself. With all the hauteur of a Southern lady, the phrasing of her refusal was admirable: 'To hurt innocent people whom I knew many years ago in order to save myself is, to me, inhuman, indecent and dishonourable. I cannot and will not cut my conscience to fit this year's fashions.' This was in a letter to the committee which was read out at her hearing and passed round. A voice from the Press benches said loudly of this rather elementary point of honour: 'Thank God somebody at last had the guts to say it.' The flustered Committee did not have the chivalry to accept her terms, so instead of answering questions about herself she pleaded the Fifth Amendment against self-incrimination and was discharged. It did not save her from the Black List. She lost her six-figure Hollywood income. She had to sell her farm and work for a time in a department store. These penalties, to be sure, fell far short of what she might have expected for speaking out in Stalin's Russia, which she had continued to admire for far longer than many people.

In her book, *Scoundrel Time*, she put the blame for the lack of guts shown during 'this sad, comic, miserable time of our history' on two things: the funk of the studio bosses and the selfishness of the entertainers they paid so well. 'The loss of a swimming pool, a tennis court, a picture collection, future deprivation, were powerful threats to many people and studio heads played heavy with it . . . Only a very few raised a finger.'

In fairness, more than a very few did stand up to the committee in spite of the danger to their swimming pools and their popularity. Lionel Stander, who played the heavy in innumerable films, stormed on unstoppably at 'informers, stool pigeons and psychopaths who come here beating their breasts and saying "Please, I want absolution, get me back into pictures,"' until the hearing was hastily adjourned. Zero Mostel told the chairman, 'My dear friend, I believe in the antiquated idea that a man works in his profession according to his ability rather than his political beliefs.' In that year, 1955, when McCarthy was of no more consequence, twenty-two witnesses plucked up courage not to testify, including the folk singer, Pete Seeger, who got a year in jail for his stand. In 1956 Paul Robeson was summoned. He was already 'blacked' and refused a passport – possibly because of his Lenin Prize and the fact that a Soviet mountain had been named after him. Having explained that his Communism was an aspect of his campaign for black equality he thundered at the committee: '*You* are the non-patriots, *you* are the UnAmericans and you ought to be ashamed of yourselves.' He finally got his passport and left for Russia in 1958. Charles Chaplin left for London, to present his film *Limelight*, and chose exile when he was told he would be examined on his fitness to re-enter the country he had lived in for forty years. Chaplin's non-appearance before the UnAmerican Activities Committee was one of the great lost opportunities of both their careers. The committee decided not to summon him, according to Chaplin, when they heard he planned to appear in the costume, boots and battered bowler of the Chaplin tramp.

There was passport trouble also for Arthur Miller. He was not allowed to go to Brussels for the European premiere of his play *The Crucible*. The loud calls for the author, by a curious irony, were taken for him by the U.S. ambassador. When Miller appeared before the UnAmerican Activities Committee in 1956, he actually did what Lillian Hellman had proposed. He admitted his previous contacts with Communist and Marxist writers but refused to say who else was present. 'I am not protecting the Communists or the party,' he said, 'I am trying to, and I will, protect my sense of myself.' He was duly cited for contempt, received a thirty-day sentence to jail and a fine, which were quashed two years later on appeal. That is what the record shows. Miller says now that he was offered a deal too, one of the most remarkable even in that committee's history of deals. 'I was approached with an offer to call the hearing off if the Chairman, Representative Walter, could have his photograph taken with my wife.' Mrs Miller at that time was, of course, Marilyn Monroe. What do you say in answer to a proposition like that? 'You laugh,' he said.

Miller was quite used to finding that his work fitted into the elusive category of 'UnAmericanism'. 'UnAmerican had numerous meanings depending on the level of sophistication to which it was addressed. Broadly, of course, it meant pro-Russian or pro-Communist but it could also mean an opponent of big business or of big unionism or a proponent of birth control or atheism. It was a catch-all for every kind of opinion which was literally in any way remarkable.'

In 1952 *Death Of A Salesman* had been filmed. Columbia Pictures were so worried by its implications – that for a man like Willy Loman salesmanship did not bring happiness and fulfilment – that they made a documentary short to precede every showing of the picture. This proved that, in reality, a salesman's lot was a happy one both emotionally and financially. Thanks partly to Miller's threat to sue, the short was scrapped.

The Crucible, the play which showed the clear parallel between the McCarthy mentality and the Salem witch-hunt of 1692, was perhaps the only enduring work of art to come out of the period. When it opened on Broadway, in Miller's words,

a sheet of ice formed over the first-night audience when it sensed the theme. In the lobby afterwards, acquaintances would pass as if I weren't standing there at all. It was dismissed by the critics until McCarthy and the Terror were safely passed. One was a hunt for witches, the other for Communists, but they involve the same function of the human mind. Once you develop a siege mentality, anything is believeable. The enemy is wily and therefore the more unlikely a person looks, the more likely he is to be the secret enemy. Once he is under suspicion he can't win. If he protests his innocence, he is doing just what he would do if he were guilty. If he doesn't protest he is admitting guilt. The most disheartening part of the Terror was the way the intellectual, creative, artistic people chickened out as if nothing special was happening. It was not just a failure of courage or conscience. It was also a lack of knowledge – 98 per cent of the people didn't know what the arguments were really about. The American Left has never had a solid basis. It is not working class. Any radical critic of society has always come from an unattached group of artists and intellectuals. So when the Left was attacked – by the old trick of imputing treason to it – they had no allies.

It was our holocaust. One got to understand very well how the Germans could have made their peace with Hitler. We weren't shooting the writers, we were only disgracing them – and look how few people came forward in their defence. Yet we blame the Germans for not defying a regime which would melt you into soap. A little humility is necessary.

Then Arthur Miller added: 'The thing to remember is that it has not gone away for ever.'

CHAPTER FOUR

The Bomb

On 30 January, 1950, after five months of agonized discussion and contradictory advice, President Truman gave the go-ahead for a crash research programme into the hydrogen or 'super' bomb, as it was then called. With that decision people came face to face with the expectation known to the early Christians soon after the Crucifixion and to the deeply religious who shivered at the approach of the year A.D. 1000 – the expectation that they might indeed see the end of the world in their lifetime. This fear of a new apocalypse began in deep secrecy the previous August when the fall-out from what could only be a Russian atomic test was detected. All estimates of the balance of post-war power were thrown into confusion. It was believed that the Soviets already had superiority in conventional armies and weapons. Now, in an unbelievably four short years, they had caught up with the atomic bomb which alone guaranteed the security of the much-disarmed United States.

It was a month before the President announced the news. In the next few weeks the scientists of the West were split into two groups: should or should they not try to make an H-bomb? J. Robert Oppenheimer, the government's chief scientific adviser and head of the Los Alamos laboratory which had produced the atom bomb, called a meeting of the General Advisory Committee on atomic energy. Edward Teller, in particular, believed the fusion bomb to be theoretically possible. Oppenheimer was full of doubts. He wrote to James Conant, President of Harvard, before they both attended the meeting: 'I am not sure the miserable thing will work nor that it can be gotten to the target except by ox-cart. It would be folly to oppose the exploration of this weapon. But that we become committed to it as the way to save the country and the peace appears to me full of dangers.'

The committee's unanimous advice was to shelve the project. 'We all hope,' ran its report, 'that by one means or another the development of these weapons can be avoided. We are reluctant to see the United States take the initiative in precipitating this development.' In other words they hoped that by self-denial the Americans could dissuade the Russians from attempting it. They were also uncertain whether it would work. But the chief argument was an ethical one: 'We see a unique oppor-

tunity of providing by example some limit on the totality of war, thus
eliminating the fear and arousing the hope of mankind.' And a minority
of two physicists, Doctors Fermi and Rabi, added: 'It is necessarily an
evil thing considered in any light . . . We think it wrong on fundamental
ethical principles to initiate the development of such a weapon.' No one
can say that the scientists showed no conscience at that moment. But
Teller, a large Hungarian with a leather foot (he had lost one under a
tram as a student in Munich), felt betrayed. Those who shared his
belief in the ultimate weapon, Pentagon chiefs and Congressional hawks,
put pressure on the President. Truman played for time by appointing a
brains trust of three to advise him. And then, in January, Klaus Fuchs
was arrested and revealed that, thanks to him, the Russians knew far
more than had ever been suspected. Four days later Truman cast the die.

The question whether this brought the world nearer to inevitable self-
destruction or, paradoxically, made it stabler and safer from major war
than ever before was to occupy the best minds of the decade. The conun-
drum is still as insoluble as ever. But it has never since been debated
as solemnly, as urgently or as hysterically as it was in the 1950s. The
debate was confused by a tangle of contradictory emotions generated by
moral and religious ideology, patriotism, self-righteousness, anxiety for
the species, economic and military self-interest and naked fear. Crudely
simplified, majority opinion passed through two well-defined phases in
the West: first, it was assumed that war was unthinkable and impossible
as a continuation of policy; later, it was suggested that within certain
limits nuclear war might still be winnable, if you were sufficiently prepared. Both beliefs were hedged with doubt. It took more optimism than
most people could summon to believe that man could renounce the
time-honoured outlet of war utterly and at a stroke. But it also strained
credulity to believe that any sort of war where any sort of nuclear
weapons were available would not eventually lead to full-scale atomic
destruction. Hence the stalemate between the two camps, the Deterrers
and the Disarmers, which is still the position. The Fifties saw the evolution of both points of view. There is a third point of view: that of weary
or wilful ignorance, which has since banished the question almost entirely from intellectual discussion among ordinary, concerned people.
It seems that human attention can only be sustained for a very limited
time by any subject, even the prospects of its own destruction. But, to
their credit, the Fifties sustained its interest at maximum heat. It was
a very frightened and concerned decade indeed.

A brief résumé of the order of events helps to illuminate the course of the arguments about them. It took two years, until 1 November, 1952, to produce Teller's first thermo-nuclear explosion. It was not a bomb but a 'device' with the force of 10 megatons of TNT fixed to a tower. It vapourized Eniwetok Atoll in the Marshall Islands, turning it into the many-coloured mushroom cloud, 25 miles high and 100 miles wide, which became the symbol of anxiety for mankind. Nine months later, to the horror of Western scientists, the first Russian H-bomb proper was exploded in Siberia, well ahead of Teller's 'improved' version. This was an actual 15-megaton bomb working on the principle of fission-fusion-fission and exploded on Bikini Atoll, on 1 March, 1954. Three months earlier, Dulles had warned the world that 'local defence must be reinforced by the further deterrent of massive retaliatory power'. Bikini showed how massive this would be. Both sides seemed appalled for a while by the race they had started.

In 1955, the year of the Geneva summit conference, there were conciliatory gestures towards nuclear disarmament on both sides. In May the Soviet Union proposed the abolition of 75 per cent of the existing stocks of weapons and offered unimpeded inspection. In effect Russia was adopting previous Western proposals almost *in toto*. The British delegate to the U.N. Disarmament Subcommittee said 'We have made an advance that I never dreamed possible.' The U.S. delegate was 'gratified' that his country's proposals 'have been accepted in a large measure by the Soviet Union.' There seemed to be nothing to stop nuclear disarmament that summer, when Eisenhower arrived at Geneva and made his 'open skies' proposal as a confidence-building measure. But in September there were obviously fresh instructions: 'The United States does now place a reservation upon all of its pre-Geneva substantive positions,' said the delegate. In other words it was off. This drew the comment from Bertrand Russell that both East and West did not really want disarmament. 'Each is only concerned to find ways of advocating it without getting it.'

In January 1956, Dulles, still apparently comforted by his country's nuclear armoury, made his 'brinkmanship' speech: 'The ability to get to the verge without getting into the war is the necessary art. If you are scared to go to the brink you are lost.' It did not reassure his European allies as much as it did him that their continued existence, as sitting targets in any exchange of fire, depended on his skills as a bluffer. By any standard 1956 was not a reassuring year. It saw the defeat of Adlai Stevenson whose demand for a suspension of tests brought an offer of immediate agreement from Prime Minister Bulganin . . . to which

'If you are scared to go to the brink you are lost.' John Foster Dulles defending his brinkmanship policy in January 1956

Eisenhower responded by accusing the Russians of 'internal interference' in his re-election campaign. It heard blithe announcements from two military eminences which were hardly reassuring. U.S. Defence Secretary Charles Wilson said, with a shrewd businessman's satisfaction, that the new type of H-Bomb tested at Bikini gave 'a bigger bang for the buck'. Field Marshal Montgomery wrote breezily in a services journal: 'If we are attacked, we use nuclear weapons in our defence. The only proviso is that the politicians have to be asked first. That might be a bit awkward, of course, and personally I would use the weapon first and ask afterwards.' All such confident talk from the West was, however, answered in November by four little words from the East: 'We will bury you!' declared Mr Khrushchev. Though he later reinterpreted them, in an economic sense, they sounded an ugly threat.

It was also in 1956 that Teller and scientists from the Massachussetts Institute of Technology assembled at Woods Hole Oceanographic Institute, Cap Cod, to solve the problem of firing a nuclear missile from a submerged, and virtually invulnerable, submarine. The solution – Polaris – took time to be developed. Before it could be, the Russians trumped the aces being developed by the U.S. military-industrial complex by sending up a Sputnik, on 4 October, 1957, closely followed by two bigger ones. It was the clearest possible demonstration that they had mastered the problems of the Inter-Continental Ballistic Missile. The Russian ICBMs, designed by the brilliant engineer Sergei Karolyev, had been tested, according to Tass, over nearly 5,000 miles. Not with accuracy, it was true. As Khrushchev later admitted: 'It always sounded good to say in speeches that we could hit a fly at any distance with our missiles. But pinpoint accuracy was necessary and it was difficult to achieve.' He also admitted that Sputniks did not solve the problem of how to defend the country. For the H-bomb, carried in long-range bombers which took several hours to fly from base to target, was already outdated by the end of the Fifties. The bombers could be brought down or exploded in the air by Surface-to-Air Missiles and SAMs were being turned out like sausages, according to Khrushchev, in order to ring Moscow and other cities. But missiles like Polaris and Minuteman and the Russian ss could make the journey within half-an-hour and arrive at 10,000 miles per hour, rendering the SAMs impotent. Development had started in 1958 on multiple warhead rocket vehicles (MRVs) which separate in flight and could be aimed at several different targets simultaneously. They were virtually unstoppable.

By 1960 there were enough nuclear missiles and bombs on either side to achieve the state known as Mutually Assured Destruction – or MAD for short. The state of MADness was a considerable advantage, according to the theory of deterrence, and one should have faith in its beneficent qualities. Mutually assured destruction, or the balance of terror, rested on two assumptions. First, that both sides had 'second strike capability', i.e., enough weapons buried in silos or submerged in submarines to hit back devastatingly after a nuclear attack. Second, that no side had 'first-strike capability', that is, the ability to knock out the other side completely in a surprise attack. Given this state of affairs, everyone should, in theory, be able to relax with a tranquil mind, secured by the logical impossibility of anyone winning a nuclear war. In fact the United States boasted of its capacity for 'overkill' – another euphemism in the nuclear vocabulary – as if to wipe out one's adversary several times over could only make the world a safer place. Khrushchev's dry comment on the Soviet lack of 'overkill' was: 'What good does it do to annihilate a country twice? We are not a bloodthirsty people.' But they acquired overkill in their turn.

There was one flaw in the logical perfection of the balance of terror which began to trouble the public mind. If you want to be sure of having deterred the enemy, you have to fire first. If your rockets are aimed at the rocket bases on the other side – a strategy known as 'counter-force' – there is no point in firing second, after those enemy rockets have been launched. In any case, you cannot destroy all the mobile launchers, such as Polaris submarines. The alternative is massive retaliation by missiles aimed at the enemy's cities, which will stay put. But, as people began to ask, in what circumstances would such an act of out-and-out mass annihilation be justified? Anyway, there is no way of confining nuclear fall-out to enemy territory. The U.S. Army's chief of research and development, General Gavin, casually revealed the vagueness of the calculations to a congressional committee: in the event of a nuclear strike against the Soviet Union, he said, the estimated casualties were 'several hundred million deaths – that would be either way, depending on which way the wind blew. If the wind blew to the South-East they would be mostly in the U.S.S.R. . . . if the wind blew the other way they would extend well back up into Western Europe.'

The British Defence White Paper of 1958 laid down with surprising confidence the circumstances in which it would unleash nuclear weapons: 'It must be well understood that if Russia were to launch a major attack, even with conventional weapons only, the West would have to hit back with strategic nuclear weapons.' ('Strategic' means the biggest missiles; 'tactical' weapons, which are supplied to NATO forces, include weapons up to the size of the bomb that 'took out' – to use another euphemism – Hiroshima.) Obviously they were assuming that the wind would blow in their favour. But would the United States go over the nuclear brink to save Britain, France, Germany or any other NATO member from a conventional attack? And if not, what was there to stop such an attack being made? The Korean War and several other border wars, backed by the super-powers, had been judged not worth pressing the nuclear button for and it was this consideration which had produced the British H-Bomb in 1957. The British atom bomb, tested in 1952–3 in Australia, gave simple satisfaction to Churchill ('We had one and let it off – it went off beautifully'). Mr Macmillan echoed the same thinking about the H-bomb: 'When the tests are completed we shall be in the same position as the United States or Soviet Russia . . . It will be possible then to discuss on equal terms.' His anxiety for equal terms in the nuclear club was echoed a few months later by, of all people, Aneurin Bevan, who urged his fellow left-wingers at the Labour Party conference not to vote for Britain to give up nuclear arms with the famous plea: 'Do not send the British Foreign Minister naked into the international conference chamber!' He spoke for a large part of the population. 'It's OUR H-Bomb!' screamed the *Daily Express* headline after the British test at Christmas Island, which put paid to the still lively hope that the nuclear club would not extend beyond the two super-powers. *Amour propre* ensured that France would emulate Britain (its first test in the Sahara came in 1960). Simultaneously the Chinese waxed more belligerent. At the Communist world conference in 1957 held in post-Sputnik euphoria, Mao Tse-tung declared that the East wind was prevailing over the West wind and that nuclear war would mean the end of capitalism but not of communism: if 300 million Chinese were killed, there would still be 300 million left alive. Khrushchev, however, showed that he had learned the nuclear facts of life in a speech in July 1958: 'If other countries fight amongst themselves they can be separated. But if war breaks out between America and our country, no one will be able to stop it. It will be a catastrophe on a colossal scale.' He quite possibly made that catastrophe recede by denying the aggressive Chinese access to Russian secrets. The proliferation of nuclear weapons was given the title of 'the Nth power problem.' The question was which would be the Nth power to acquire the bomb which would also be irresponsible enough to start the holocaust. Few doubted that sooner or later one would. Nevil Shute, in his scarifying novel *On The Beach* (1957, filmed in 1959), foresaw the extermination of the human race in a war started by a minor power. As a mathematician, Bertrand Russell pointed out that while there were two nuclear powers, only those two powers could quarrel. But with four nuclear powers, six pairs could quarrel, while five powers provided ten possible pairs and so on, the likelihood of war increasing faster than the number of nuclear players. Hence his proposal of a 'non-nuclear club', to be led by a disarmed Britain, to confine the danger within limits. 'It is not so long ago,' Russell reminded his readers, 'since a great power was controlled by a madman.'

The possibility of nuclear war through madness was much on people's minds in the Fifties, together with the spectre of war by error. 'Dr Strangelove' was not to be imagined for a few more years but it was not

'It went off beautifully,' said Winston Churchill of the
British H-bomb test in 1953 in Woomera, South Australia

Robert Oppenheimer, fired for his reluctance to make the H-bomb

reassuring to learn that nuclear submarine crews were supplied with pistols with which to shoot any shipmate who showed signs of wanting to fire an unauthorized missile. It was perhaps even more alarming to learn that the Distant Early Warning System, the chain of radar stations ringing the Soviet Union from Greenland to Alaska, had more than once given the alarm which put Strategic Air Command into the air *en route* to the target thanks to picking up a moon echo or a flock of geese migrating in formation. Error, miscalculation or madness seemed perhaps the most likely cause of nuclear war in the early days, before the coming of the 'hot line' connecting the Kremlin and the White House in 1963.

The Deterrers were gradually drawn into the relentless escalation of the weapons race by the logic of their beliefs. Nobody in government seriously considered there was any alternative. But meanwhile the Disarmers grew in numbers and in influence. The Fifties was a great time for moral stands, at least on this subject, accompanied by high-level debate and quixotic, brave, sometimes eccentric gestures of persuasion. Scientists were deeply split on the uses to which the discoveries of atomic physics were being put. Many felt that, in the words of Robert Oppenheimer, 'in some sort of crude sense the physicists have known sin – a knowledge they cannot lose.' It was also a knowledge that could not be unlearned or removed from the human stockpile. Disarmers were uneasily aware that, even if all existing nuclear weapons were destroyed, the knowledge of how to make them would be revived fast enough in the event of a future global war. But, on the whole, most distinguished Western scientists, from Einstein downwards, were Disarmers not Deterrers. They wished to restore the good name of physics. No such luxury was permitted to the scientists of the Soviet Union but even there Andrei Sakharov, the Russian Oppenheimer, was trying to persuade Khrushchev to abandon testing by 1958. 'I felt myself responsible for the problem of radio-active contamination from nuclear explosions', he wrote later. But, like his brother scientists in the West, he found his advice was ignored. 'Khrushchev said, more or less, Sakharov is a good scientist, but leave it to us who are specialists in this tricky business to make foreign policy.' Similarly, the clock on the front of the American *Bulletin of Atomic Scientists* stood at a few minutes to midnight, but the American government did not heed it. The scientists did try. Many of them refused to work on nuclear projects. Teller did not succeed in attracting more than a handful of Oppenheimer's brilliant team back to Los Alamos to work on the H-bomb.

Oppenheimer himself was refused security clearance in December 1953, four months after the first Russian H-bomb was exploded. He had actually been denounced to J. Edgar Hoover as 'more probably than not an agent of the Soviet Union.' The accuser, a certain William Borden, was a dedicated propagandist for strategic air power – that is, the H-bomb, over which Oppenheimer dragged his feet. The long hearing of the case before a board of inquiry finally confirmed the ban on the revered 'Oppy' in June 1954. The scientific community was profoundly disturbed by the finding. Oppenheimer's 'defects of character', the political indiscretions and Communist Front connections of his past, were seen to be an excuse for the real reason for his suspension: that the father of the A-bomb was 'lacking enthusiasm' and 'lukewarm' about the H-bomb. He had opposed it along with the rest of the General Advisory Committee but it was no clear-cut moral stand: 'I never urged anyone *not* to work on the hydrogen bomb project,' he told the inquiry.

Nevertheless a brilliant scientist was being fired from government service and his reputation as a patriot clouded (although he was affirmed a 'loyal citizen') – because of what? Because of his concern for the survival of the human race. This implication was hardly lessened by the evidence of personal hostility between Teller and Oppy which came out at the inquiry. 'Do you believe Dr Oppenheimer is a security risk?' Teller was asked by the board. 'I thoroughly disagreed with him on numerous issues,' said Teller, 'to this extent I would like to see the vital interests of this country in hands which I understand better and therefore trust more.' It was hardly a statement in the highest traditions of scientific objectivity. Henceforward the split between the Teller and Oppenheimer camps in the scientific community became total.

The next few years saw several appeals for sanity from top scientists who were Disarmers – in 1955 an appeal to renounce force because radio-activity could wipe out 'whole nations, neutral or belligerent' was signed by fifty-two Nobel prizewinners. The same year brought the Pugwash manifesto, written by Bertrand Russell and signed by Einstein two days before he died, as well as by Professors Max Born, J. F. Joliot-Curie and Joseph Rotblat. It put the stark question: 'Shall we put an end to the human race: or shall mankind renounce war?' The professors went on: 'We are speaking not as members of this or that nation, continent or creed but as human beings, members of the species Man whose continued existence is in doubt . . . a biological species which has had a remarkable history and whose disappearance none of us can desire.' After this the 'Pugwash Conference' of scientists from East and West – so named after the site of their first meeting in Nova Scotia – was held annually. They found little difficulty in agreeing with one another on the current dangers but an insuperable difficulty in communicating enough anxiety to Eastern and Western governments to make them seriously disarm. Albert Schweitzer appealed for the same cause the following year, and in January 1958 Professor Linus Pauling, the Nobel prize-winning chemist, presented the signatures of more than 9,000 scientists to the United Nations secretary-general, Dag Hammarskjöld, warning the world of the genetic dangers of tests and calling for their immediate end – it was this which immediately influenced Sakharov to make the same appeal to Khrushchev.

But the reasoning of the leading scientific intellects of the age had nothing like so much effect as an obscure little Japanese fishing boat named the *Lucky Dragon* which was 85 miles from Bikini Atoll when Dr Teller's H-bomb went off. In the darkness before dawn one of the crew of twenty-three watched the ball of fire, changing from white to yellow to flaming orange-red, and dashed below to tell his shipmates 'The sun rises in the West!' About five minutes later as they watched its dying effects a great sound wave enveloped the ship. Two hours later, as they were hauling in their lines, a light drizzling snowstorm of ash began to fall. When they reached port and had sold their catch on the market, radio-activity was discovered all over ship, crew and catch. Japan was hysterical. Overnight the Japanese stopped eating fish. The crew fell ill with radiation sickness and after six months, despite intensive care, the radio operator died, the first known victim of the H-bomb.

People throughout the world suddenly became much better informed about radiation hazards. They learned that the fall-out from the Bikini explosion had covered 7,000 square miles. Strontium 90, which is absorbed via plants and milk into the bones of growing children and can cause leukaemia, became the best-known radio-active substance. Even the rain was supposed to be radio-active after the long series of 1954–5 tests. At first the governments tried to brazen out the dangers. Eisenhower claimed in 1955 that the tests were not a health hazard. Macmillan in 1957 claimed the hazards were 'negligible'. There was talk of developing a 'clean' bomb with little fall-out, a chimera at that time, which simply produced a lot of Carbon-14 which does not decay for literally thousands of years. But by August 1958 both sides realized that world opinion was turning against them, partly as a result of the scientists' warnings, partly out of revulsion and fear, partly because nuclear disarmament had begun to be a popular political issue – and nothing makes a politician have second thoughts faster than the awareness that he might be losing votes. So, after that year's very comprehensive tests were finished, Eisenhower announced he would suspend American tests for a year, with extensions if the Russians and the British followed suit. The pause was to last for three years.

It was not as altruistic as it may have looked. Both sides were finding it ruinously expensive to keep up in the race. The American defence budget increased to 12 billion dollars in 1958. There was some attempt made to reach agreement at the continuous disarmament talks but the only real progress was a pledge not to test in the Antarctic, a gesture of more value to the species Penguin than the species Man.

But it was in late 1957, when the nuclear race was at its most reckless, before the test suspension, that the nuclear disarmament campaign finally germinated. It was helped by the obvious inadequacy, indeed fatuity, of the governments' plans to protect their populations by civil defence. Atomic shelters had been on sale in the U.S. (at a cost of $1,995 in 1951) since the first Russian atomic bomb. Weekly shelter drill became a routine in American schools ('Bring a woolly toy' advised one leaflet). In 1954 a campaign to build fall-out shelters for big American cities was announced though nobody was sure how to do it. The director of Civil Defence, Mr Val Petersen, suggested concrete pipes sunk alongside main roads, into which the populace should crawl in case of an attack. But his official estimates of the effects of a 2,500-megaton attack were 36 million deaths on the first day and 72 million by the 60th day, without reckoning on the effects of a breakdown of organized services. 'Life is going to be stark, elemental, brutal, filthy and miserable' for the survivors, admitted Mr Petersen, who was in a position to know. The United States had hopes of at least twenty-five minutes' warning of a nuclear rocket attack. Britain could expect only four. The 1957 government White Paper on Defence baldly admitted: 'It must be frankly recognized that there is at present no means of providing adequate protection for the people of this country against nuclear attack.' So there. 'I would have you know,' said one of the four protagonists of the Oxbridge revue *Beyond The Fringe* in 1960, 'that some people in this great country of ours can run a mile in four minutes!' It was not surprising that it was in Britain that the most effective campaign against nuclear weapons began.

When the British H-bomb was tested, a solitary Quaker couple, Harold Steele and his wife, volunteered to make a suicide voyage into the test area at Christmas Island. For his pains he was christened 'H-Bomb Harold' and ridiculed by the popular press when he reached Tokyo only in time to find that the test had already been held. Not everyone, however, thought his intended martyrdom was a laughing matter. In November 1957, after the news of the first Soviet ICBM and Sputnik, and Aneurin Bevan's 'naked into the conference chamber' speech, the *New Statesman* published an article by J. B. Priestley called 'Britain and the Nuclear Bomb' which started a wave of reaction of tidal proportions. Letters of approval and calls for action of some kind flooded into the magazine, especially from the Left Wing whose natural leader, Bevan, had just slammed the door on them. Bevan was the spur to Priestley's powerful pen: 'The sight of a naked minister might bring the conference to some sense of our human situation,' he wrote, 'What should be abandoned is deterrence-by-threat-of-retaliation. There is no real security in it, no decency, no faith, hope nor charity in it . . . If there is one country that should never have gambled in this game, it is

Britain. Our bargaining power is slight; the force of our example might be great.' And he ended with a call to the hearts and consciences of his countrymen to 'reject the evil thing for ever.'

The force of Britain's example: that was the moral appeal of Priestley's polemic. It was a form of patriotism – could we still lead the world in moral, instead of military and economic power? It was some such hope which united the movement that now coalesced from all points of the spectrum. When the Campaign for Nuclear Disarmament emerged from the discussions that followed Priestley's article, it was chaired by a Canon of St Paul's, the gaunt non-conformist cleric John Collins, and presided over by the foremost sceptic and humanist of the day, Bertrand Russell. On its executive could be found such skilful publicists as Michael Foot, M.P., Kingsley Martin (editor of the *New Statesman*), James Cameron, a leading journalist of protest, and Priestley himself. It was sponsored by a galaxy of British artistic talent: Benjamin Britten, E. M. Forster, Barbara Hepworth, Doris Lessing, Henry Moore, Michael Tippett, Edith Evans and Peggy Ashcroft among them, as well as Sir Julian Huxley and the future Lord Chancellor, lawyer Gerald Gardiner. The inaugural meeting overflowed the Central Hall, Westminster, where 5,000 people listened to the historian A. J. P. Taylor listing the effects of an H-Bomb explosion. Then he asked, 'Is there anyone here who would want to do this to another human being?' There was a long-drawn hush in the hall. 'Then why are we making the damned thing?' he demanded to thunderous applause.

On Good Friday 1958 the first march set out for Aldermaston, the atomic research establishment in Berkshire, under the CND symbol, a black circle forked with a white 'drooping cross', the semaphore symbols for N and D, which became the membership badge not only for the campaign but for a certain kind of non-conformity among young people. Five thousand of them covered the last mile of the march through the Berkshire fields in silence, despite the coldest and wettest Easter for forty years. The next Easter, when the march sensibly reversed its direction, it stretched for four miles as it wound its way into Trafalgar Square, which held a crowd ten times as big. Those who marched were a coalition of wildly different elements: pacifists and Christians, Trade Unionists and Little Englanders, anarchists and rationalists, Beats and ravers, the barefoot and the long-haired and also a great many quiet and concerned young parents pushing prams or carrying infants on their shoulders. There were steel bands and folk singers. The large proportion – estimated at forty per cent – of the marchers who were under twenty-one sang 'Ban, ban, ban the bloody H-Bomb' (to the tune of 'John Brown's Body') or 'When the Saints Go Marching In' and welcomed the fact that there was something different to do for Easter.

The CND was a sort of emotional hold-all. Most people joined it for humanitarian reasons but it was an outlet for all kinds of disgust. Some were impatient of disarmament talks which never resulted in the abandoning of a single weapon; some were appalled by Civil Defence pamphlets which advocated spending your last four minutes on earth whitewashing your windows and by planners who talked blithely in terms of 'megadeaths'; some were convinced that Armageddon would be next week: the immensely influential film of *On the Beach* showed the last survivors, in Melbourne, waiting for death in 1963. Many were appalled by the thought that a global build-up of radiation was silently threatening the health of their children, present or to come. They also responded to the idea of Britain asserting a moral lead in the world after the soul-scarring debacle of Suez. They did not want to play the 'great power' game any longer. They wanted the world back as it was before Hiroshima. They were marching for a lost innocence.

It was not really a political movement (the Communist Party began by opposing it) but it aimed first to convert the Labour Party to unilateral disarmament and, by getting Labour elected, changing government policy. Its effectiveness grew through 1958 and 1959 to reach its peak in 1960 when both the Trades Union Congress and the Labour Party Conference passed resolutions in favour of unilateral disarmament. But they were just resolutions. By then Labour had lost its chance of power and the militant rank and file of the Disarmers were growing impatient with the lack of results. A new technique of 'direct action', with Bertrand Russell's blessing though not as yet his participation, began in December 1958, with a march through the muddy fields of Norfolk leading to the obscure American rocket base at Swaffham. This time they marched behind not Canon Collins but a fiercer cleric, the Reverend Michael Scott. The militants trudged along the empty lanes unobserved except by the Chief Constable of the county and his forces. He met them at the gates of the airfield (still a debris of contractors' equipment surrounded by barbed wire) and informed them gravely that if they entered – no difficult matter – they would be breaking the law. They replied formally that that was exactly their object. Civil dis-

OPPOSITE *The first Aldermaston Marchers on their way, April 6, 1958*

MARCH FROM
LONDON
TO
ALDERMASTON
NUCLEAR DISARMAMENT
THE BOMB OR THE HUMAN RACE?

obedience on the Gandhian pattern was still strange to Britain and no one knew exactly what to do next. Both sides were scrupulously polite, as if participating in a chess tournament. The demonstrators pushed their way in and sat down and were lifted out again, limp and unresisting, by the police. There was a council of war, a pause for prayer ('Quiet time, Quakers!' called someone) and they scrambled past the wire once more. This time they got their desire. Some forty were arrested, refused bail by a puzzled magistrate and sent to spend Christmas in prison for drawing attention to their preference for peace and goodwill rather than nuclear threats towards men.

Tiny as the demonstration was by subsequent standards, it won the attention of the country. The jails where the demonstrators were held were deluged with letters and Christmas food parcels. But it was also the beginning of the split between law-abiders and law-breakers which was to cripple the movement within a few years and lead to its decline.

While CND concentrated on the aim of British nuclear disarmament, the American Committee for a Sane Nuclear Policy – Sane for short – campaigned for general disarmament. Though this was a less contro-versial aim it had less emotional kick. Launched in 1957, it claimed 25,000 supporters by 1958 and by 1960 pacifist members had sailed into the Pacific testing grounds, boarded nuclear submarines or missile bases or simply refused to take shelter during bomb drills. But during the Fifties the impact of the Disarmers on American public opinion was 'very marginal' according to David Riesman, the Harvard sage. 'Ameri-cans envy the ease with which Englishmen discuss alternatives to nuclear war.' If Americans thought World War III was inevitable, they seemed curiously unbothered by it. A Gallup Poll taken in the last three weeks of 1959 found that only one person in fourteen listed among their major worries the international situation. In Britain at about the same time another Gallup poll showed 30 per cent of the populace were in favour of giving up the British H-bomb. And this was the very winter when Khrushchev announced that Russian scientists were hatching 'a fantastic weapon' which turned out, when tests were resumed in 1961, to be the 57-megaton bomb. Hardly a time for complacency, yet either that or fatalistic resignation seems to have put America to sleep.

The Disarmers' efforts were the only serious attempt made by ordinary citizens to influence policy on this matter of their own life and death. On the face of it they were an utter failure. But that is too simple. Clearly they failed to bring about disarmament, though they may have had a con-tributory effect on the decision to suspend tests in 1958 and later on the partial test ban treaty. In Britain they failed to convert more than a faction of the Labour Party, which was outvoted the year after it won its victory at the party conference. But they did educate the public on a subject which it would have preferred to ignore. 'At a time when political parties couldn't get twenty people in a room, we had to hold overflow meetings everywhere we went,' recalls Priestley, 'I don't think we.were ineffectual. At one point it nearly came off. We changed the climate of opinion. Before we started, nuclear bombs were sacred objects. The Labour Party talked of them as if they were filled with caramels.' Canon Collins now credits the movement with two achievements – 'public awareness of what the nuclear threat was in reality and of the danger from the tests. Khrushchev explicitly stated to me that one of his reasons for suspending tests was because he had studied the effect of the CND on the British public. If you believe that, there was a positive result.' It should also be credited with the fact that within a few years very little more was heard from politicians about the importance of the much-vaunted 'British independent nuclear deterrent' against which CND had originally campaigned. It simply became less credible by the light of educated common sense. No Prime Minister after Macmillan would maintain the fiction that Britain was on equal terms with the super-powers. Could anyone imagine Britain unleashing its bomb all alone, and, if so, on whom?

It was in the summer of 1959 that a man with untidy hair, a crumpled suit and pens clipped to his outside breast pocket, looking like a school-master who had fallen on hard times, boarded a plane at London Airport for East Berlin. He was the man who had started the race for thermo-nuclear superiority or, if you looked at it another way, prevented America from attaining such superiority. His name was Klaus Fuchs and the penalty he incurred for his epoch-making betrayal of atomic secrets was already paid, after less than ten years in prison. He left without a word. He betrayed no feelings to anyone in the country that had given him asylum. But that same summer thermo-nuclear war was the subject of a remarkable series of lectures being given at the Princeton Institute of Advanced Study by the futurologist, Herman Kahn, which showed how far human values had been changed during the years Fuchs had been in prison. Fuchs went to jail leaving behind him a world shocked and horrified by the prospect of atomic warfare. When he came out, Kahn was advancing the thesis that thermo-nuclear war had to be made into a practical proposition, because a totally disarmed world which renounced war was unbelievable. People had hitherto talked of the aftermath of nuclear bombing as 'catastrophic'; he introduced the concept of 'acceptable damage'. 'The effects of nuclear war vary greatly', he asserted, 'Do you survive with half or less than half your population and productive capacity? How many years would it take to recuperate?' His discussions of what was 'acceptable damage' in return for striking the first blow was 'somewhere between ten and sixty million dead. No American believed that any action would be justified if more than half our population would be killed in retaliation.' There the thinking at Princeton contradicted the thinking at Harvard where Tom Lehrer, the sardonic mathematics lecturer, put the point in a hectically hopeful ditty:

> We will all go together when we go
> What a comforting fact that is to know
> Universal bereavement,
> An inspiring achievement,
> Yes, we all will go together when we go.

'There'll be nobody left behind to grieve,' carolled Lehrer, looking on the bright side. Kahn, on the other hand, advocated massive investment in deep shelters so that at least the lucky half – or should it be the un-lucky half? – would be left behind to grieve, and to prove that war need not yet be quite abandoned as mankind's most addictive sport.

On Thermonuclear War, as Kahn's lectures were called, was to be published the following year with much effect on military-political thinking. The optimism of 1959 which runs through them is quite breathtaking at this distance in time: 'Some experts insist on talking as if the only choices were immediate surrender, immediate preventive war or eventual world annihilation,' Kahn declared. 'We must have an "alternative to peace" including a limited war capability ... We must at least make preparations to fight wars "carefully".' Presumably his vision of a careful war was fulfilled in Vietnam.

His assurances that it was still possible to declare war and survive were appreciated most of all by the 'military-industrial complex' – the Pentagon, the RAND Corporation (for which Kahn's research was done) and the thriving weapons industry. Deterrence always had and will have one decisive advantage over Disarmament as a policy: it makes some people a fortune. Between 1953 and 1960 the Pentagon defence budget swallowed $350 billion. Britain, with a defence budget of £1,500 million a year, was actually spending an even higher proportion of its wealth on arms – between 8 per cent and 10 per cent of the Gross National

Product, a third of its tax revenue. Those who wanted to know afterwards why British economic recovery was so poor by comparison with
that of Germany and Japan in those years need have looked no further.
They were not spending their resources on obsolete weaponry. A
nuclear arms race is a good recipe for national bankruptcy but it is very
profitable for those who design and manufacture the weapons. Each
escalation perpetuates the struggle by forcing the other side to match or
overtake the enemy's latest threat. In 1959, at their man-to-man talks at
Camp David, Eisenhower and Khrushchev admitted this to each other.
The conversation, according to *Khrushchev Remembers*, went like this:

> EISENHOWER: How do you decide military funds?
> KHRUSHCHEV: How do you?
> EISENHOWER: My military leaders say 'We need such and such.' I say
> 'Sorry, we don't have the funds.'
> They say 'The Soviet Union has already allocated funds
> for such a programme so we shall fall behind' . . . So I
> give in. That's how they wring money out of me. How is
> it with you?
> KHRUSHCHEV: Just the same.

Eisenhower made the elementary point that they really should agree
to stop such wasteful rivalry but they failed. It was this conversation,
most probably, which made Eisenhower so suspicious at the end of his
presidency of the armaments lobby and its effect on policy. No doubt it
was behind the sudden volte-face of the American position on disarmament when agreement came within its grasp in 1955. As he prepared to leave office five years later he warned the nation to 'guard
against the acquisition of unwarranted influence by the military-
industrial complex.' No one has yet been able to stand up to that complex and refuse to give it the money. The paradox continues that each
side's military-industrial complex guarantees the prosperity of the other
side's.

So the continued existence of the species, Man, remains in doubt.
The curious thing is that though the facts are the same as they were in
the Fifties and the risks are higher, the level of anxiety about them has
markedly fallen. Can this be called an advance? Hardly. There is no
good reason for it other than that given by Bertrand Russell in that more
troubled decade: 'The world in which we are now living would have
seemed, before 1945, too horrible to be endured. But we have got used
to it.'

CHAPTER FIVE

The Man from Moscow

It is a salutary exercise to turn around and look at the Fifties and the Cold War from the East instead of the West. From the Communist point of view the witch-hunts and loyalty tests of the United States must have looked like the little puffs of smoke and flame of a stage dragon which fooled nobody. Far more seismic events were giving shocks to the Communist world. We now know from Russian eyes, particularly from Khrushchev's much suspected but surely authentic memoirs, how precarious and nerve-ridden the future looked to the Communist high command when Stalin succumbed to his stroke on 5 March, 1953. For years they had lived with his mounting paranoia, the ever-more-irrational purges of his intimates, then entering an even more extreme phase with the totally imaginary 'Doctors' Plot'. In *Khrushchev Remembers* the misery of those telephoned summons to share Stalin's nightly loneliness is vividly caught: the Westerns they had to watch with him, the dinners they had to endure with him, the drinking they had to keep up with him until breakfast time (even Beria arranged to be given coloured water, until Stalin found out). 'Once Stalin made me dance the Gopak, squat down on my haunches and kick out my heels,' writes Khrushchev, an image hard to call up in view of his shape, but – 'When Stalin says "Dance", a wise man dances,' added the peasant proverb-spinner in his accustomed vein. It was a very scared bunch of men, announcing the death of the Dear Father of the Soviet People, who appealed to those people to avoid 'panic and disarray'.

The next major event was the emergence of Nikita S. Khrushchev as the dear chairman of the Soviet People. It took a little while to dispose of the competition. First, the appalling Beria had been arrested at pistol point in the Kremlin and executed as privily as his victims. Next the collective leadership were ousted under the taint of being an 'anti-Party group'. The most memorable thing about the complex power struggle that had this result was the fate of the losers. They were not shot. They were not dropped into the oblivion of the Gulag archipelago or the Lubianka. They were rusticated like naughty undergraduates to remote provinces – Molotov as ambassador to Ulan Bator, Malenkov to run a power station, Kaganovich to run a cement works, while Marshals Zhukov and Bulganin in due course followed them into retirement. After a few years' disgrace they were back living quietly but comfortably in Moscow. Perhaps it was a reversion to humane behaviour after Stalin's terror techniques. Perhaps it was self-interest. Khrushchev may have been perspicacious enough to imagine the day when his turn would come and he would become Special Pensioner Khrushchev. But for the remainder of the Fifties the initiative was seized in the Soviet Union, and often the world, by this gifted peasant, a copy-book proletarian, a metal worker who did not read or write until he was in his twenties and who summed up in his character so many of the strengths and weaknesses of the Communist system. Ruthless as he was, Khrushchev gave the Soviet Union a more human face. He was crude and shrewd, he was belligerent and boastful, but he was a realist. As he finally demonstrated over Cuba, he did not think Communist domination was worth the ruin of civilization. Having risen from Ukrainian coal mines through the party ranks as a tough and brutal Stalinist, once he achieved personal power he wasted no time in opening his mind to the ways of the rest of the world. He travelled on an unprecedented scale for a Russian head of state – unprecedented, that is, except by Peter the Great. It would be too much, given his limitations, to talk of Nikita the Great, but there was uncommon ability in him for which the world could eventually breathe more easily. He broadened the dogmas of Communist orthodoxy in several important respects. First, he threw the worship of Stalin overboard in his celebrated secret speech at the twentieth Party Congress in 1956. By the time Khrushchev sat down, Stalin stood revealed not as the dear father but as the mass murderer of his people. A liquidator of the best men thrown up by the Revolution, a torturer, a racialist on a Hitlerian scale, a defeatist when war was going badly, and a mind of insatiable vanity and paranoid suspicion was exposed. The statues came tumbling down all over the Soviet Union. Factories, streets and towns, right up to the hero city of Stalingrad, were hurriedly renamed. And the corpse in the holiest of Communist Holy Places, the Red Square mausoleum, was hurriedly removed from Lenin's side. The greatest shock Khrushchev delivered that day was to read Lenin's letters suggesting that the party should remove Stalin for abuse of power and threatening to break off all relations with him because of his affronts to his wife, Nadezhda Krupskaya. There was commotion in the hall when it was realized that Lenin's heir had been adulated for so long against Lenin's own better judgment.

At the same congress Khrushchev profoundly modified Lenin's tenet that world revolution would come about through inevitable war with the capitalist powers. War, he said, was no longer 'fatally inevitable'. Indeed, there could be peaceful co-existence between different political systems. He had already accepted 'different paths to socialism' within the Communist bloc itself when he healed the breach with Tito in 1955. All these were heresies from a Marxist standpoint but then Marx had not foreseen the coming of nuclear war.

In the same year, 1955, Khrushchev had got his first close view of his adversary, Dulles, at the Geneva summit conference, passing notes to Eisenhower who, Khrushchev decided disapprovingly, was letting Dulles do his thinking for him. In the end he looked back on Dulles as 'a worthy and interesting adversary – he always kept us on our toes'. At least he behaved as Khrushchev expected a capitalist to behave, as a 'chained cur of imperialism'. You knew where you were with curs. But Khrushchev's next visit to the West was one of sweetness and light, to Britain at the invitation of Eden. He and his straight man, Bulganin, came by battle cruiser, which was the target of much curiosity in Portsmouth harbour, especially since the body of a naval frogman, Commander 'Buster' Crabbe, had been found floating there during another Russian naval visit the previous autumn. No special secrecy was attached to the cruiser – indeed, Khrushchev told the disconcerted Admiralty that he would be glad to sell it to them because cruisers had been out-dated by missiles. Mr K, as the headlines called him, was pleasantly enough impressed by the hospitality of Eden's dacha, Chequers, by tea with the Queen, and by learning from Winston Churchill how to eat oysters. He also watched Churchill nodding off in his seat in the Commons. It was a peaceful scene of *bonhomie*, but it was shattered by the Parliamentary Labour Party. The dinner they gave him ranks among the epic brawls which regularly give the brotherhood of socialist solidarity a bad name. Hugh Gaitskell, the party leader, presented a list of Social Democrats imprisoned in Eastern Europe. Khrushchev asked truculently why he should care what happened to the enemies of the working class. George Brown shouted, 'God forgive you', Aneurin Bevan shook his finger at the guest with the warning 'Don't try to bully me!' and Khrushchev roared above the din: 'I haven't met people like you for thirty or forty years!' Unused to the rough and ready answering-back of British socialism, he remarked next day that if he lived in Britain he would be a Tory. There might be many roads to socialism but the Labour Party was not one of them.

Secret police being shot during the Hungarian rising in 1956

After the contents of the twentieth Party Congress speech sank in, there was a general revolt, logically enough, among the East European satellite regimes which Stalin had held in contemptuous subjugation. Russian tanks were called out against striking East Germans and then against the 'defiance of Poland' in 1956, when the Russian divisions marching on Warsaw almost found themselves fighting the Polish army and the armed workers of the capital. They were pulled back just in time. Within days Hungary was in open revolt. The Soviet leadership was thrown into panic. It was one thing to back down before the Poles. If they gave way in Hungary too, where would it stop? When 200,000 demonstrators marched through Budapest on 23 October and the imprisoned leader, Imre Nagy, was swept to power, the Army refused to act against the demonstrators and the police handed their batons to the students. Soon the hated secret police were being hunted down and shot in the streets. The Russians changed their minds about intervening 'I don't know how many times,' wrote Khrushchev. Frantic consultations went on with the Chinese, the newly-established Gomulka in Poland, with the Romanians, Bulgarians, Czechs, even with Tito. Only after that did the order go to the waiting troops to smash the uprising on the transparently false grounds that they had been asked to assist in quelling a 'counter-revolution.'

After three days of violent resistance, with 3,000 dead on the Russian side and 7,000 Hungarians, Budapest fell silent. General Pal Maletar of

Red Tanks in Budapest photographed by Erich Lessing

the freedom fighters, who was negotiating with the Russians under a safe-conduct pass, was arrested and shot. A puppet government was moved in behind the Russian tanks. Imre Nagy, the rebel premier, was assured of his safety if he left the Yugoslav embassy and was promptly seized and later executed. The naked cynicism of Russian power politics was manifest. Soviet control was preserved – but at a terrible psychological cost. All over the West party members resigned in horror. In Britain, where the *Daily Worker* refused to publish its own correspondent's eye-witness reports from Budapest, Harry Pollitt, the party secretary, resigned, ostensibly from ill-health. Young enthusiasts drove across the border to join the freedom fighters who had appealed to the world to help, but the world in general looked on in anguished impotence as the rebels were extinguished.

Britain's only response was to cancel the Royal Ballet's visit to Moscow. The British government was too embroiled in its Suez adventure to take a stand, or to have any moral ground to stand on. But it was the moral pretensions of Dulles and his policies which lost most credibility. For all his lofty declarations of the Christian mission to liberate the enslaved subjects of Communism, when they pleaded for liberation he remained deaf, if it meant risking war. He could not have asked for a clearer-case of his anti-Christian enemy 'trampling on the moral law' than in Hungary. But he showed no sign of carrying out his threat that 'they can and should be made to pay'.

The following Spring, a still shaken Khrushchev called a group of writers to his dacha outside Moscow and told them that the Hungarian rising could have been avoided if a few writers had been shot in time. If this situation arose in the Soviet Union, he warned them, 'my hand would not tremble'. The literary 'thaw' which set in after the secret speech was now going too fast for him, as he admits in his memoirs: 'We were scared – really scared – that the thaw might unleash a flood which could drown us.' One of its chief fruits was the submission of *Dr Zhivago* to the literary magazine *Novy Mir* in July 1956. Boris Pasternak, who had published nothing since the Thirties because he refused to submit to censorship by the party, had his manuscript rejected all the same. That year he gave it under cover to a Milan publisher, Feltrinelli, and in 1958 it appeared in English. Subsequently Pasternak won the Nobel prize. In the West its enormous popularity was as a love story set against the epic background of the Revolution and its aftermath. In Russia, it was the background that caused the sensation. Here there were none of the accustomed party cant or heroics about the Revolution.

After the Nobel announcement, *Novy Mir's* letter of rejection of two years before was hastily published to lend justification to Pasternak's expulsion from the writers' union as a traitor: 'The spirit of your novel is that of non-acceptance of the Socialist Revolution, that it brought the people nothing but suffering and destroyed the Russian intelligentsia ... that the Revolution was a mistake and that all that happened afterwards was evil.' It was too much for the rigid party mind.

Weary with the struggle to be understood, and fearful, like Solzhenitsyn after him, that to collect his prize in Stockholm might prove to be a one-way journey, Pasternak declined his honour, writing to Khrushchev that, for him, exile would mean death. Khrushchev appears to have taken Pasternak's side – when it was too late. The book should have been published, he told the writers' union, in a small edition and 'allowed to be forgotten'. Khrushchev, who had not read it, was no great judge of what would live; nor did he have any artistic education. 'Sometimes,' he cries in one of his disarming bursts of candour, 'You turn on the radio and say to yourself "Who wrote this junk?". Then you find out it was written by Tchaikovsky.' But he was not taking any more chances on writers who might turn out to need shooting.

There was another reason for caution – to the East of him. Mao Tsetung had played second fiddle to Stalin as senior revolutionary but Khrushchev was a different matter. By the mid-Fifties he considered himself the natural leader of world Communism. Despite all the fraternal banqueting, Khrushchev had returned from his first visit to Peking in 1954 and told his colleagues 'Conflict with China is inevitable.' 'We used to lie around a swimming pool in Peking chatting like the best of friends,' he later recalled, 'But it was all too sickeningly sweet ... Some of Mao's pronouncements struck me as being much too simplistic and others as being much too complex.' Such Maoisms as 'Let a hundred flowers bloom' and 'Imperialism is a paper tiger' were anathema to Khrushchev. In one of the sessions round the pool he was horrified to hear Mao apply kindergarten arithmetic to war. Between them they had many more divisions and better rockets than the West: so why didn't Khrushchev go ahead and provoke the war? That was only the first occasion that Chairman Khrushchev reminded Chairman Mao that the paper tiger had nuclear teeth. In doing so he was being made to look like a 'revisionist', one of the dirtiest words in the Communist vocabulary, their equivalent of 'UnAmerican' or worse. Just as in Washington the favourite McCarthy taunt was that the administration was 'soft on Communism', so Mao would accuse him of being 'soft on imperialism'. After he refused to supply the Chinese with atomic secrets, Chinese propaganda began to be openly anti-Soviet. The Kremlin leaders were 'bourgeois pacifists' who were betraying the revolution by seeking 'peaceful co-existence', which was a contradiction of Marx and Lenin. Soviet technicians, supervising the building of new factories in China, were harassed and their rooms ransacked and searched. Chinese students sent to university in Russia demonstrated noisily on their cross-country train journeys and, on one occasion that shocked Khrushchev deeply, defecated all over a Mongolian station platform. By 1960 all Soviet technicians had been recalled, taking their blueprints with them and leaving the factories to be finished as best they could be. Beneath it all lay Khrushchev's hostility to the 'cult of personality', declared at the twentieth Congress and afterwards at the very time that Mao's personality cult was endowing him with almost divine status. 'When I knew him,' writes Khrushchev, 'he was bursting with an impatient desire to rule the world. "Think of it," he said, "You have 200 million people and we have 700 million." His chauvinism and arrogance sent a shiver up my spine.'

Towards the end of the decade the long-frozen Cold War postures of East and West began to relax a little. In 1958 confrontation was avoided. The Red Chinese were persuaded to call off their bombardment of the Nationalists' offshore islands of Quemoy and Matsu. In a typically devious climb-down they announced they would bombard the island in future on only the odd dates of the month, as though the rain of shells was a form of parking restriction. In 1959 Macmillan became the first Western head of state to visit Moscow in time of peace, sporting a white fur hat (a psychological mistake, since white was only worn by Finns). Khrushchev lavished banquets, ballets and banter on him and took him tobogganing – then, with mysterious abruptness, withdrew his favours and gave the British a public drubbing over the Suez adventure and the Berlin question, where he was demanding the evacuation of allied troops. When they were due to fly to Kiev together he snubbed Macmillan by staying at home 'to have a tooth filled'. A day or two later he resumed the courtesies by paying mischievous tribute to the new British drill which his dentist had used to cure him. 'A mixture of Peter the Great and Lord Beaverbrook,' was Macmillan's somewhat bemused assessment.

The upshot of the visit was the withdrawal of the Berlin ultimatum in favour of a conference. Perhaps it was to exploit this slight sign of thaw that Eisenhower immediately afterwards invited Khrushchev to the United States. The fact that Foster Dulles had been removed from his

The two most powerful men in the world at a moment of détente

side by cancer (he died that May) only made this easier. When he saw the invitation, Khrushchev tells us he could not believe his eyes. So cold was the Cold War that America had been boycotting the import even of Soviet crab meat, let alone a live and wily Soviet leader. But he felt a tremendous sense of awe at the invitation to visit the President as an equal. 'I admit I was worried. I felt as though I were about to undergo an important test.'

Remembering the humiliation of arriving at the Geneva summit in 1955 in a plane with only two engines, he took the biggest and longest-range jet of its day, the TU 114, to New York. When it landed, the Americans had no steps tall enough to reach it, a gratifying start except for the fact that the Chairman of the Council of Ministers and his party had to climb down an emergency ladder hand over hand. The guard of honour, the 21-gun salute, and the reception party overawed Khrushchev, bringing with him an inferiority complex towards the West which was often the cause of his bluster. The visit hardly went like a breeze from start to finish. At gatherings of businessmen he was most often asked, 'Why should we trade with you? What do you have to sell us?' He was met with extreme suspicion and often a rudeness that was doubtless considered patriotic, like Gary Cooper's in Hollywood. He lounged over on the studio lot to deliver the not very perspicacious remark that he was glad to have heard Khrushchev promise the Russians would surpass the Americans because competition was a capitalist idea. As Khrushchev began to reply, he walked away. 'I wasn't going to stand there and listen to that stuff,' explained Cooper graciously. Nothing went right that day. At lunch at the commissary of 20th Century Fox, Spyros P. Skouras (he who had insisted that his movie makers clear themselves of Communist taint) asked in his speech where else in the world but in America could a poor Greek boy have become so important a person as president of 20th Century Fox? Khrushchev was ready to trump that one. As a poor boy in the Soviet Union he had, he pointed out, become chairman of the Supreme Council of Soviets, a job whose responsibilities compared even with those of running 20th Century Fox.

Then came the visit to the shooting of a dance sequence from an un-remembered film called *Can-Can*. Frank Sinatra, pacing the sound stage in his elevator shoes, explained they had all been up late the night before and that their performance might leave something to be desired. It did. As a cunning demonstration of the superiority of a free culture the scene required the girls to expose their pantied behinds to the visitor and a chorus boy to run his head beneath Shirley MacLaine's petticoat and emerge with her underwear. All of this led to Khrushchev's best-remembered comment of the tour: 'Man's face,' he said, 'is more beautiful than his backside.' Just to round the day off, the Mayor of Los Angeles, Norris Poulson, told Khrushchev at the banquet in his honour that he was well-known to Americans as the man who had promised to bury them. This remark had haunted Khrushchev, who had several times explained he did not mean it literally, and finally got that famous goat. Khrushchev rose with dignity and asked his audience to stop reducing the life and death of whole peoples to a joke. 'One should not play on words,' he said, 'We hold positions of too much responsibility.' The audience applauded. Back at his hotel Khrushchev raged that he would cancel the rest of his tour, though he was ranting, he explained in his memoirs, for the benefit of the microphones he was sure were concealed in his room, relaying what he said to Henry Cabot Lodge, his ambassador-escort. But eventually he was mollified and went on his way, drawing all eyes, swapping his watch for a cigar from a factory worker, feeling the maize cobs in the Iowa corn belt, stuffing himself with hot dogs before the television cameras. This uninhibited tourist did not look like the Frankenstein monster whom many Americans had expected and some of them began to wonder if they had got Khrushchev and his modest and dignified wife wrong.

So he reached Camp David, the presidential dacha which he had first suspected of being an outpost of the American Gulag. As the president's weekend guest he discovered that Ike had one thing in common with Stalin – they both expected him to watch Westerns. But the talks themselves were a virtual stalemate. Khrushchev decided he liked Eisenhower, 'a reasonable and modest man', and the much discussed 'Spirit of Camp David' meant that a lot of smiling went on in public. But, though they both admitted they desired it, they could find no way of ending the arms race. 'Some people might say nothing came of our talks,' Khrushchev remembered later, 'My answer to that is yes and no. We broke the ice which held our relations in a paralysing grip. The Americans recognized the failure of their past efforts to discredit and humiliate us.' Was the shade of Foster Dulles listening?

Nobody who had looked at the bald bullet-head and roly-poly self-confidence of the visitor, or heard his folksy repartee, could fail to have been reminded of an *American* grass roots politician on tour. He hardly lived up to his Dullesian billing as an emissary of Satan. Was this what the Cold War was all about? Although the flight of the U2 spy plane and the debacle of the summit the following year were to put everybody back on guard once more, there were some moments at the end of the Fifties when the fog of ideology cleared enough for realism to creep in. At such moments it did not seem better to be dead than Red, neither did it seem plausible that there was a godless conspiracy at work wherever one looked. There was a balance of power – but there had always been a balance of power. Now it was shifting eastward to include China in the equation.

CHAPTER SIX

Youthquake

Holden Caulfield, a sixteen-year-old reject from American private schools, with a red hunting hat whose long peak he pulled round to the back, captured the imagination of English-speaking readers in 1951 in a book mysteriously entitled *The Catcher In The Rye*. Its author, J. D. Salinger, was and remains a recluse who seldom breaks silence by publication and never by giving public explanations of his work. He had an ear finely tuned to certain faint vibrations in the generation raised in or just after the war. Holden Caulfield, who narrates the book in one long confidence to the reader couched in his own fractured vernacular style, became a hero in universities and colleges around the country for telling the young what they were feeling before they knew it. It turned out to be what the young were feeling in Britain too. He spoke an international language of disaffection. Holden's message was that he had weighed up the adult world and found it crumby – to use one of his favourite words – and, to use another, *phoney* through and through.

In his odyssey through New York on his way home from the fourth private school to throw him out, he finds 'the phoneys are coming in the goddam window' almost wherever he looks. Phoneys include his headmaster who was nice to the smart parents but ignored the rest, preachers and ministers with Holy Joe voices, old boys who declared that school was the happiest time of their lives, and anyone who pretended to give a damn if the football team won or lost. 'Learning to be smart enough to buy a goddam Cadillac' does not appeal to Holden. He also dislikes actors who let you see that they know how good they are and night club pianists who turn round and give 'this very phoney, *humble* bow.' He does not care for sophisticated New York bars where singers with overdone French accents are admired by people with 'tired, snobby Ivy League accents'. Naturally he is always trying to pass himself off as an adult (he is six-foot-two) with barmen, waiters, hotel porters and prostitutes, but in the end finds the charade insufferable.

Though Holden has his naive and sentimental streak, his young sister puts her finger on it when she says, 'You don't like *anything* that's happening.' That was his appeal to the young. He rejected the adult world in its entirety. His ambition was never to have to join it: 'I thought what

I'd do was, I'd pretend to be one of those deaf mutes. That way I wouldn't have to have any goddam stupid useless conversations with anybody.' To some extent this is a feeling recognizable to all adolescents throughout human history, but this was a specially propitious moment to open up the generation gap. For Holden, it couldn't be wide enough. In the Forties there had been no such thing as a teenager. In 1951 it was still assumed that to be sixteen was to be waiting around to 'join the game of life' as one of his mentors put it. 'Game my ass,' is Holden's succinct comment, 'Some game'. Alongside the phoney, materialist adult world pretending to be nice, Salinger placed the innocence of children, exemplified by Holden's younger sister, Phoebe, who understands him and wants to run away with him to a cabin in the West. Holden's vision of the ideal life is of children who really *are* playing a game in a big field of rye on the edge of a cliff. His task is to catch them just in time to save them from falling over the edge, presumably from innocence into experience. It was an impossible dream, which is why he is addressing the reader from a vaguely hinted-at sanitarium or loony bin. The gulf he is pointing to between childhood and adulthood is not yet a separate stage of life. It is a precipice comparable to the fall of Man.

Three themes in this book – distrust of elders, distrust of adult values and distrust of the still prevailing conspiracy of silence over sex (Holden is a very reluctant virgin) – grew more and more insistent in the early Fifties until they converged in one crucial year, 1956, in the explosive discovery of teenage identity – a Youthquake.

The adult world first became aware of the process as a puzzling and disturbing increase in juvenile crime and delinquency. Crimes by offenders under twenty-one in England rose from 24,000 in 1955 to 45,000 in 1959. Early in the decade Britain produced the first Teddy Boys, a not very numerous but very colourful minority of unskilled, unregarded urban working-class boys who sought an identity through draped jackets, velvet collars and drainpipe trousers. They pursued violent gang warfare and vandalism in the streets and dance halls. The remarkable thing is that very soon parallel styles were evolved by delinquent gangs in Germany ('Halbstarken' – half strong), Sweden (Skinnnuttar – leather jackets), France ('Blousons Noirs' – blackshirts), Japan ('Taiyo-zoku' – children of the sun) and even Soviet Russia ('Stilyagi' – style boys). It was a youth movement almost as international as its

OPPOSITE *A characteristic Teddy Boy of 1954, in drainpipe trousers and Edwardian jacket, outside the Mecca Dance Hall in Tottenham*

opposite, the Boy Scouts. Scouting – good deeds in eccentric uniform – had its greatest appeal after the first war 'to end war'; delinquency in eccentric uniform appealed to the generation that did not quite remember the second war to end war. And twenty-five years later, the Teddy Boy style was to be revived by a generation to whom the first Teddy Boys were as historical a phenomenon as the original Edwardians.

One of the international symbols of revolt was a hairstyle, long (for the time), greasy, curly and sideboarded. A rash of elaborate variations broke out among boys who had hitherto been made to wear a wartime 'short back and sides': the 'Tony Curtis' and the 'D.A.' (for Duck's Arse or Duck-ass according to which side of the Atlantic it was on) were the most popular. The style owed much to America. Even the Teddy Boy uniform, which was supposed to be a copy of smart Edwardian gentlemen's wear owed more to the look of Baddies in a Western – especially the sideburns and the bootlace ties – rather than the Knuts of the Gaiety Theatre stage door or the Empire promenade.

There was nothing gentlemanly about their anti-social behaviour. They did not deign to dance but went to dance halls to break up the decorum and the toilet fittings. Their Edwardian finery concealed coshes, bicycle chains, razors and flick-knives which they pulled on one another in the streets of south and west London. There was no dandyism about their behaviour. In 1954 a gang of Teds murdered a defenceless youth on Clapham Common and in 1958 they were prominent among the provokers of the Notting Hill race riots. Their originality compared to street gangs of the past was their narcissistic absorption in their appearance, 'It was a point of honour among the Teds,' wrote T. R. Fyvel in *The Insecure Offenders*, 'to be more interested in themselves than in girls.' They were using clothes to assert their right to have attention paid to them.

In the United States the same motive led to the adoption of more sinister fancy dress, the motor-cyclists' black leather, brass studded jackets. Again it was the outcasts – the Negroes of Harlem and Puerto Ricans – who set the style. When the latter were romanticized as the 'Jets' and the 'Sharks' in the musical *West Side Story* in 1958 it was against a background of a New York where there were estimated to be 150 gangs with 6,000 followers. They had no motor cycles. The idea of the motorized adolescent gang began in spacious California where the first gang raid occurred in 1947 on the hamlet of Hollister. First recorded in detail in a magazine article in *Harper's*, it was, after long hesitation, converted into the film, *The Wild One*, released in 1954. In the film the

Precursor of 'Hell's Angels' – Marlon Brando in THE WILD ONE

gang ride into 'Wrightsville', commandeer the town, break into the jail,
terrorize a girl hostage (gang rape was intended but any suggestion of it
was vetoed by the production code) and finally kill an old man – by
accident. They get away with nothing worse than a severe telling-off
by the sheriff.

Originally the film's intention was to analyse the reasons for gang
violence. Marlon Brando, who played the gang's 'president', stated their

attitude: 'These guys are nameless, faceless fry-cooks and grease monkeys all week, working at dreary jobs they hate. They've got to break out and *be* somebody, they've got to belong to something. They do violent things because they've been held down so long.' But at the height of McCarthyism, any idea that American society might be blameworthy, indeed anything less than perfect, seemed too daring to the movie producers, and consequently the film turned into a display of violence for its own sake and was banned in most towns in Britain. A disenchanted Brando said afterwards: 'Instead of finding out why young people bunch in groups that seek expression in violence, all we did was show the violence.' *Time* magazine dismissed the picture as 'too overdrawn to engage credulity' but life was already catching up with art. Some gangs existed. In ten years they would break into the headlines, committing rape and mayhem in California towns under the title of 'Hell's Angels'. Meanwhile in the cities they persisted with their 'presidents', their hierarchies of power, their nicknames for gang members like those in the film – 'Chino', 'Gringo', 'Mouse', 'Red', 'Crazy' – and a private language in which they talked of having 'heart' (reckless courage), minding their 'turf' (territory), 'bopping' and 'japping' (fighting and beating up). Significantly, they called one another 'man'. Harrison Salisbury of the *New York Times* studied them like a naturalist observing a new sub-species and reported in *The Shook-Up Generation* on their 'rumbles': Montagu and Capulet skirmishes conducted with the modern equivalent of the rapier, a snapped-off car aerial.

It was in this climate of emergent self-consciousness, allied with a taste for violence and speed, that youth found its first satisfying symbol in the person of James Dean. He had all the ingredients that make a myth. He was an outsider from the Indiana backwoods. He lost his mother and home when he was nine. He ran away to prove himself to the world. He was rejected in love. He found release in speed. He had an extraordinary capacity for looking injured and wronged. And by the time most young people had heard of him he was dead. Death, at 24, in fitting circumstances – the seat of a smashed-up racing car – made him, for his contemporaries at least, immortal. Dean distilled the essence of youthful non-belonging – in the same sense as Holden Caulfield meant it – for everyone between fourteen and twenty-four. His life was as

OPPOSITE *James Dean – 'the resentful hair, . . . the deep eyes floating in lonesomeness, the bitter beat look, the scorn on the lip'*

The wreckage of the Porsche in which James Dean died

alienated as his films. He summed up his refusal to join the Hollywood star system by his behaviour before Hedda Hopper, queen bee columnist and chief toady to the studios. He slouched in for the arranged meeting in his dirtiest clothes, put his feet up on a commissary chair, jumped up and stared at one of the framed portraits of the studio's stars on the wall, spat on the glass, wiped it with his handkerchief, sat down again, still ignoring Miss Hopper, and wolfed his lunch.

He was also half in love with death, obsessed with men who risked it in war, in the bull ring, on the motor racing circuit. 'Death is the only thing left to respect,' he said, 'The one inevitable, undeniable truth.' When his Porsche Spyder collided with another car at a crossroads *en route* to a motor racing meeting – it was never settled who was to blame or whether the short-sighted Dean was wearing his spectacles – an amazing hysteria gripped the young. Within two weeks, in September 1955, his second picture, the emotively named *Rebel Without A Cause*, was released, and adolescents everywhere identified with its delinquent, hurt hero.

For three years afterwards his fan mail of 2,000 letters a week outnumbered that of any living actor. Many of the letters stated 'I know you are not dead'. There were rumours that he had been shut away in a sanitarium, terribly disfigured from the crash. In a macabre echo of Gethsemane, his grave in Fairmount, Indiana, though guarded by police, was said to be empty. His crumpled car was exhibited in Los Angeles and 800,000 people went to see it, many of them paying extra for the macabre thrill of sitting in the driving seat in which he died. Chips from his tombstone were set into rings, and pieces of bloodstained and twisted metal alleged to come from the Porsche were sold as souvenirs. Thousands made pilgrimages to the cemetery and two years after his death a film biography, *The James Dean Story*, was distributed. Buttons and brooches appeared with advertisements like this:

> JAMES DEAN FANS! ! ! Keep the memory of Jimmy Dean alive by following the craze that is sweeping America: wear this BEAUTIFUL PHOTOGRAPHIC REPRODUCTION of an Original Oil Painting!

John Dos Passos wrote a poem that talked of 'the resentful hair . . . the deep eyes floating in lonesomeness, the bitter beat look, the scorn on the lip.' What was it that made the scornful lip, the lonesome eyes, the resentful hair inspire such powerful necrophilia? Unlike Valentino, his obvious forerunner, he had no reputation as a lover, on screen or off. His appeal was not to a sex but to an age-group. What he offered, again like Holden Caulfield, was a rallying point against the adult world of corruption. In all three of his films adults, especially parents, exist to reject, hurt and warp the young. In Steinbeck's *East of Eden* Dean was cast as a lonely boy, Cal, whose help is rejected by his bankrupt father and whose mother has deserted him to run a brothel. 'Talk to me please, mother,' he begs as he is dragged away. His next, most satisfying film, *Rebel Without a Cause*, showed him as the alienated teenage son of well-to-do middle class parents. His domineering mother bickers with the weak and gutless father until the boy screams at them: 'You're tearing me apart!' His two bosom friends share his isolation: Judy (Julie Harris) is rejected by her father while Plato (Sal Mineo) lives apart from his divorced parents. Jim (Dean) begins the film drunk and in custody, continues by challenging the local gang leader – the famous 'chicken run' sequence in which both drive for the cliff's edge and the last to jump is 'chicken' – and ends as a fugitive, trying but failing to protect his friend Plato from the police bullets. In every possible way it is the story of a loser, kicked in the face by an unconcerned world but responding heroically to the different values of his own age-group– courage, loyalty and innocent calf love.

In his last picture, *Giant*, Dean's character is rejected by a surrogate family, the owners of half a million acres of Texas ranchland on which he is the despised, semi-articulate hired hand, Jett Rink. There is a memorable scene of role reversal: when his tiny patch of land strikes oil for him, he exultantly gate-crashes their garden party in his truck, covered in the black crude oil from the gusher that will make him as rich as them. The least effective part of the film comes afterwards, when Dean is required to play a millionaire instead of a victim. Whether, had he lived, he could have made the transition to such parts is a matter of guesswork. He would have been noticed at any time in cinema history because of his troubling good looks, his expressive body, his ability to walk magnificently. But the time at which he appeared was exactly right for him.

The blandness of Hollywood's acting styles had already been shattered by Marlon Brando, whose meteoric career began in 1950 with *The Men*, a tough film about paraplegics, and reached worldwide fame in 1952 with the Mexican heroics of *Viva Zapata!* followed by *A Streetcar Named Desire*. It was the part of the vulgar, sadistic but perversely attractive brute, Stanley Kowalski, who fascinates and destroys Blanche du Bois, which more than any other set the style of Brandoism. It was a kind of super-realism which was to become the norm for film acting within a few years but which raised outraged hackles in a Hollywood accustomed to polish and elegance of diction, movement and grooming. 'I don't understand a goddam thing the sonofabitch says – can't you stop him from mumbling?' said Daryl Zanuck at his screen test. The 'scratch-and-mumble' school of acting it was dubbed by critics fixated on the past. Young actors like Dean and Paul Newman paid Brando the compliment of imitating it and were taken to task for it. *East of Eden*, like *Streetcar*, was directed by Elia Kazan, who was ultimately responsible for the style of both Brando's and Dean's performances. Dean, who used to watch Brando at work whenever possible, said 'It is impossible not to carry around the image of so successful an actor.' Both had attended the Actor's Studio and both were exponents of 'whole body acting' such as Brando had demonstrated so powerfully in *Streetcar*.

Dean carried his warming-up methods to lengths that were not appreciated by his fellow actors of the older school. According to Rock Hudson: 'He never stepped into camera range without first jumping into the air with his knees up under his chin or running round the set shrieking like a bird of prey.' He even used the bladder as an aid to his performance. In *East of Eden* he played the tense, uncertain love scene with Julie Harris on the fairground big wheel with a bursting bladder, after a day spent refraining from relieving it, to achieve greater intensity and unease. And when he was due to play his first location scene in *Giant* with Elizabeth Taylor watched by a large and curious crowd, he broke the tension by advancing towards the onlookers, unzipping his trousers, letting fly, and walking back to rejoin the actors. According to a friend who asked him why, he said 'he figured if he could do that in front of four thousand people, he could go back and do anything with Liz Taylor in front of the camera.' Kazan, who did not like Dean, said his body was more expressive than Brando's – 'It had so much tension in it'. He saw no resemblance between the reaction to Brando and to Dean: 'The main thing you felt about him is hurt. And the main thing the girls felt and the boys felt and the faggots felt about him was that you'd want to put your arm around him and protect him and look after him . . . Don't cry kid, I'm on your side.'

Dean was a natural victim, Brando a natural victor, with a touch of the truck driver about him, the physique of a boxer and the broken nose that, in the words of his make-up man, 'dripped down his face like melted ice-cream.' Dean's rebelliousness was that of a small, slight and spectacled boy, moody but vulnerable and above all, immature. His power was over the immature, besides bringing out the protective instinct in their elders. The two men maintained a wary distance from each other, an undeclared rivalry. After Dean took to arriving at the studios on a motorbike in a dirty jerkin and jeans, Brando, who pioneered that style, promptly gave it up for neat shirts and slacks. 'He had an *idée fixe* about me. Whatever I did, he did.' Brando told Truman Capote after Dean's death. 'He was always trying to get close to me. He used to call me up . . . I'd listen to him talking to the answering service, leaving messages. But I never called him back.' Brando finally met him at a party and recommended him to an analyst. But despite his rather patronizing tone, they were both on the same side against the Hollywood of bourgeois, show-business values. Dean spat for Hedda Hopper, Brando refused to do more than grunt for her or for her crony, Louella Parsons. He maintained his aloofness from the world of fan magazines, premières and award ceremonies. He took out waitresses and secretaries rather than screen goddesses. 'I had every right to resist turning my private life into the kind of running serial you find on bubblegum wrappers,' he said. Both refused to play the star game by the rules observed by a Ronald Colman or a Cary Grant. Sudden, violent death froze Dean for ever in the role of the teenage rebel while Brando lived on becoming plumper and less aggressive, reaching his high tide in *On The Waterfront* (1954) before declining into such costumed exotica as Napoleon in *Desirée*. At the end of the Fifties it seemed (wrongly) that the Wild One had been tamed indeed. He returned from France with a fisherman's daughter as his fiancée and he was wearing *a hat*.

In 1955, the year of James Dean's death, the anti-adult, anti-bourgeois heroes were already in place but as yet the combustible element was

ROCK AROUND THE CLOCK *Bill Haley and the Comets*

missing. That element was a new kind of music, which was first heard that year accompanying the title of a film called *Blackboard Jungle*:

One-two-three o'clock, four o'clock rock!
Five-six-seven o'clock, eight o'clock rock! –
Nine-ten-eleven o'clock, twelve o'clock rock! –
We're gonna rock around the clock!

The effect of those words shouted to a deafening, pistol-cracking beat unlocked the floodgates of a generation's self-awareness. It was a crude sound. It was a young sound. And, once again, it was a sound stolen by white musicians from blacks. It expressed very forcibly the contempt of teenage minds for middle-aged, middle-class, middle-of-the-road music. Above all it vibrated with highly-charged adolescent sexual energy. The film itself, set in an American slum school where a classroom of thugs beat up their teacher, was not the stuff by which cinemas are normally packed. It contained one symbolic scene in which the kids smashed a friendly teacher's collection of jazz 78 records. But the magic moment was the assault of the title music played by the then little-known band of Bill Haley and his Comets. As soon as it exploded from the sound track, the teenage audience rose from their seats and bounced or jived in the aisles as if by spontaneous combustion.

By May 1955 'Rock Around The Clock' was the anthem of dissident youth of all classes. It stayed at the top of the record charts for five months and by the next year was the title of a cheap quickie movie. Haley and his band rocked their way through it to fame and fortune with the bass player lying on top of his instrument straddled by the saxophone player who removed his tartan jacket to reveal his braces. The picture took a million dollars in American cinemas in 1956 but curiously the riots it was famed for causing occurred mostly in Britain. At the Elephant and Castle, the home ground of South London Teddy Boys, riots in the cinema were reported by excitable newspapers to have led to two thousand young people taking to the streets in an orgy of vandalism. By subsequent standards it seems to have been a mild sort of riot: nine arrests, two policemen injured, some cups and saucers thrown about the streets and one or two £1 fines awarded. But wherever the film was shown afterwards there was further trouble and ripping out of cinema seats (they got in the way of the dancing). Many towns banned the picture. Pundits discussed it in newspaper and pulpit. The Queen sent for a print in Scotland. In Bombay it ran for eleven weeks. In Moscow it was given underground showings. Rock 'n' roll had arrived.

In the next two years Bill Haley's band sold twenty-two million records. Compare that with the figure of twenty-seven million which was the entire output of the very popular Victor Silvester and his strict-tempo ballroom orchestra· in its whole career up to that time. Haley himself, a plumpish, thirtyish, dance band leader with a kiss-curl plastered damply on his forehead, had spent years playing for high school hops. He had realized that no band was providing what the high school audience wanted, which was a strong, indeed stupefying, beat. He began to record numbers which were a hybrid of country music and black Rhythm and Blues, previously known as 'race' music. By then the words 'rock' and 'roll' were occurring frequently in the very limited vocabulary of the lyrics: 'Shake, rattle and *roll*', 'Ma Daddy *rocks* me with one steady *roll*', 'You've gotta *rock* with me, Henry, all night long,' 'Let the good times *roll* . . . ' It took a disc jockey called Alan Freed to put the two words together and christen the new music, which he broadcast in a programme called *Moondog's Rock and Roll Party*. By 1955 he had promoted an also-ran among New York radio stations, WINS, to the top of the audience ratings with his music, now folksily shortened to 'rock 'n' roll'. Record companies were not slow to sense that a market of enormous potential had been discovered. Haley went on to record a string of numbers whose titles tell their own story: 'Rip It Up', 'Rockin' Through The Rye', 'Don't Knock The Rock' and 'See You Later Alligator'. This became such a popular catch-phrase with its response, 'In a while, crocodile' (exchanged, so it was said, as a greeting by Princess Margaret and her set) that there was a sudden vogue for baby alligators as pets. The rumour ran that when people became bored with keeping the creatures in their baths they flushed them away and the New York and London sewers were becoming infested with lethal amphibians of ever-increasing size and snappishness – a picturesque thought for which no evidence, such as a disappearance of sewermen, was ever forthcoming.

In 1957 Bill Haley announced his imminent arrival in Britain to a breathless public whom he greeted through the columns of the *Daily Mirror*: 'Yeah, man, we are on our way, waiting to dig that crazy train at Southampton. Oh man, we really are hopping to dig you British cats.' As it turned out the British cats were not hopping for long to dig the too-too-solid, ample and ageing flesh of Mr Haley, whose image did not match the sound he had pioneered. The new music was clearly labelled 'Under 21s Only' and he was over thirty. Rock 'n' roll was the music of youthful revolt or it was nothing. Its crude, simple, deafening vigour was its point. By comparison all previous popular music had been middle-aged. Until then the Fifties had been the heyday of ballad singers, especially the long succession of Italian-Americans following in the wake of Frank Sinatra's success – Frankie Laine (born Lo Vecchio), Perry Como, Mario Lanza, Vic Damone, Al Martino and many more with anglicized names like Dean Martin and Tony Bennett. The top-of-the-pop charts in the mid-Fifties were dominated by Sinatra's 'Three Coins In The Fountain', and 'Love And Marriage', Doris Day's 'Secret Love' and 'Que Sera Sera', Eddie Fisher's 'Oh! My Papa!', Rosemary Clooney's 'Hey there!', Perry Como's 'No Other Love' and Frankie Laine's 'A Woman In Love'. It was a reassuring world of sentimental conformism that was presented to the young, for the most part by singers old enough to be their fathers. Mr Wonderfuls still promised them some enchanted evenings with a stranger in paradise who might well turn out to be Oh! My Papa! England also produced its tenor balladeers from factory bench and milk round and building lot – Dickie Valentine, Frankie Vaughan, David Whitfield, Dennis Lotis, Ronnie Hilton – and its songstresses of restrained charm such as Petula Clark, Alma Cogan, Anne Shelton and Ruby Murray, who at one time was selling one out of every four records in Britain, most of them of a hit called 'Softly, Softly'.

Apart from Johnny Ray, who sobbed out 'Cry' (if your sweetheart sends a letter of goodbye) with his hearing aid clearly visible to an audience of screaming bobby-soxers, there was little here to appeal to anyone under twenty-one. The music was too languid to support anything but a slow smoochy fox-trot or occasionally a stiff-tempo quickstep. Rock 'n' roll swept away the formalities of having to learn the steps. Gone was the waist-grip, the outstretched hand-clasp. Contact between the partners was reduced to the minimum, a quick grab, a flick of the wrist into the girl's pirouette. Sometimes only the finger-tips were in contact. Boy and girl no longer looked at each other but danced in a trance with inscrutable expressions of aloofness, even boredom, like clockwork animals gyrating to some hidden spring. It was the transition stage to complete separation of the partners in the Sixties. But there was always the relief of a slow, usually mournful, set of numbers to which the rockers would stand motionless propped against one another. This enabled the ballad to survive and indeed the two years of the rock 'n' roll explosion also saw the rise to fame of the too-good-to-be-true all-American college boy, Pat Boone, who sang 'I'll Be Home' and 'Don't Forbid Me' and 'Friendly Persuasion' in as healthy and wholesome a manner as could be wished by any mother in the land. He smoked not, neither did he drink. He took two showers daily, was a pillar of his suburban church and the father of three by his marriage to his high school sweetheart. He sang, he explained, to help pay his way through Columbia University and must have had a certain amount of change to spare out of his earnings from a sale of ten million records. One of the Top Ten hits of the decade (computed by the trade paper *Billboard*) was Pat Boone's 'Love Letters In The Sand'. No true rock 'n' roll number was anywhere on the list.

But though its reign was for a limited period, it was rock 'n' roll which produced the phenomenon no other form of popular music has ever equalled: a husky young truck-driver from Memphis, Elvis Aron Presley. It is possible that as much attention was paid to Mao Tse Tung or Fidel Castro or John F. Kennedy, among post-war figures of world renown, but they are the only contenders. In Elvis teenagers at last found a model who looked and acted the way they felt. Presley had asked to record a song for his mother's birthday one day in Memphis in 1953 and chose the studio of Sam Phillips, manager of the small, independent Sun Records. Some time before this Mr Phillips had announced 'What I need is a white boy who can sing coloured.' Now he thought he heard the sound he wanted and invested twenty months in nurturing it. He was right, for many people on first hearing Presley assumed he was black.

Had he been black it is not likely that within three years he would have been appearing only from the waist upwards on television at record fees of 50,000 dollars an appearance. The waist-upwards rule was to avoid the dangerous pelvis which so shocked the white world. 'He moved,' wrote a critic, 'as if he was sneering with his legs.' Even above the waist he gave offence to the *New York Times* which noted: 'He injected movements of the tongue and indulged in wordless singing that was singularly distasteful.' There were constant protests at Presley from Catholics, critics and guardians of public seemliness. In Miami he was charged with obscenity. In Des Moines he was declared 'morally insane'. In Oakland, California, a policeman said: 'If he did that on the street, we'd arrest him.' Official disapproval, of course, only increased his appeal to teenagers everywhere, and it was music to the ears of 'Colonel' Tom Parker, his manager, who had bought him from Sam Phillips for the very considerable sum for that time of 35,000 dollars.

The 'colonel' (a courtesy title but by whose courtesy was not clear) was not a military man but a showman, a veteran of country fairs and carnivals who had not been above peddling hot dogs and lemonade in his

An unusual photograph of an unusually relaxed Elvis, 1957

early days, nor painting sparrows yellow to pass as canaries. He might well have been a living version of a W. C. Fields role. One of his most successful sideshows had been a dancing chicken act. The chickens began to hop and gyrate when the Colonel turned on a radiator concealed beneath their straw. Now he had a chicken of a different kind whose gyrations turned on a radiator of sensuality beneath an hysterical mass of teenage girls to the extent that, as the phrase cynically had it, 'there wasn't a dry seat in the house'. Presley's first nationally released record, 'Heartbreak Hotel' ('Ah'm-ah sah lonelah baybah') appeared in January 1956. It sold three million copies and topped every record chart around the world. In the next two years Elvis and the Colonel between them grossed a hundred million dollars. Elvis made four box office hit films in quick succession, and the inventive Colonel sold franchises for Presley T-shirts, Presley jeans, badges and diaries, even lipsticks ('Hound Dog Orange') and toilet paper. Elvis himself, already acquiring Cadillacs by the garage-full, bought the former presidential yacht *Potomac* as a Presley yacht.

The simple reason for this sensational success was that Elvis, unlike Pat Boone and the crooners, did not moon about April Love, Secret Love, Love And Marriage, or promises of Friendly Persuasion. He was the first white singer to sing about naked lust. Everything about him said 'stud'. He left his audience in no doubt of the meaning of 'Good Rockin' Tonight'. His lyrics were sub-literate, truculent aphrodisiacs helped out with rutting noises, animal grunts and groans. He manipulated his hips and guitar together into an explicit paraphrase of the sexual act. His looks were the most provocative in show business: surmounting the gold *lamé* ensembles, the suede shoes and jewelry, was a face noticeably similar in type to those of Brando and Dean – someone called him a 'guitar-playing Marlon Brando' – with grease-gleaming, duck-tailed hair and a plumed quiff. With his sideburns, heavy-lidded eyes and slightly cruel lips, he looked *common*, an essential part of his bad-boy appeal, an unusually spruce and dazzling example of the rough trade. And his movements left no doubt that he could be as rough and vigorous as a young stallion. The most exciting singer, someone called him, since Al Jolson – and it wasn't his Mammy he was singing about. And yet off-stage, for publicity purposes at least, he was a model citizen, as god-fearing as Pat Boone, who called his elders 'Sir' and 'Ma'am' with Southern courtesy. 'God gave me a voice,' ran one of his rare utterances, 'If I turned against God I'd be finished.' And there was no denying his deep-throated, blue voice that could turn from a war-cry to dripping treacle and back again, was the most original sound to come out of the rock 'n' roll era.

By 1958, for many of his worshippers, Elvis's best years were over – the years of 'Hound Dog', 'All Shook Up', 'Jailhouse Rock' and 'Hard-Hearted Woman'. Then he sailed for Germany to do his military service leaving several recordings ready in the larder for release by the provident Colonel Parker. But he came back a changed man – a loyal servant of Uncle Sam who had put on plenty of weight in his service and now only wanted to be a 'family entertainer'. And so he became, in a series of movies of stunning banality. He even put on tails to sing with Sinatra. It looked like a steady decline into flabbiness and decadence, and yet, by dying of a heart attack at the age of forty-two, the overweight idol proved that he had never lost the world's affection. His death commanded more attention that any since President Kennedy's and the scenes of mass mourning recalled those for Valentino. The President of the U.S.A., a fellow-Southerner, called him 'a symbol of the vitality, rebelliousness and good humour of the country.'

Many meteors of early rock 'n' roll met sudden ends. Buddy Holly was killed in a plane crash in 1959; Little Richard believed the Russian Sputnik was a sign that he should enter a seminary to become a minister; Jerry Lee Lewis tactlessly married his thirteen-year-old cousin and was widely booed and finally banned on a tour of Britain; Chuck Berry went to jail; Bill Haley became too fat. Congress investigated the 'payola' bribery of disc jockeys in 1959. Dick Clark, the disc jockey who made rock 'n' roll hits by spinning the records on his daily TV show, 'American Bandstand' (with the artists synching their lip movements and the white bobby-soxed audience rocking to the record) was cleared but fellow-DJ Alan Freed was discovered to be deeply implicated. Rock 'n' roll ended the Fifties in a nose-dive from which it looked unlikely ever to recover. A shrewd market assessor would have dismissed it as a flash in the pan, a hectic craze in the interval between ballad singing. Besides, it was beginning to bore even the teenagers.

Girls in particular were demanding their share of romantic music, and this was supplied by the vocal close harmony ('doo-wop') groups, mostly black, who proliferated under the names of birds – Flamingos, Orioles, Robins – insects, flowers, even makes of car. The Platters revived the style of the Ink Spots of the Forties and the Coasters (originally Robins) were their nearest rivals. The emphasis of the hit songs was on true love as can only be experienced before the age of twenty, on the right side of the generation gap. The Coasters sang of

'Young Blood', the Everly Brothers sang 'Bye Bye Love' and 'All I Have
To Do is Dream', Frankie Lymon and the Teenagers asked 'Why Do
Fools Fall In Love?', Dion and the Belmonts expounded on 'A Teenager In Love', Tab Hunter suffered from 'Young Love', the baby-voiced
Buddy Holly and the Crickets promised 'That'll Be The Day' and, most
explicitly of all, Nat King Cole plaintively rebuked the middle-aged in
the song 'Too Young':

> They tried to tell us we're too young,
> Too young to really be in love,
> They say that love's a word,
> A word we've only heard
> And can't begin to know the meaning of . . .

For the first time you did not have to apologize for being young . . .
the others had to feel bad about *not* being. Their music proclaimed that
teenagers were a new species, completely different from their predecessors
who spent their early years dumbly segregated in school or awaiting
call-up to the armed forces. They had just been old people waiting to
grow up. These were dreading growing up. In Britain, teenage culture
had a network of rebel rendezvous – the coffee bars which proliferated
like tropical rain-forest amid the hiss of Gaggia espresso steam and an
undergrowth of rubber plants. Many of them also had Sieberg juke-
boxes to play the American hits to which the whole generation was
orientated. In the cellar beneath a Soho coffee bar called 'The Two i's'
was discovered an ex-cabin boy from Bermondsey called Tommy
Hicks. He was playing skiffle at the time: it was a curious spin-off from
the revivalist jazz boom of those days. During the breaks for refreshment – copious refreshment was essential to an historically correct jazz
style – the audience was entertained by some guitar singing. In the
case of Chris Barber's banjo-player, Lonnie Donegan, the guitar-
backed solos soon outstripped the parent jazz in popularity. His engine-
driving epic, 'Rock Island Line', had the distinction of having to be
promoted from an LP to a single which climbed both the British and
American charts in Elvis-riddled 1956. In England it sparked off the
national love of amateurism. Skiffle became a countrywide craze before
the rock 'n' roll wave hit the shore. Almost anyone could have a passable
shot at it, even if it was only on a kazoo. Donegan showed them how to
construct a bass from a tea-chest, broom handle and string, to which was
added a washboard and as many three-chord guitarists as wanted to join
in. A high, nasal whine served for the vocal – the more nasal, the more

folksy and 'sincere'. Jazz purists were contemptuous but Donegan went through the decade outselling all native attempts to imitate Elvis with folk numbers like 'Cumberland Gap' and 'Tom Dooley' or chirpy ones like 'Putting On The Style' or 'Does The Chewing Gum Lose Its Flavour On The Bedpost Overnight?' which took him back finally into the music hall tradition.

Tommy Hicks was renamed Steele by a New Zealand entrepeneur called John Kennedy, who offered to make him a star there and then in the coffee bar basement. He dressed him in a white suit and silk shirts designed by the tennis designer, Teddy Tinling, and got him a pair of blue suede shoes in honour of the rock number by Carl Perkins – 'Do what you want but don't step on my blue suede shoes'. A record called 'Rock With The Cavemen' and some skilful promotion at a night club where the Duke of Kent was present got him talked about as rock 'n' roller by appointment to the quality. Colin MacInnes, a hawk-eyed observer, described his appeal in *England, Half English*: 'a gold-haired Robin Goodfellow, dressed in sky-blue jeans and neon-hued shirting, who jumps, skips, doubles up and wriggles as he sings. At certain ritual gestures – a dig with the foot, a violent mop-shake of the head – the teenagers utter a collective shriek of ecstasy. Tommy has sent them!' He rose in a year at the age of twenty from obscurity to idolatry, even conquering the Café de Paris, which was still the hallowed cabaret territory of ultra-sophisticated entertainers like Marlene Dietrich and Noël Coward. He was, wrote MacInnes, 'every nice young girl's boy, every kid's favourite elder brother, every mother's cherished adolescent son.' Here was a gulf between British and American pop idols. In Britain, at that stage, you needed to appeal to Mums. Tommy Steele was soon touring the variety theatres, full of pixie charm, dropping his assumed transatlantic whine and reverting to what he essentially was – a Cockney music hall entertainer.

Other products of the skiffle world were recruited, re-styled, re-named and launched by managers like Kennedy and his partner, Larry Parnes: among them Marty Wilde (really Reg Smith), Adam Faith (Terry Nelhams) and Cliff Richard (Harry Webb). Parnes played house-mother in his flat to a stableful of hopefuls whose names, at least, were a promise of highly-strung temperaments: Marty Wilde, Billy Fury, Johnny Gentle, Vince Eager and so on. Their solos, when recording, were sustained by a backing group of usually middle-aged songsters known on their vocal parts as 'Boy One', 'Boy Two' etc. Their contribution was to interject in close harmony a 'waah' or a 'bup' or a 'sh-boom' – even a 'sha-

Tommy Steele with 'nice young girls' in an appropriate open-air setting

wadda-wadda'. But nothing would sustain most of the manufactured idols for long. Overkill – as every agent tried to do the trick of making a star with more promotion than talent – took its toll. All the rock 'n' rollers declared their ambition was to become 'an all-round entertainer' – in short, to join the Establishment and make money.

A few of them made it. Television by then was playing benevolent uncle to the rock-struck teenies. Providing they behaved nicely and didn't damage the equipment, they were allowed onto the screen, as in *American Bandstand*, as the chief attraction of the show. Jack Good, who produced *Six-Five Special* for the BBC, followed by *Oh Boy!* – 'the fastest show on television' – on the commercial channel, converted Cliff Richard into family entertainment. He persuaded him to shave off his sideburns and abandon his guitar, leaving his hands free to plead for sympathy. His biggest success of the Fifties, 'Livin' Doll', was not a rock 'n' roll number but a product of the commercial songsmith, Lionel Bart. Cliff Richard went on to send himself up – he played the talentless rock 'n' roll 'discovery' in the musical satire *Espresso Bongo*. Soon afterwards he heard the call of Billy Graham. With Cliff Richard evangelizing and Tommy Steele in pantomime (a natural Buttons if ever there was one), singing cheering numbers like 'Little White Bull', British rock 'n' roll quickly snuffed out any flickers of rebellion and danger there may have been in the air during the *Rock Around The Clock* riots. On both sides of the Atlantic the balladeers were back on top by 1959. Pat Boone's 'April Love', Paul Anka's 'Diane' and Harry Belafonte's 'Island In The Sun' were throbbing gently over millions of radios and even those purveyors of reliable soft-centres, Sinatra and Como, were back in the charts offering 'High Hopes' and 'Magic Moments' respectively.

Jazz, adopted by the young in the Forties, now became the identifying badge for a minority that thought itself more discriminating than the teeny-rockers. Scott Fitzgerald dubbed the Twenties 'the jazz age' but in truth the Fifties did more to earn that title. The line of jazz development was splitting into its separate streams. Progressive or 'cool' modern jazz was still a minor tributary, exploring the experimental language of Bop discovered by Charlie Parker and Dizzy Gillespie for a small, dedicated band of disciples. Miles Davis, the miraculous player who made the muted trumpet 'breathe' confidences in a way it never had before, was their god. John Lewis, one of the pianists who first played with him, founded the ultra-cerebral Modern Jazz Quartet, a password among the congnoscenti, and Dave Brubeck, whose record 'Take Five' was, untypically, a hit which broke through to the non-specialist audience, were the high priests. But most simple jazz lovers were left as far behind by the unsmiling, funeral-suited Modern Jazz Quartet as the Promenade Concert audience was left behind by Schoenberg.

This brought about the extreme back-to-the-roots reaction of the New Orleans revival, which spread with gospel-meeting fervour on both sides of the Atlantic. It was a revival of Negro music played almost exclusively by whites. It appealed particularly to the antiquarian enthusiasm of the middle-class young in Britain, the grammar school and provincial university student generation, often scientific, spectacled and sweatered. Lucky Jim adored revivalist jazz (like his creator) and so did Jimmy Porter, who played the trumpet to ease his frustrations and declared that he didn't think he could love anyone who didn't love jazz. In their Fair Isle knitted sweaters and their duffel coats, with submissive girls in tow, heavy pipes clamped in jaw and the air of thoughtful acolytes observing time-honoured rites, they would stand in groups in smoky clubs living a new version of the *Vie de Bohème*. Their first hero, Humphrey Lyttleton, with his club at 100 Oxford Street, was always pointed out to be an Old Etonian and a Guardsman (which was socially comforting but far from typical) and brought in each of his band's numbers with four romantic thumps of his foot.

Revivalist jazz went through two booms – the first in the early Fifties led by Humph, as everyone knew him, the second as the rock 'n' roll wave receded in the late Fifties. This time purity was the cry, under band-leaders Ken Colyer and Chris Barber. The new revivalists, like Bible Fundamentalists, believed that only the exact sounds made by very old Negroes in New Orleans were the pure milk of the Word. Debates of theological complexity raged about the permissibility of the sounds made in Chicago, often by New Orleans musicians who had migrated there. To a purist's ear the chunk-chunk-chunk of the banjo was essential for authenticity, and the idea of a saxophone was heresy. Anything with a banjo in it was called 'Trad' and at the end of the decade came the Trad boom in which jazzmen consciously applied the techniques of show business to their art in a way that would once have been thought shameful. A Somerset jazzman called Acker Bilk achieved sudden fame with the use of a bowler hat, striped waistcoat and the prefix 'Mister', to go with the manner of an arch Victorian master of ceremonies. He had many imitators. This was the era of jokey uniforms and riverboat shuffles, solemn beer-drinking and no more improvisation. Eventually the sheer monotony and predictability of the music wore out its welcome.

The Trad audience was ultra-conservative. When Johnny Dankworth was invited to the annual Beaulieu jazz festival and began to play modern jazz, they rioted and howled for his blood. The world of the jazz clubs with their revivalist groups provided an alternative culture. It was a world away from the dance halls and theatre shows of the rockers with their luminous socks and sky-blue jeans. Jazz was always a minority music, even in its Fifties heyday, but it also had its own freemasonry, almost like an open university. Colin MacInnes's teenage narrator in *Absolute Beginners* spoke of it with awe:

> The great thing about the jazz world is that no one, not a soul, cares what your class is, or what your race is, or what your income is, or if you're a boy or girl or bent or versatile or what you are – so long as you dig the scene and can behave yourself and have left all that crap behind you when you come in the jazz club door.

There was a social gulf, however, between the aspirations of the jazz and the rock 'n' roll audiences. George Melly, the best-known British Blues shouter of the day, recalls:

> Jazz was the suburbs' escape from their lot. The audience was middle-class and suburban, with a strong element of students, particularly from art schools. Trad was the music of the Aldermaston marchers. The English rock 'n' roll audience, on the other hand, was mostly working-class and very young – it soon became teeny-bopper territory. Jazz enthusiasts despised rock 'n' roll as musically illiterate, although it produced one or two fine artists like Presley and Little Richard. It was a thinned-down derivative of Negro urban Blues reduced to their most boring element – the rhythm. Why this, which had been around for ever, should suddenly have sparked off a whole generation is a mystery. I think it had to do with military service. There was no point in getting on with your life after leaving school and while waiting to be called up. So they earned high wages in dead-end jobs and wanted something to spend them on. In this gap rock 'n' roll flourished.

Businessmen were not slow to wake up to the teenage market in the United States, where it was developed first. By the end of the Fifties it was calculated that each teenager had an average of 400 dollars a year to spend. *Life* magazine did a survey which found they owned 1,500,000 cars and spent 20 million dollars on lipstick. The cigarette industry recovered most of its sales after the first lung cancer scare thanks mainly to the rise in teenage smoking. Obviously it was a market too big to miss. In Britain five million teenagers, four million of them at work at an average of £8 a week, were spending £830 million by 1959, on clothes, cigarettes, records and cosmetics, in that order. Colin MacInnes's hero again put it succinctly in 1959:

> The teenage ball had a real, savage splendour in the days when we found that no one couldn't sit on our faces any more because we had loot to spend at last and our world was to be *our* world . . .

In America, of course, they had made this discovery several years before. They became mobile so much sooner and so much younger. Drive-in restaurants, movies and burger palaces – not coffee bars – were the rendezvous for the tribal rites of the American teenager. Tom Wolfe recalls:

> All over the world people were in love with the life of the American teenager. It was so much freer than it was anywhere else. Anything the young wanted to do they would do in an automobile. On Saturday nights the drive-in was the automobile meeting ground where carloads of boys and girls would go to do anything from picking up each other to picking a fight.

A flash of the lights or honk of the horn would normally bring the girl car-hops to the driving window to serve on a clip-on tray the food that had been ordered through a microphone beside each parking space. This signal could mean more than a call for service. In Lisa Alther's *Kinflicks*, the high school audience at the Fifties drive-in movie (*The Ten Commandments*) is described like this:

> Mixed with the dialogue were the various sighs and gasps and sucking sounds from the front seat and blasts from car horns throughout the parking area as, in keeping with Hullsport High tradition, couples signalled that they'd gone all the way.

From this time onwards, the young would never again revert to what they had been in previous ages – a group without rights, without money, without a music and a culture of its own, a group to which nobody bothered to listen. But for the moment they were still rebels without a cause, except their common refusal to join the grown-up, bourgeois world. It was a cosy time to be a rebel. No violent sacrifices were demanded. It was enough to hold up to scorn the phonies that Holden Caulfield had first identified. The very fact that the adult atmosphere was so stifling enabled the young to breathe.

CHAPTER SEVEN

Shedding the White Man's Burden

Some days seem to be selected by destiny to attract synchronized disasters. They are days on which Yeats's celebrated couplet seems to be coming true:

> Things fall apart; the centre cannot hold;
> Mere anarchy is loosed upon the world.

Such a day was Sunday, 4 November 1956. This was the day which began at 2 a.m. in Budapest with the thunder of Russian tanks rolling into the city, firing their shells at their fellow-communists who actually lived there. At noon Moscow announced that the 'counter-revolution' had been crushed but for hours afterwards despairing SOS broadcasts were picked up from the Freedom Fighters of Hungary calling for rescue by what they hopefully addressed as 'the civilized world'.

Much of the civilized world was preoccupied with the Anglo-French invasion of Egypt. In Cyprus that day the paratroops prepared to drop on Port Said at dawn the next morning and other forces embarked by sea to join the convoy which had been steaming with maddening slowness for the same objective from Malta for nearly six days. British and French planes, having already destroyed the Egyptian air force on the ground, overflew the Suez Canal unopposed, firing cannon at Egyptian tanks returning from the rout in the Sinai desert. They hit a ship loaded with concrete and beer bottles. It sank and blocked the canal just as the Egyptians intended. Meanwhile the Iraq Petroleum Company's pipeline was set on fire in Syria and the oil supply cut off.

In New York the United Nations Assembly, having demanded a cease-fire and a withdrawal that Britain and France had refused, was debating a Canadian plan for an emergency U.N. force to be sent. It now called, with even less effect, for Russia to withdraw its troops from Hungary. So did Eisenhower, on the last day of his presidential election campaign, after calling on his secretary of state, Mr Dulles, who had just undergone a major cancer operation. In London Sir Anthony Eden sat with his cabinet ministers in Number 10, Downing Street, that evening, able to hear the roars of 'Eden Must Go!' from an angry mass meeting in Trafalgar Square. It ended in a pitched battle between a mob charging down Whitehall and eighty mounted police charging the mob while being pelted with fireworks. It was the most violent street demonstration London had seen in the peaceable Fifties, ending with eight injured policemen and thirty-two arrests. Feelings had not run so high against the government since before the war.

That night, in the teeth of Eden's resistance, the Opposition leader, Hugh Gaitskell, insisted on answering his prime ministerial radio and television broadcast of the night before. 'He is utterly, utterly discredited,' he declared and offered Labour's support to the Conservatives if they would change both their leader and his policy. Aneurin Bevan, the voice of the party's left wing, put it even more trenchantly to the angry crowd in Trafalgar Square that evening: 'If Eden is sincere,' he began and paused dramatically – 'He is' cried a voice. Bevan leapt: 'Then he is too *stupid* to be Prime Minister!' His final crescendo worked up to a high Welsh bark: 'There is only one way in which they could try to restore their tarnished reputation. And that is to get out . . . get out . . . GET OUT!' That night after dinner the French foreign minister, Christian Pineau, arrived at Downing Street for talks with Eden. It was announced afterwards that the landings would go on. What was not announced was that the intense moral and financial pressure from Washington was already giving Eden and his cabinet, particularly Macmillan, the Chancellor, serious doubts as to how long Britain could afford to act against America's out-and-out hostility. A few hours before the seaborne invasion at last arrived, at dawn on 6 November, Eden was to tell the French premier, Guy Mollet, that the game was up: there would be a cease-fire at midnight.

So 4 November 1956 ended in confusion and doubt – except for the Hungarian rebels who knew quite well what their fate would be, if they had not already met it. It was a bad day for empires of all kinds: for the feudal brutality of the Russian empire which earned it the disgust of the rest of the world; for the wavering of the British empire on the brink of dissolution, as it discovered that Britain's will could no longer be imposed against determined opposition; and for the emerging American empire, based on a covert imperialism of aid and trade, which proved itself helpless to control its Communist enemies, able only to sabotage its former friends and allies. It is this American empire which must be examined in order to understand how the Suez affair came about.

At a distance of more than twenty years, Suez seems an act of almost incomprehensible folly. The very place-name has become a shorthand symbol for utter defeat, like Brutus's Philippi or Napoleon's Waterloo. This was the place where history banished the British empire from the stage and gave the *coup de grace* to Britain's pretensions as a great power. At the time, however, it did not seem like that. A large – and sane – part of the British nation enthusiastically supported the invasion, until it failed. Had it succeeded, even in the short run (and the Israelis were to demonstrate later how successful such operations could be in the short run), it would have been a wildly popular stroke of policy, even with some of those who were quick to denounce it as immoral when it failed. Success would have greatly enhanced Britain's waning prestige in the Middle East. The British empire might even have lasted a bit longer than it did, though this would not necessarily have been to Britain's benefit.

The single and sufficient reason that none of this happened was the policy of the United States. The American 'empire' has been mentioned. Colonialism was still officially a dirty word in the American lexicon. But in the Fifties, under the guise of 'containing Communism', American policy subtly shifted towards unannounced, unacknowledged imperialism. The Truman Doctrine, announced in 1947 at the time of the Greek civil war, began the change with these words: 'It must be the policy of the United States to support free peoples who are resisting attempted subjugation by armed minorities . . . to assist them to work out their destinies in their own way.' The very far from free peoples of Greece, Turkey, Spain and Portugal were among the first to benefit from this irreproachable-sounding doctrine. In the Fifties billions of dollars were spent on aid to autocrats like Franco and Salazar and on establishing American bases on their soil. Soon there were four thousand bases encircling the Communist bloc in a hundred aided countries, many of them patrolled by the Sixth or Seventh Fleet as a reminder whose writ it was that ran in their territory. 'Not for one minute,' said John Foster Dulles to Congress with brutal frankness in 1958, 'do I think the purpose of aid is to make friends. The purpose is to look out for the interests of the United States.' The Truman Doctrine had the Dulles Doctrine added unto it: in the holy war against world communism, it was 'immoral' to be neutral. Communism, of course, was partly detested as a threat to liberty, but in its zeal to befriend an anti-communist regime the State Department did not inquire how tenderly it cared for freedom. Dictatorships by generals or juntas on the Latin American pattern were in many ways easier to handle or bribe with dollars and weapons. They were what American diplomacy knew best. It was an immense advantage in 1953 for Foster Dulles to have the cooperation of his brother, Allen Dulles, as head of the Central Intelligence Agency. The CIA trebled in size between 1950 and 1955. It reached a strength of 15,000 and spent a billion dollars on subsidies to approved political parties and in what it called Clandestine Services, the department of internal subversion which attempted to ensure that America's interests were always served by the party in power. One of its earliest successes was the overthrow of the Iranian premier, Dr Mossadeq, in 1953. Since he had nationalized the Anglo-Iranian Oil Company in 1951, oil had ceased to flow out of the Abadan refinery. Now, when he appealed to Washington for loans, the Dulles brothers instead sent Kermit Roosevelt, the CIA's Middle East expert, to eliminate him. On his advice the Shah dismissed Mossadeq and appointed General Zahedi prime minister, but the short term result was that the Shah and his Empress Soraya had to flee for their lives to Rome. Three days later came the counter-coup. The industrious Roosevelt had bought the support of the Teheran street mobs.

Gangs of young men led by a champion athlete (called Sha'aban the Brainless) walked through the bazaars 'persuading' people to demonstrate for the Shah. Anyone who shouted 'Long Live The Shah' was paid in banknotes. Ten million dollars was distributed. Teheran changed sides, thanks to American money, and a tank demolished half of Mossadeq's house with a well-aimed shell. The Shah was restored with $250 million in American aid to help keep his throne stable.

It was not an altruistic investment. A consortium of five of the American oil companies came out of the crisis the richer for owning forty per cent of Anglo-Iranian. Thereafter the Shah ruled with the tacit presence and support of the CIA, and the Persians, whom only an optimist would describe as a free people, continued to work out their destiny, not in their own way but in the Shah's. The same could be said of the Saudi Arabian people, whose King was so conscious of his debt to Aramco that he made it a crime against the state for any of the oil company employees to strike. Aramco in turn showed its gratitude by supplying Saud's palace at Riyadh with air conditioning in the harem and a Swiss chef. When the King went to Washington he was one of the few heads of state whom the President went to the airport to meet.

In Guatemala there was no oil, or Aramco, but there was, instead, the United Fruit Company, the republic's largest landowner. When a land-reforming president, Arbenz, in 1951 expropriated the company from a quarter of a million acres they did not bother to farm, the U.S. ambassador, the CIA and the company became extremely active in looking for an alternative president. They found one in Colonel Castillo Armas. A full-scale military invasion was mounted from the compliant neighbouring territories of Nicaragua and Honduras. Guatemala City was bombed by American planes. The Colonel was flown in by U.S. diplomatic plane, dissolved parliament, returned its acres to United Fruit and, as a bonus, abolished taxes on the profits of foreign investors. He got $90 million in aid.

If the hallmark of colonialism is the economic exploitation of the territory colonized on the most favourable terms to the colonizer, then the Dulles Brothers were possibly the most successful colonists since Cecil Rhodes. Nor did they let the democratic process of free elections stand in their way. The Shah's decrees went on as before. There was no one to oppose Colonel Armas when he was 'elected' president. When the French withdrew exhausted from Indo-China after their defeat by Ho Chi Minh's forces at Dien Bien Phu in 1954, and Vietnam came into being, temporarily divided into North and South, the Geneva peace accords specified that elections should be held in 1956 to reunify the country. They would, by all calculations, have resulted in a sweeping victory for the Viet Minh and for Ho – if they had been held. Instead the Dulles Brothers installed the Diem Brothers, with the covert help of the CIA's Colonel Edward Lansdale, the model for Graham Greene's *The Quiet American*. In the rigged elections which gave Ngo Dinh Diem the presidency in 1955, he designed the ballot material red (for good luck) for Diem and green (for a cuckold) for his opponent.

Brother Nhu and his secret police arrested anyone who might have opposed this solution – estimated to number between 50,000 and 100,000 political prisoners, a remarkable yield for a small country. It is possible to be thankful that Dulles did not do worse. At the time of the French collapse, he and certain Pentagon chiefs were all for direct military intervention, which implied a nuclear strike if necessary. Eisenhower should be given credit for resisting this. He showed himself, not for the only time, wiser than his Secretary of State. For this was the height of Dulles' 'brinkmanship' period, the period when Churchill called him 'the only case I know of a bull who carries his own china shop with him.'

'It is now being realized that in spite of the atmosphere of complacency and torpor at the top of his administration, Eisenhower was a very cunning, calculating and crafty man,' says the historian Arthur

Schlesinger, Jnr, 'He ran what Americans call a very "coony" foreign policy' ('Foxy' would be the English equivalent). 'Ike abandoned the American army and substituted the C.I.A. as the instrument of American intervention abroad. It was kept very quiet. Hardly anyone realised it.'

Against this perspective, the Suez affair can be seen as another example of undercover imperialism brought about by a combination of Dulles' duplicity and Eden's vanity. When the Egyptian army Free Officers' Movement put King Farouk aboard his yacht on a one-way voyage to Naples in July 1952, it ended an era of British dominance which had lasted seventy years. The bemedalled expanse of the King had been a façade for the real power of the British ambassador. On one famous occasion in 1942 the ambassador had surrounded the royal palace with tanks to force the King to accept the Prime Minister he had chosen. But it was deeply rooted in British mythology and history books that the Suez Canal had to be protected as the lifeline of the empire. When there first was talk of evacuating 80,000 British troops that guarded it, to placate Nasser and Egypt's new-found nationalism, there was shocked and bitter opposition in Parliament from the 'Suez Group'. Its most eloquent spokesman, Enoch Powell, did not exaggerate the traditional awe of the importance of this waterway when he said in November 1953: 'The removal of our forces would have almost illimitable repercussions in the Mediterranean, the Middle East and in Africa. In the Middle East all our positions would thereby become insecure . . . by the fact that we have been eliminated from the focal point.' And he went on ominously: 'American policy over the past decade has been steadily and relentlessly directed toward the weakening and destruction of the links which bind the British Empire together. American imperialism is advancing in this area.' Three years later, many more people would have agreed with him that indeed, the chief threat to the British Empire was the American Empire.

Despite these misgivings the Canal was duly evacuated under an agreement negotiated by Sir Anthony Eden himself. Ironically enough, the last British troops were withdrawn in July 1956, three months before the operation was launched to put them back. Eden by then had met Colonel Nasser at a dinner at the British embassy and the two men had taken an immediate and fateful dislike to one another. Dulles also viewed Nasser with mounting disapproval. He was not pleased when Nasser refused to join the Baghdad Pact, part of his tier of alliances encircling the Soviet Union. He was furious when Nasser bought $80 million-worth of arms from Czechoslovakia (having been refused them by the Americans). His anger was further provoked in April 1956, when Nasser recognized Communist China – comparable to committing the sin against the Holy Ghost in Dulles' dogma. This nationalist leader was not answering to the leading rein. He must be taught a lesson with the curb.

So, in July 1956, the American loan to help finance the Aswan High Dam on the Nile, vital to Egyptian agriculture, was curtly withdrawn by Dulles. Along with it went the smaller British loan. It was typical of high-handed Dulles imperialism – more far-reaching than anything British ambassadors used to do. There is evidence that even Dulles paused to wonder if he was being rash. He phoned Eisenhower at the golf course about it and told him that the Egyptians were not playing ball. Eisenhower, who was, replied 'Whatever you think, Foster, whatever you think.' Nasser's next move was premeditated. He had had plenty of warning of the likely cancellation of the loan through his spies at the Baghdad Pact meetings. He made a speech in Alexandria announcing that Egypt would pay for its own dam out of the dues paid to the Canal Company, which was now nationalized. Its offices were taken over as he was speaking.

Nasser said later that he had calculated it would take Britain two or three months to prepare to retaliate. He thought by then it would be too late. He was right about the three months. He underestimated the spleen and vengeance with which Eden would react. When the news of Nasser's speech arrived in London, Eden was at dinner with King Feisal of Iraq. 'How can he do it?' he demanded of his guests, turning white with fury. To him, who had negotiated the evacuation of the canal, despite the Suez Group, it was a personal affront and betrayal. Also, like most of his countrymen who had served out there, he believed the Arabs were quite incapable of running an international waterway – which they soon disproved by increasing the traffic that went through it.

Eden, a vain man with a petulant temper, was in a highly unstable emotional state that summer. He had already been taunted in the Press as an ineffectual successor to Sir Winston Churchill, in whose shadow he had waited so long. In the *Daily Telegraph's* wounding phrase, he had failed to deliver 'the smack of firm government'. Eden responded to this by deporting Archbishop Makarios from Cyprus, then in the grip of EOKA terrorists seeking union with Greece. If Makarios was to be his Napoleon, banished to the Seychelles, Nasser was to be his Hitler – or, at least, as he once called him, a 'Moslem Mussolini'. It became his personal obsession to topple him from power. Anthony Nutting, junior

Fruitless invasion – British tanks entering Port Said

minister at the Foreign Office until he resigned over Suez, recalled in his account of the crisis, *No End Of A Lesson*: 'The world was not big enough to hold both him and Nasser.' At about this time Eden shouted down the open telephone to Nutting: 'What's all this nonsense about neutralizing Nasser, as you call it? I want him destroyed, can't you understand? I want him removed.'

There followed a futile farce of London Conferences at which Dulles suggested forming a Suez Canal Users' Association, which would avoid having to pay dues to Nasser, but nobody believed it would work. Force would be needed and Dulles only offered endless talk. Eden's wife, Clarissa, conveyed her weariness of the subject with the unfortunate remark that at times she felt the Suez Canal was flowing through her drawing room. In reality, neither the British nor French governments treated this as more than a smokescreen for their military plans. The French had put out feelers to the Israelis about a combined operation against Nasser, who was their enemy for supporting the nationalist rebels in Algeria. On 22 October there was a meeting between the Israeli premier Ben-Gurion, his chief of staff, General Moshe Dayan, and the French under Pineau, the foreign minister, to settle the timetable of the Israeli attack on Egypt across the Sinai desert. Britain and France would issue an ultimatum, calling for their temporary occupation of the Canal to 'separate the combatants'. This was the collusion that was flatly denied by British ministers at the time and concealed for many years afterwards until General Dayan inconsiderately exposed it in his memoirs, *The Story Of My Life*. The British representative at this secret meeting, at Sèvres, was the Foreign Secretary, Selwyn Lloyd, who appeared to be holding his nose while conspiring with such associates:

> His whole demeanour expressed distaste – for the place, the company, the topic. His opening remarks suggested a customer bargaining with extortionate merchants. He said Her Majesty's Government considered that Nasser had to go. It was therefore prepared to undertake military action.

As everyone knows, the Israeli attack was totally successful. The Anglo-French ultimatum duly expired on 30 October and their invasion force plodded across the sea from Malta into a rising storm of world disapproval and ever-increasing division of opinion at home, ignoring a United Nations resolution demanding a cease-fire and, most effective of all, the determination of President Eisenhower 'to do everything we can to stop this thing'. In the words of Macmillan, one of the keenest promoters of the Suez Adventure (known to his colleagues as 'the Lady Macbeth of Suez because of her line 'Give *me* the daggers!'), there had been 'a profound miscalculation of the likely reaction in Washington . . . For this I carry a heavy responsibility. I knew Eisenhower well from the war years and I thought I understood his character. I believed that the Americans would issue a protest, even a violent protest in public; but that they would in their hearts be glad to see the matter brought to a conclusion . . . The Secretary of State and, to a lesser degree, the President seemed to regard the actions of Britain and France as a personal affront.' That makes three personal affronts – that of Dulles to Nasser, of Nasser to Eden and then of Eden to Dulles, to complete the circle. In his memoirs, *Riding the Storm*, Macmillan concludes: 'They particularly resented the fact that we had acted on our own without American permission or concurrence . . . Dulles showed in the vital period a degree of hostility amounting almost to frenzy . . . He clearly lost his temper; he may also have lost his nerve.' Of course, American permission had not been sought, particularly on the grounds that it would almost certainly have not been given. As Sir Harold Wilson later commented in *A Prime Minister On Prime Ministers*:

Of all the laws of politics, one which had never previously been questioned is that nothing provocative must be allowed to happen in an allied country in the year leading up to an American Presidential election . . . The Macmillan–Eden challenge was at its height in election week. Even the tolerant Eisenhower could not forgive that.

But it was also a matter of national pride to men of Eden's and Macmillan's stamp and generation that Britain still could take decisive military action in the world without anybody's permission, even their old friend Ike's. One of the bitterest lessons of the affair was to find that they were wrong.

The invasion got twenty-five miles down the canal before the midnight cease-fire, at the cost of six hundred Egyptian lives and fifty British and French ones. The canal was blocked and petrol was later rationed in Britain. The Aswan dam was eventually built with Russian aid. It was not, as politicians obsessed with misreading history kept claiming as their justification, 'another Munich'. It is true that Nasser emerged as a hero to the Arab world and with an international stature he never had before – but although he dreamed of a pan-Arab empire, he showed none of Hitler's megalomania. Nothing could disguise the fact that it was Nasser who survived and it was Eden who was destroyed. At the height of the hopeless gamble, his appearance in the Commons was tellingly described by J. W. Mallalieu:

> The Prime Minister sprawled on the front bench, head back and mouth agape. His eyes, inflamed with sleeplessness, stared into the vacancies beyond the roof. His hands twitched at his horn-rimmed spectacles. The face was grey except where black-rimmed caverns surrounded the dying embers of his eyes. The whole personality seemed completely withdrawn. One day he announced the surrender of Port Said (later withdrawn), the next a cease-fire, and was cheered on both occasions.

After Eden's health, like Britain's dollar reserves, had collapsed and there was nothing for it but to climb down and withdraw the troops, Selwyn Lloyd and the British ambassador called at the Walter Reed hospital to see the stricken John Foster Dulles, the man who had done most to bring about the whole affair. He gave them this amazing greeting in his slippers: 'Well, once you started, why didn't you go through with it and get Nasser down?' 'Foster, why didn't you give us a wink?' Selwyn Lloyd is reported to have replied. 'Oh,' said Dulles, 'I couldn't do anything like *that*.'

Once again, the devious currents of Dulles' thinking defy rational

explanation. He probably calculated, as usual, on backing both possibilities. If a swift invasion had succeeded behind his back and *had* got
Nasser down, he could have accepted it as a *fait accompli* that suited
American policy very well; as it did not, he paraded the virtue that he
enjoyed parading most – self-righteousness. Once more the moral issue
of the Suez action was obscured: Eden's real miscalculation, folly or
crime, according to taste, was that he didn't pull it off. That, at least,
was where most people were content to leave it.

It took only two more years before American Marines were engaged
in their own Suez operation on the beaches of the Lebanon. The difference was that they and their atomic howitzers were met only by surprised
girls in bathing costumes. The murder of the King, Crown Prince and
Prime Minister and the establishment of a military dictatorship in Iraq
had made the regimes in the Lebanon and Jordan insecure. After Suez,
the Eisenhower Doctrine had pronounced that the vacuum in the Middle
East must be filled by the United States before it could be filled by
Russia, and Congress had given the President a blank cheque to inter-
vene with troops wherever a Middle Eastern ruler requested aid against
Communist aggression. True, the Lebanese president had requested
help, but Macmillan, on hearing that the Sixth Fleet was approaching
Beirut, was amazed by the turnabout in American attitudes to inter-
vention. 'The new American policy could hardly be reconciled with the
Administration's almost hysterical outburst over Suez.' He telephoned
Eisenhower. 'I said "You are doing a Suez on me", at which the President laughed.' The difference was that Britain stood by America and
shortly dispatched paratroops to bolster up the rule of King Hussein in
Jordan. This time there were no recriminations.

But the United States had not yet met its Nasser. That was to happen
on 1 January 1959, when Fidel Castro marched back into Havana, a city
where he had been a conformist, grey-suited, clean-shaven lawyer only
three years before. Now his guerrilla fatigues, peaked cap and luxuriant
beard, like those of his lieutenant, Che Guevara, created the image of
revolutionary gallantry for years to come. Under dictators like Fulgencio
Batista, Cuba had been Egypt all over again. Since 1898 the American
ambassador had been the second most powerful man in Havana, sometimes the most. American businesses owned ninety per cent of the
minerals, all of the oil and forty per cent of the sugar which sustained
Cuba's economy and general employment – or rather, general unemployment – for most of the year. Since he seized power in 1952 Batista
had enjoyed the benevolent protection of the United States, which

trained and supplied his army of 43,000 men, the army that had now lost to a small and dedicated band of amateurs. Castro had only 1,200 guerrillas with him when he entered Havana. Batista's regime had been described by Senator John F. Kennedy as 'one of the most bloody and repressive dictatorships in the long history of Latin America.'

But Dulles' State Department was used to supporting tyrants. In Formosa they were committed to Chiang Kai-shek, whose pig-headed and pathetic pretensions to be the real ruler of China almost dragged them into a war for the singularly uninteresting off-shore islands of Quemoy and Matsu. In South Korea they poured billions into the shaky and corrupt regime of Syngman Rhee. In South Vietnam they paid the bills for Diem and his brother Nhu's concentration camps, his army and eighty per cent of government expenses. In Latin America they propped up one hated military dictatorship after another – as Vice-President Nixon discovered on his 'goodwill' tour of 1958. Such was the ill-will demonstrated by the mobs which stoned his cavalcade of cars that, finally, his rescue from Caracas was planned by no less a force than six destroyers, a cruiser, an aircraft carrier with a full complement of fighters and a thousand paratroopers and Marines. Luckily they did not in the end have to send them in against the stone-throwing crowds. Nixon simply cancelled the rest of his tour and caught a plane back to genteel Washington.

And now, with Batista gone, they were faced on their own doorstep with a genuinely popular leader who had not taken office to protect American business investment. Even so, Castro was no doctrinaire Communist at first. He talked of nationalization with compensation in Cuban bonds, which was not surprising in a country so poor, so illiterate and so exploited. But he repeatedly asked for American aid for economic development and was curtly refused. Nixon met Castro and reported he was a Communist who should be put down by force. Such were the simplicities of Dullesian doctrine. Now the parallel between Castro and Nasser became uncanny. The United States threatened to cut the quota of sugar allowed to reach the u.s. market. Castro nationalized the sugar industry. Soon he was forced to exchange Cuban sugar for Russian oil and machinery. The American oil companies refused to handle Russian oil. Castro nationalized the refining industry and began full-scale nationalization.

OPPOSITE *New image of the gallant revolutionary: Fidel Castro leading his men in the Cuban mountains*

By March 1960 Eisenhower took the decisive step down the road paved with the mistakes of Suez: he authorized the training of an invasion force of exiles that was to culminate in the humiliating embarrassment of the Bay of Pigs. Once again, the assumption was that Castro, as Nasser had been supposed to do, would fall in an internal revolution. But Castro, like Nasser, was only strengthened in his popularity by the attack. It is remarkable that two great and sophisticated powers could make the same simple miscalculation twice over within five years of each other.

The long-term effects of mishandling Cuba were to include a missile crisis which was possibly the most traumatic event of the Cold War for the United States. For Britain, the mishandling of the Suez affair was deeply traumatic, possibly even more so than Dunkirk or Singapore. After those defeats, it could even the score. Here there was no score to even. The Suez Canal proved, in the event, not to be worth fighting for. The following year it was back in operation under perfectly capable Egyptian control. Britain paid its dues on Nasser's terms and the Suez Canal Company changed its name and went on to prosper in business elsewhere. The empire which the Canal had connected was no longer a reality. Suez helped to speed the process of dismantling it by giving heart to nationalists everywhere in Africa. It changed the thinking of many politicians, particularly that of Harold Macmillan. He succeeded the discredited Eden with the delicate task of saving the country and his party from the shipwreck by diverting their attention from it, indeed by acting with the calm assurance of a world statesman as though the facts justified such a role. Hence the legend of 'SuperMac' the unflappable. By the end of the Fifties independence had come to Ghana, the Federation of Malaysia, Singapore and Cyprus and was imminent in much vaster territories so that, when Macmillan said in Capetown in February 1960, that 'a wind of change is blowing through Africa', howling would not have been too strong a word. 'Was I destined to be the remodeller or the liquidator of the British Empire?' he asked himself in his memoirs. 'The old Pax Britannica, which had brought to about a quarter of the globe the inestimable advantage of order and good government, was being replaced by a new and untried system. It was doubtful how far we could hope to maintain the mystique which had held the old organization (the Commonwealth) together.'

It was and remains extremely doubtful but, for the time being, mystique still blinded Britain and Macmillan to the significance of the 1957 Treaty of Rome which, at the beginning of 1958, brought into existence the European Economic Community. Britain's destiny, it was felt, could not possibly lie with Europe rather than with the Commonwealth or the American alliance, battered though both of them were. This was a costly inflexibility of mind. Suez, after all, had dealt less serious a blow to British prestige than the loss of first Indo-China, then Algeria, dealt to France. Yet the wiliness of the recalled national hero, General De Gaulle, who became prime minister in 1958 and President in January 1959, saved France from psychological defeat by substituting his and his country's dominance over the six members of the Common Market. It was not surprising that he would later refuse to allow Britain to join since that dominance would then be challenged.

So British credibility as a great power was destroyed and nothing was put in its place. Suez clearly demonstrated that none but the two superpowers could take independent action on a world scale. The inability to accept this unpalatable fact divided the nation at the time morally and emotionally, friend against friend, brother against brother, readers against their newspapers. The disgrace of world censure, the shock of not having 'beaten the Wogs', was profound. The reaction was an unspoken agreement to erase the memory of Eden and of the humiliation he represented. No prime minister dropped into a swifter oblivion since, ironically enough, Neville Chamberlain.

Cancer removed John Foster Dulles from the scene in 1959 before the full consequences of his policies had come to roost. His concept of a Pax Americana to replace the Pax Britannica involved him and his country in picking up the White Man's Burden, which Britain was dropping as quickly as it gracefully could. It is arguable that it led down the road to the inevitable disaster in Vietnam. Certainly it proved a much heavier burden than even Dulles ever imagined in his self-righteous self-confidence. Once you embarked on the path of empire, you needed bigger and bigger forces and bags of gold to keep the natives loyal. 'No one dreamt in Teddy Roosevelt's day,' wrote the sceptical Washington commentator, I. F. Stone, 'that we would seek to impose a *Pax Americana* on the whole world or wield a stick as big as our present Pentagon.' The Dulles policy escalated in spite of him, wider and yet wider over palm and pine until, in Adlai Stevenson's succinct comment: 'The sun never sets on American commitment.'

CHAPTER EIGHT

The Establishment Loses Face

'Top People,' proclaimed the hoardings in London, 'read *The Times*'. The flattering suggestion was that only those who read *The Times* were Top People, whatever that meant. Another term had been coined for roughly the same group: the Establishment – a shorthand symbol for the people who ran Britain and, it was sometimes implied, ran it ineptly. The label was derived from the Establishment of the Church of England. But it was, and is, a slippery concept, for the Establishment does not mean the Government or the party in power, even if that happens to be the Conservative Party. The point of the Establishment is that it continues to look after itself whatever party is in power. It is not so much a power bloc or trade union for Top People as a ruling class mentality, a set of attitudes and assumptions, objectives and opinions about English society and who should press the buttons that operate it. The prime attitude and assumption of the Establishment is that it knows best what is good for the rest of the country. Certainly the upper ranks of the Church and the Bank of England, of Whitehall and the City, the governing bodies of the public schools and the BBC are impregnated with this attitude.

The vital lubricant of the Establishment is personal intimacy, the word in the ear or over the telephone, over lunch or a drink in the club. What 'the old boy network' really means is that the right members of it can be steered into the right jobs in which they will pursue the right policies and nothing need be put in writing. England can work such a nebulous system smoothly because the ruling class normally goes to one of only two universities, Oxford and Cambridge. This is more impor- tant than the contacts made at school, although Eton and Winchester confer a sort of tribal identity which often lingers on. It is virtually impossible for America to run an Establishment in the English sense; the Ivy League colleges are too numerous to produce a closely knit group. Richard Rovere, the *New Yorker* writer, attempted as a spoof to construct an American Establishment of the Fifties with the *New York Times* as its daily bulletin and a combination of Wall Street and Washington names as its members. As he admitted, it didn't really work out. Americans are less inclined to form *élites* who believe they know best what is best for other people. A perfect American Establishment figure of those days, said Rovere, was John J. McCloy, president of the World Bank, chairman of Chase Manhattan, chairman of the Council on Foreign Relations and of the Ford Foundation. Pillars of the English Establishment in the same period were such people as the head Civil Servant (and Fellow of All Souls), Sir Edward (later Lord) Bridges, or the banker-ambassador-academic, Sir Oliver (later Lord) Franks. These are not exciting names. Their owners prefer not to be known to the public at large. No one could be more of an Establishmentarian than an editor of *The Times* who was a former Director-General of the BBC, yet Sir William Haley, who achieved this double, was interviewed by one journalist under the impression that he was Bill Haley the bandleader. It must have been a baffling session for both of them but it is typical of the publicity-shrinking habits of the Establishment. (Sir William Haley, it must be added, was not at all typical in his path to the top: instead of being reared as a Top Person he left school at sixteen and made his way as a ship's wireless operator and later a telephonist on *The Times'* switchboard.) Generally speaking, when an Establishment figure makes headlines it is because something has gone badly wrong. So it was with Alger Hiss. So it was with Donald Maclean and Guy Burgess – for a long while after their disappearance in 1951 many in the Establishment still declined to believe they were traitors, any more than they believed it of Philby when his connection with Burgess forced his resignation from the Foreign Service.

These incidents and the Suez disaster of 1956 lowered the esteem the British traditionally accorded to the Establishment and within the year the ramshackle and elderly structure was under progressive attack. The divine right of Oxbridge men virtually to monopolize certain areas of authority such as the senior civil service no longer seemed self-evident. The monopoly of the BBC had been broken by commercial pressures: Sir Kenneth (later Lord) Clark, who became the first chairman of the Independent Television Authority and had an impeccable public service background in the arts, was booed in the Athenaeum for deserting to the enemy. In Establishment circles feelings can scarcely run higher than that. Finally the monarchy, the fountain of honours which mean so much in Establishment circles, was itself attacked, something which had not happened in England since the early years of Queen Victoria and seemed as unthinkable to the devout as the sin against the Holy Ghost.

What on earth had happened to the English reverence for good form? The pennants which first announced this shift in the prevailing wind were flown by a group of writers labelled Angry Young Men, a theoretical concept as artificial as the Establishment itself but an equally convenient shorthand symbol. Though the Young Men constantly complained of being grouped together there was some justice in it. They were mostly under thirty and, if not always angry, they were certainly rude about their 'betters'. They had something more significant in common, too. To a man they wrote about the newly-educated meritocracy emerging from the grammar schools and the redbrick provincial universities. By 1956 three-quarters of university students were dependent on state grants subject to the means test, so this was a numerous class. But it had no place in the existing class hierarchy. The children of the Butler Education Act of 1944, which threw open the university doors regardless of wealth, were the misfits of the time and no one till now had written about them. Then, quite suddenly, there was a rush to portray them.

Kingsley Amis, son of a City clerk who went to Oxford on a post-Army grant, begat *Lucky Jim* Dixon (1954), a grammar-school-bred ex-Corporal who was now a disaffected junior lecturer in a provincial university. John Osborne, expelled from a minor public school for slapping the headmaster, turned from acting to writing and begat Jimmy Porter of *Look Back In Anger* (1956), a provincial university drop-out running a sweet stall in a Midlands town. John Braine, son of a sewage works supervisor, grammar school boy and library assistant, begat Joe Lampton of *Room At The Top* (1957), a self-educated ex-sergeant in a Northern borough treasurer's department. To these bottom-drawer protagonists could be added Charles Lumley, university drop-out of John Wain's *Hurry On Down* (1953); John Lewis, Welsh provincial librarian of Kingsley Amis's second novel, *That Uncertain Feeling* (1955); Arthur Seaton, bicycle factory worker from *Saturday Night and Sunday Morning* (1958) by Alan Sillitoe, who also worked in a Nottingham bicycle factory; and *Billy Liar* (1959), a Walter Mittylike undertaker's apprentice from a small Yorkshire town, begotten by Keith Waterhouse, a Leeds journalist.

Now that distance lends disenchantment to the view, it can be seen that all these immensely influential, anti-heroic young heroes, who also became familiar through films, were variations on the theme of the misfit who needs to find his feet in a society he despises. He either defies it, like Jimmy Porter, compromises with it reluctantly and resentfully, like Lucky Jim, or cynically exploits it, like Joe Lampton. All of them are up against class barriers symbolized by some character who is the concentrated essence of all that the hero and, one assumes, the author, hates most in Fifties England. In Jim Dixon's case it is the phoney culture of his departmental professor, who entertains, if that is the word, at weekends with parties devoted to pseudo-artistic chatter and recorder ensembles. For Jimmy Porter it is the world of middle-class convention represented by his wife and her disapproving Mummy and Daddy. For Joe Lampton it is the ex-officer rival who takes, without earning it, what he wants from life. These resentments rang bells all over the country as though a new, suppressed generation had heard the echo of its own voice. The authors were catapulted from obscurity into publicity, controversy and affluence overnight. Whether they deserved it or not, no group of writers has received such concentrated attention since the days of Shaw, Wells and Bennett. They were interviewed and photographed, invited to broadcast and pontificate, pursued and spied upon by newspapers as if they were footballers or singers. They were the first pop stars of literature and perhaps also the last, for the appetite died with the Fifties and, losing their 'angry' label, they returned to the indifference with which writers are normally treated in England.

Doris Lessing wrote at the time that their work was 'an injection of vitality into the withered arm of British literature.' What was this vital fluid? Kingsley Amis, whose novel took a year to catch on with the public, refused to participate in the declarations of the Angry Young Men with whom he was retrospectively grouped. He passed the Fifties in Swansea in an academic backwater not unlike that in which he sets Jim Dixon, whose acts of defiance are very stealthy and circumspect, lest he lose the job he dislikes so much. His method of keeping boredom at bay is to pull mocking faces in secret – his ape face, Eskimo face, crazy peasant or lemon-sucking face – to write insults in the steam on his professor's bathroom mirror, to make obscene gestures behind his back and to encourage the professor's cat towards anarchy: 'Scratch 'em. Pee on the carpets.' The professor and his family are the enemy because they are phoneys and bores and his social superiors. Until the very end, when fate hands him his escape ticket, *they* are the ones who have all the luck. The strength of the book lies in its ridicule of the enemy, the fraudulence of the academic world that requires a paper called 'The Economic Influence of the Developments in Ship-building Technique, 1450–1485' and its recorder-tooting, madrigal-singing weekend culture feasts. Despite his crude tactics, his drunkenness and philistine provoca-

The first Angry Young Men – John Osborne, on the right, with Kenneth Haigh, the original 'Jimmy Porter', outside the Royal Court Theatre in 1956

tions (he talks about 'filthy Mozart'), Jim contrasts with this as a relatively honest and decent sort.

Looking back on it all, Amis says:

> I was only trying to write a funny novel, while having a few knocks at groups of people I disliked, people who are entrenched in power through no merit of their own. *Lucky Jim* was isolated in enemy territory, making faces to signal that these people were idiots. It's the kind of thing I used to do myself. The sort of hero I wrote about would previously have been treated either as a comic character pure and simple with no serious identity or as a working class boy who comes up in the world only to find the world has done him down.

Jim Dixon was a solitary sniper picking off his cultural and academic targets. John Osborne's Jimmy Porter opened up with a tommy gun sweeping the entire horizon from left to right. In his opening barrage in his dreary flat in a dreary provincial town he rattles away at the English Sunday, the 'posh' papers, the Church of England, the upper classes, American influences, and gradually, inflated with his own rhetoric, homes in on his real emotional target all along, his unresponsive wife at the ironing board. (Why she has so much ironing to do on Sunday evenings is never apparent, since they are childless.) His rage takes in her father, the retired Indian army colonel, her chinless wonder of a brother at Sandhurst, while 'Mummy' aggravates him most of all.

'That young man was rotten with self-pity,' barked J. B. Priestley, voicing a typical reaction to the insufferable, unstoppable monologues. But he is really ranting away to obtain not sympathy but a hot-blooded reaction from his wife. It is really a very conventional play about calf love and English inhibitions which ends with them playing erotic nursery games of squirrels and bears together. But it was a fact that Jimmy was an eloquent proletarian who did not desire to rise to middle-class standards. That was original. He exerted a spell like a writhing snake on the very people he declared to be his enemies, the predominantly middle-class intellectuals who formed the Royal Court audiences. Everyone theorized about his anger. Was it caused by disappointment in the revolution that had never happened? Was he enraged that the welfare state had been born without the promised millenium of socialist brotherhood and equal shares? Or was he simply frustrated by a sexually passive woman? He is best remembered for his cry that 'there aren't any good, brave causes left. If the big bang comes and we all get killed off . . . it'll be just for the Brave New Nothing-very-much-thank-you.' He had no coherent point of view, still less a political objective. He dealt in gut reactions.

Kenneth Tynan, the only theatre critic of stature who was in his twenties like Osborne and Porter, admired the play for presenting 'postwar youth as it really is'. If he was right, there was a lot of muddled thinking about and a lot of unspecific fear and dislike of life under the mushroom cloud. 'The Porters of our time deplore the tyranny of "good taste" ' he added, cautiously endorsing it as 'the best *young* play of its decade.' In this he was surely right. Good taste was the hallmark of Establishment thinking as far as the arts were concerned. Osborne had broken the middle-class grip on the drama, exemplified in 1950 by T. S. Eliot's *The Cocktail Party*, an inhibited Establishment play if there ever was one. Until Jimmy Porter came along, emotional anaemia was far advanced and spiritual torment was discreetly hinted at in tones that would not transgress the bounds of taste as they are understood in

Belgravia or Kensington. 'By putting the sex war and the class war onto one stage, Mr Osborne gave the drama a tremendous nudge forward,' wrote Tynan later. This was his true achievement. Whatever the dramatic merits of *Look Back In Anger*, it did open up the stage to a range of completely neglected, anti-Establishment characters. The Royal Court's success with such plays as Osborne's and Arnold Wesker's *Roots* opened up the stage also to a new species of actor. These young men and women nurtured their native regional and lower-class accents, scorning to assume the brittle upper-class vowels traditionally taught at drama school. Fired by the example of Albert Finney, Peter O'Toole, Alan Bates and Kenneth Haigh (the original angry duo of *Look Back*), Tom Courtenay and Joan Plowright, the students at the Royal Academy of Dramatic Art were soon busy *acquiring* working class accents. They needed them in order to get work.

A kick at the Establishment is not necessarily aimed to demolish it. In the case of John Braine's hero, Joe Lampton, it was more a matter of kicking at the door in order to be let in. Joe does not lacerate himself about good causes. As a working class upstart, unashamedly on the make, it is good pickings he is looking for. As he arrives from the darkest industrial West Riding of Yorkshire in the market town of Warley (just as his creator moved from Bradford to Bingley as a librarian) he immediately sees what he wants. From a tea-shop window he watches a suntanned girl driven away in a green Aston Martin by a young man with an open-necked shirt (collar *inside* the jacket) whose hair, unlike Joe's, has no oil on it. Braine has an acute eye for small but tell-tale class indicators like these. 'For a moment I hated him,' Joe confesses, 'I wanted an Aston Martin, I wanted a three-guinea linen shirt, I wanted a girl with a Riviera suntan – these were my rights.' The rest of the book is the story of how he got the girl, spoiled daughter of a rich manufacturer, and through her the job that would provide the rest, although he gets it at the cost of his only genuine love which is for an older woman. An important part of the triumph for ex-Sergeant Joe Lampton, as for ex-Corporal Jim Dixon, is getting the officer's girl. In Jimmy Porter's case it is the colonel's daughter.

It is as if the class battle is being fought out in sexual terms. The anger in *Room At The Top* is directed downwards at the drabness near the bottom. In a telling passage Joe reflects on a working class face:

With that solid mass of brilliantined hair and mass-produced face, bony, awkward, mousy, the face enjoying itself at Blackpool with an open-necked shirt spread out over its jacket – Len or Sid or Cliff or Ron – he'd never explore in another person the passion and innocence which a hundred thousand in the bank could alone make possible.

This simple equation – money buys a superior experience of love – made some people take Braine to be a radical critic of the class system. Nothing could have been less accurate, he now says:

> I never thought of myself as belonging to any particular class. My only ambition was to get the hell out – out of being a librarian, out of local government, out of the whole system. Joe doesn't want to do away with the class system. But he would say that from now on it's achievement that counts. It shouldn't matter who your father was.

Braine wrote the book between 1952 and 1955 and was conscious that he was making a break with the traditions of English fiction at the time.

> I realized that a novelist didn't have to live in the Home Counties or make the hero a sensitive middle-class liberal any more. If you made him working-class, he didn't have to be portrayed as a victim. Joe Lampton was called ruthless because English literary critics were still concerned to classify characters either as cads or as gentlemen.

The literary mandarins were especially concerned with the distinction between cads and gentlemen when Joe Lampton appeared in February 1957, because the previous Spring they had become headily infatuated with a real specimen of an angry young upstart, Colin Wilson, and the affair had ended in tears. Wilson, product of a Leicester secondary school and shoe factory, had come up with the unlikeliest of best-sellers at the age of twenty-four, a book of quasi-philosophical-religious-artistic commentary called *The Outsider*. The outsiders referred to in the book were a heterogeneous bunch who included as specimens of the physical, intellectual and emotional variety Nietzsche, Blake, Sartre and even Van Gogh and Nijinsky. The theoretical web which Wilson wove to connect them all was intricate and confused in the extreme. But the title of Outsider seemed apt enough for the author himself. He was acclaimed not so much for the content of the book (which was understood cloudily, if at all) as for getting it written and past the post against such long odds. In particular this self-taught and penniless philosopher was celebrated for having slept out on Hampstead Heath – the most convenient open space, he explained, for the British Museum Reading Room. This is where he spent every available moment between necessary bouts of navvying or washing up in coffee bars to avoid starvation. *Life* magazine posed him with his bicycle, his rucksack and his sleeping bag under the very tree where he had bivouacked while pondering the intellectual problems explored in the book. 'Fuss Over English Egghead' was the headline . . . and the fuss was considerable. Only a fortnight after Jimmy Porter took the stage and was called an 'angry young man' by the theatre's publicity material, here was a real-life example of the species. 'He's a major writer and he's only 24' ran one headline in the popular papers while what Jimmy Porter called the posh Sunday papers rushed to prostrate themselves before this provincial Dick Whittington who had conquered literary London. 'Luminously intelligent . . . truly astounding,' proclaimed the *Observer's* Philip Toynbee, while Cyril Connolly, the *Sunday Times* critic and the very embodiment of the middle-class, Oxbridge domination of English letters, pronounced it 'one of the most remarkable first books I have read for a long time' and hoped that Mr Wilson's 'sanity, vitality and typewriter are spared.' Victor Gollancz's total print of 5,000 copies was exhausted on the day of publication and 20,000 more were sold in six months. 'Not since Lord Byron woke up and found himself famous,' ran one fanciful paragraph, 'has an English writer met with such spontaneous and universal acclaim.' But Childe Colin was very unlike a Byronic hero. His classless lick of floppy hair surmounting earnest glasses over a fisherman's heavy-knit sweater was soon copied in hundreds of coffee bars where 'angry young men' congregated and sometimes were discovered and lionized. Osborne and Wilson were clubbed together, though they detested each other's work, and Amis and Wain were retrospectively elected as fellow members, while many lesser names revolved like satellites around these stars. Along with the 'kitchen sink' painters like John Bratby and the film-makers like Lindsay Anderson who were turning out 'social conscience' documentaries, they represented the protesting malcontents who, as Tynan put it, 'came of age under a Socialist government and found that the class system was still mysteriously intact . . . A lot of unequal talent is exploding in many directions.' Indeed it was unequal. Young writers and artists were front-page news for once and for a while you could get farther on less talent than in any period in memory, providing you were against the Establishment, literary or artistic.

Even more human interest was generated in the movement when Osborne married his leading lady in *Look Back In Anger*, Mary Ure, as his second wife, and Colin Wilson crashed back into the headlines in

The polo-necked philosopher – Colin Wilson at his typewriter

early 1957 because of a girl he had not yet married, Joy Stewart. The pair of them were pursued to London by her father brandishing a horsewhip and intent on dragging her away from him. A supper guest in their flat that evening, by a curious coincidence, was Gerald Hamilton, the original model for Christopher Isherwood's 'Mr Norris'. Thanks to his opportunist eye for drama and his instinct to telephone the newspaper offices in Fleet Street, a full account of the scene, with pictures, was available to all the next morning. Life had copied fiction in a way that was almost too good to be true. Not only was Colin Wilson possibly the last young Englishman to be publicly threatened with horsewhipping by a girl's irate father, but the father, an accountant, actually burst in upon them with the classic line: 'The game is up, Wilson! We know what's in your filthy diary!' This already had a period charm, the period of John Buchan or Bulldog Drummond. There was a struggle during which Wilson was belaboured with an umbrella (the horsewhip, it appears, was not employed) and writhed on the floor – because, he later said, he was laughing so much. Miss Stewart refused to be dragged away – she later became Mrs Wilson – and the police arrived as well as reporters and photographers. Once again there was the now-familiar sexual challenge: the outsider had carried off the daughter of an outraged middle-class father. From then onwards the angry young men symbolized the desire for a new, frankly acknowledged sexual freedom among the under-thirties.

But the game *was* up in another respect. The lionizing of Colin Wilson, egged on no little by his own habit of claiming to be a genius, began to rebound until the sequel to *The Outsider* appeared later that year to the deafening splash of critics jumping overboard. 'Deplorable . . . inferior . . . a rubbish bin,' wrote the same Philip Toynbee of the new book, *Religion and The Rebel*. Other reviewers were even more contemptuous: 'Half-baked Nietzsche', 'highly embarrassing', 'Folie de Grandeur' were the phrases used. 'By less charitable American standards,' said the *New York Times Book Review* sharply, 'Mr Wilson is quite simply brash, conceited, pretentious, presumptuous, prolix, boring, unsound, unoriginal and totally without intellectual subtlety, wit and literary style.' *Time* magazine captioned his photograph 'Egghead, scrambled'. What a rise and oh, what a fall was there – and all inside the space of eighteen months! It was as if the critics were seeking to excuse their previous enthusiasm by exceptional virulence – yet, with all its faults, *The Outsider* had been an exciting event at the particular moment it appeared, though nobody could now remember why. If not back to the sleeping bag, it was back to a Cornish cottage well out of the literary limelight for Colin Wilson. There he stayed with a hard fifteen years ahead of him before he made a comeback, to a different readership, as a writer on the occult.

Looking back now on the fuss over his so-called eggheadedness, he sums it up with disarming simplicity:

The whole *Outside~* thing sprang from the fact that I was born into a working-class environment, was too clever for it and wanted to escape. I felt an outsider. I found a whole lot of other people felt that way too . . . people who were too clever for the niche to which they are assigned. I expected to be rejected but, for a short time, I was accepted. I found myself thrown in with this group to which I was totally opposed emotionally. I felt totally misunderstood.˙ I hoped to found an intellectual movement but England didn't want intellectuals, it wanted

Angry Young Men sleeping with girls they weren't married to. The ideas I stood for were élitist but I found myself promoted, absurdly, as a sort of pop philosopher and then demoted as someone who had taken in the intellectuals and been found out. If I had committed suicide they would all have been satisfied. In spite of the backlash, I feel I have been very lucky. I got out. I could have still been enslaved to the factory. I still wake up sometimes feeling, My God, I'm free!

There could scarcely be a better illustration of how an Establishment operates. Having taken a naive and over-confident young writer at his own valuation, with one accord the literary mandarins made him a sacrificial scapegoat and reasserted their natural prejudice against anyone who had come up from the ranks. It is the unanimity which is sinister and unreal.

Meanwhile attitudes were very different among those who came out of the top drawer educationally, the Oxbridge where the Appointments Boards were at least as important as the Examination Boards and where the undergraduates tidied their not very long hair and changed into unaccustomed suits to offer themselves to the polite, sedentary buyers from industry who came to look them over as potential management trainees. Frederick Raphael (Cambridge 1950–53) has described them as

a grateful generation, eager to please and willing to conform . . . We were a generation eager to be recruited, the eternal examinees of life, asking only to be asked. If my contemporaries were ravenous, it was with unremarkable appetites: the BBC, the law, Parliament, the Foreign Office, the Treasury; Shell and ICI and J. Walter Thompson; weekly journalism and publishing and, above all, the Academy itself – these were the niches that held the glittering prizes.

Contrast that with the feelings of a Redbrick graduate and novelist, Malcolm Bradbury (University of Leicester), looking back on his far from angry novel of 1959, *Eating People Is Wrong*:

It is true that the Fifties saw a cult of provincialism, that the Redbrick university became an appropriate subject, but most of the writers who wrote about them did not go there. Indeed, to my eyes, writers, if they went to university at all, went to Oxford and Cambridge. Leicester did not offer glittering prizes: what it offered was sober futures in low or middle management or schoolteaching.

The novel itself described the rather limp conformity of the grammar-school-educated, Redbrick student of the mid-fifties:

They appeared each year to eat for three years in the university refectory, to join sports clubs and attend the students' union dances held each Saturday night . . . tempting girls out into the grounds in order to kiss them on damp benches; to throw tomatoes at policemen on three successive rag days . . . finally passing on into teaching or business seemingly untouched by what the university stood for – whatever that was.

Seemingly untouched also by any desire to emulate the Angry Young Men, who were in reality an untypical coterie of London's bohemia, given undue attention by the media. Anger and protest at a sober future in middle management or schoolteaching did not come readily to those who might otherwise have expected, like Colin Wilson, a future on the factory floor.

Nevertheless the old class barriers were crumbling at the edges and in the mid-Fifties a counter-attack, or at least a cavalry skirmish, was mounted against the noisy upstarts with neither birth nor breeding nor the manners to defer to those who had them. The 'U and Non-U' battle was one of those Tweedledum and Tweedledee conflicts which no one enjoys as much as the English with their obsession for the niceties of placing one another socially. It began in the obscurest possible way in a Finnish learned journal: A Birmingham professor, Alan S. C. Ross, contributed a paper entitled 'Linguistic Class Indicators in Present-Day English'. Its style was as dry and as far from humorous as the title and it remained resolutely academic when later republished in the magazine *Encounter* in 1955 as 'U and Non-U – an Essay in Sociological Linguistics'. But it was fallen upon with enjoyment by the novelist Nancy Mitford, one of the five celebrated daughters of Lord Redesdale and thereby owed the prefix of 'The Honourable'. The chronicler of the 'Hons' was the first to bring the good news to a wider public: 'The professor,' she wrote, 'pointing out that it is solely by their language that the upper classes nowadays are distinguished (since they are neither cleaner, richer, nor better educated than anybody else) has invented a useful formula: U (for upper class) speaker versus non-U-speaker.' Useful, that was, to Miss Mitford and her fellow aristocrats for it put a name to a distinction between themselves and those who were, in her phrase, N L O (not like one), even if they were nowadays as clean and possibly cleverer.

Tested against this audible equivalent of litmus paper, the best people showed up blue in blood and the rest red in face. Society and the newspapers were diverted for months by earnest discussion of whether it really was Non-U to say 'sweet' instead of 'pudding' or 'cycle' instead of 'bike'. Such euphemisms as 'toilet', 'dentures' or 'serviette' and such expressions as 'Pardon!' or 'Pleased to meet you' had been well-known class giveaways for years but it came as a flash of unwelcome revelation to many to learn that every time they spoke of a mirror or notepaper or the 'phone or passed the cruet or sat in the lounge or raised their glasses to say 'Cheers!', Miss Mitford and friends were exchanging looks across the social gulf. Miss Mitford, with tongue in chic, went even further: 'In silence one must endure the use of the Christian name by comparative strangers and the horror of being introduced by Christian and surname without any prefix'. (No Hon among thieves?) 'This unspeakable usage sometimes occurs in letters – Dear xx – which, in silence, are quickly torn up by me.'

She went on to declare that the landed families who opened their country houses to the public did it not because of want but because they unashamedly enjoyed it ('shame is a bourgeois notion'). The great virtue of the English aristocracy was that their minds were not occupied with money and in this the nation to a large extent followed them:

> Our outlook is totally different from that of our American cousins who have never had an aristocracy. Americans relate all effort, all work and all of life itself to the dollar. Their talk is of nothing but dollars. The English seldom sit happily chatting for hours on end about pounds.

This is especially true, of course, if they have enough pounds for their needs. It is piquant to realize that the pages of *Encounter* in which these romantic, anti-republican and inaccurate notions appeared were heavily and secretly subsidized by the CIA as valuable propaganda for the free democracies. Soon after that they were subsidizing the high spirits of Mr Evelyn Waugh, who believed in the aristocratic virtues with all the fervour of a convert, being himself the offspring of a middle-class home in the non-U suburb of Golders Green. His rejoinder to Miss Mitford reminded her that 'all nannies and many governesses, when pouring out tea, put the milk in first' with the consequence that to be 'rather MIF, darling' was to be cast out from their circle. At tea tables all over the country, one imagines, hands froze guiltily on the milk jug handle, attempting to eradicate the habits of a lifetime. The fish knife, a Victorian invention, was also touched on by Mr Waugh, once 'U' but now 'Non-U' though, he added consolingly, 'at some of the really august stately homes fish knives have been in continuous use for nearly a hundred years.' They were, however, good enough for a laugh at the expense of the would-be genteel. John Betjeman whose poem 'How To Get On In Society' concluded the book of U and Non-U collected papers, *Noblesse Oblige*, placed them first among the Non-U solecisms:

> Phone for the fish-knives, Norman,
> As Cook is a little unnerved;
> You kiddies have crumpled the serviettes
> And I must have things daintily served . . .

But somewhere in Evelyn Waugh's teasing there was a genuine note of peevish outrage which showed that the Establishment was rattled: 'Have you heard of the Butler Education Act?' he demanded of Miss Mitford, 'In it he provided for the free distribution of university degrees to the deserving poor . . . I could make your flesh creep by telling you of the new wave of philistinism with which we are threatened by these sour young people who are coming off the assembly lines in their hundreds every year and finding employment as critics, even as poets and novelists. *L'Ecole de Butler* are the primal men and women of the classless society.' *L'Ecole de Butler* was, of course, the school of Amis and his many followers who were invading the enclosed pastures of English letters which would otherwise have been only lightly grazed. Evelyn Waugh had, according to his lights, correctly identified the enemy. So had Somerset Maugham when he said succinctly of *Lucky Jim* and his fellows, 'They are scum.'

The first American drop-outs, the Beats, alias Beat Generation or, sometimes, the Beatniks, would have been proud to be called 'scum' by an Establishment writer. Their manifesto by Kenneth Rexroth was accurately entitled 'Disengagement'. They were not particularly delinquent. They refused to join wage-earning, rat-racing society and sought freedom in unplanned, impromptu treks across the face of the United States, going nomad with the rejects of society, the migrant workers, Negroes, prostitutes, alcoholics and bums. Most of them had dropped out from the security of middle-class college-educated life. Jack Kerouac, whose wanderings produced the Beats' Bible, *On The Road*, in 1957 was in the habit of sending his French Canadian mother a request for fifty dollars when the going got rough. The Existentialists of Left Bank Paris of the Forties were their nearest predecessors. The Hippies of the Sixties were their obvious successors. But in the Fifties the Beats were the ultimate bohemians. Their music was the modern jazz of Charlie Parker, Miles Davis and Thelonius Monk. From modern jazz musicians they picked up their *argot* and the habit of smoking marijuana. Their spoken communication was often minimal – they did not trust words but preferred the non-rational insights of Zen. But what vocabulary there was was the language of the hipster, borrowed from the black ghettos of jazzmen. They addressed each other as 'man', referred to themselves as 'cats' (if female, 'chicks'), 'dug' what they liked and were 'bugged' by what displeased them. What they dug was 'groovy' and the rest of the world was 'square'. At moments of high excitement they 'flipped'. They despised but needed 'bread' and called a spade a spade. Eldridge Cleaver said perceptively that they were 'a bunch of white, middle-class kids adopting the life-style of "niggers".' Norman Mailer, similarly, classified them in a well-known phrase as 'White Negroes'. His explanation of hipsterism in an essay of that title (1957) was tortuous in the extreme: 'It is essential to dig the most for if you do not dig you lose your superiority over the square and so you are less likely to be cool . . .' Jack Kerouac put out an almost religious gospel of universal love which seemed to dig everything: 'We love everything,' he declared, 'Billy Graham, Rock 'n' Roll, Zen, apple pie, Eisenhower – we dig it all.' A critical faculty was one of the pieces of intellectual equipment which Beats discarded as not wanted on voyage. Allen Ginsberg, who published the best-known Beat poem, 'Howl' (1956), obtained his effects by primitive incantation, like a witch-doctor cursing in a rain of exclamation marks:

> Moloch! – Solitude! Filth! Ugliness! Ashcans
> and unobtainable dollars! Children
> screaming under stairways! Boys
> sobbing in armies! Old men weeping
> in the parks!
> Moloch! Moloch! Nightmare of Moloch!
> Moloch the loveless! Mental Moloch!
> Moloch the heavy judge of men!

Kerouac's book *On The Road* describes his rides by bus and hitch-hiking across America in pursuit of 'Dean Moriarty' – in reality Neal Cassady, a parking attendant of rootless and ruthless mobility, whose sex life thrived on a variety quite sensational for the time in which it was written. Cassady disappeared with Kerouac's friend Allen Ginsberg (Carlo Marx in the book) and later with Ginsberg's friend, William Burroughs. This enthusiastic homosexuality did not prevent him from marrying three times and producing numbers of children. William Burroughs wrote an account of his life as a drug addict in 1953 (*Junkie* was

its uncompromising title) and as a homosexual (*The Naked Lunch*, 1959). Their frank amorality was the chief distinction of Beat works but Kerouac achieved a romantic half-poetic intensity with the story of his odyssey. It proclaims him an inefficient traveller or hobo but extraordinarily open to whatever experience comes along, good or, more usually, very uncomfortable. Having worked on it over several years, in 1951 he shot it out in three weeks in one unbroken stream of 'spontaneous prose' typed on 120-foot rolls of teleprinter paper. 'It isn't writing,' commented Truman Capote, 'it's typing.' But half a million copies can't be shrugged off so easily. This highly romantic, rhapsodic, rambling narrative which plunges into set-pieces and confessions like verbal jazz breaks, portrays an alternative America, the sort that did not like Ike, nor commute nor compete, nor play Canasta, but lived intensely, travelling onwards, having visions, seducing girls, getting into fights, but caring about the uniqueness of the people found along the road. 'The only people for me are the mad ones,' ran its best-known passage, 'the ones who are mad to live, mad to talk, mad to be saved, desirous of everything at the same time, the ones who never yawn or say a commonplace thing, but burn, burn, burn like fabulous yellow roman candles, exploding like spiders across the stars.' Ten years later this would be the orthodoxy of the Underground.

Kerouac and Ginsberg had to go to the West Coast to find a sympathetic audience. San Francisco was the capital of non-conformist America, the Left Bank of the Mind. It was the cradle of the Beat scene (which centred round City Lights bookshop), it initiated poetry and jazz concerts, it incubated its own style of West Coast jazz as played by musicians like Shorty Rogers and Jimmy Giuffre, and it was the launching pad of the hip comedians. Mort Sahl began his long reign as resident monologuist at 'the hungry i' – a cellar seating 265 – in 1953. No one was sure whether the small 'i' stood for 'intellectual' or for 'id'. In his early days it was a brave exercise in free speech to make jokes about McCarthy, who had just accused the U.S. Army of being a Communist-front organization. Sahl said the Army had responded by redesigning its Eisenhower jacket. They called it the McCarthy jacket because they had added a flap which would button over the mouth.

In the days when night-club comedians were wont to have a dinner jacket and a line of chorus girls behind them, Mort Sahl stood at the

OPPOSITE *Mort Sahl: 'If there's any group I haven't offended, come to the next show'*

Tom Lehrer: 'So long, Mom, I'm off to drop the bomb'

microphone in a sweater and open-neck shirt carrying a rolled-up news-paper and talked about politics. He asked of Richard Nixon, 'Would you buy a used car from this man ?' and he described Eisenhower's problems of policy as 'whether or not to use an overlapping grip.' Protest, indeed the mere idea of criticism, was such a novelty then that Mort Sahl's name was soon nationally known as an 'intellectual' and his picture was on the cover of *Time*. People passing the club would shout 'Communist!' and roll garbage cans down the steps and some would wait to beat him up outside afterwards. Sahl continued to end his act by saying, 'If there's any group I haven't offended, come to the next show.' College audiences from Berkeley loved him. So did jazzmen. So in the end did a wide selection of ordinary people: 'Probably my biggest secret,' he wrote later in his book *Heartland*, 'is that most Americans look down on other Americans and think they're the only ones who understand my act . . . I was playing back the sounds of my time.'

'The hungry i' was also played by a very different kind of cult intellec-tual, a Harvard graduate student of mathematics called Tom Lehrer. Lehrer and Sahl were the sweet and sour heroes, respectively, of the student generation. Lehrer's local fame as a songwriter who performed at Harvard parties spread so widely that he made records of his songs privately and distributed them by mail order himself. Recording com-panies wouldn't look at him. The songs were not 'allowed' on the radio. It was a time when the mass media didn't like to do anything that might be complained about. In England his L Ps were a status symbol to be brought out at smart parties, since they were not released until he toured the country in 1959.

Where was the offence? It seems extraordinary that subversive menace was detected in these burlesques of the stereotypes of American popular song – cowboy songs, Dixie songs, college songs, love songs, folk songs, waltzes and tangos. Perhaps it was accounted a heresy because American song is sacred – and his blithe, genial voice concealed a macabre twist such as the missile testing ground on the cowboy's desert prairie: or, simply announced, 'So long, Mom, I'm off to drop the bomb.' It was definitely UnAmerican to mock the Boy Scouts or the Spirit of Christmas ('I have written a carol to all we most deeply and sincerely believe in – money'). He emerged from Army service (just before Elvis so ceremoniously joined it) with a sardonic number, 'It Makes A Fellow Proud To Be A Soldier' which he prefaced with the tribute: 'They have carried the American democratic ideal to its logical conclusion: not only do they refuse to discriminate on the grounds of

race, creed and colour but also on the grounds of ability.' Lehrer now
looks back on that time with mild amazement at its naivety:

> I was just saying what everybody else in Harvard's ivory towers was
> saying. It came as a surprise that some people thought it was shocking.
> What was shocking to me was that Eisenhower could beat Stevenson. It
> made me realize that times had changed: I grew up in an era when the
> best man always won. Part of the success of the records was due to the
> fact that people who bought them felt they were members of an élite
> minority, we happy liberals, the Stevenson band, living in an ivory
> tower like me and reading the *New York Times*. In the Fifties it was
> easier to laugh. There wasn't anything terrible happening. I didn't feel
> hatred or real bitterness about what was being done – it was just foolish.
> But by the Sixties, no one could sing 'Oh, what a beautiful mornin' '
> any more. I was never able to write a funny song about the Vietnam
> war or Nixon or the race riots. You could write jokes that would make
> people applaud but they wouldn't make people *laugh*. Since the Fifties
> it seems to be harder to laugh.

The most notorious comedian to scourge his audience as they laughed
uncomfortably was Lenny Bruce. Like Mort Sahl he first worked in jazz
concerts – he was an intermission act with the Woody Herman band –
until he opened in San Francisco clubs including 'the hungry i' in 1958.
Within a year he was a cult among hipsters and jazz men but had not yet
acquired the notoriety that his arrests for obscenity and drug offences
brought him in the Sixties. His reputation was the result of more substantial and courageous material than mere obscenities. He improvised
brilliantly in the character of the squarest, red-neck reactionaries, con-
fronted with such deviants as there were – falsetto faggots, black bop
musicians and junkies muttering in hipster argot. His humour came out
of their total mutual incomprehension and from saying the unsayable.
An awful lot was considered unsayable in the Fifties, even Lenny Bruce's
definition of a Flamenco dancer, to quote a mild example – 'A man trying
to catch a glimpse of his own ass'. One of his earliest and most celebrated bullseyes was his satirical sketch of a meeting of religious leaders
which sounded like a big business conference. The climax was a telephone call by the American revivalist preacher, Oral Roberts, to the
newly elected Pope John as if he were a show business agent calling his
client: 'Hello Johnny! – What's shakin' baby? Boy, it's really been an
election month, hasn't it, sweetie? Yeah, the puff of smoke knocked me
out . . . ' Having offered His Holiness the chance of a booking on the Ed
Sullivan show he signed off – 'just wave – and wear the *big* ring! No!

Nobody knows you're Jewish!' At that moment, as the laughter swelled, Lenny Bruce would duck and call to the audience: 'Watch out for the lightning!' Lightning was something the Fifties had been short of. By 1957 even the British Monarchy was being singed by lightning.

The Royal Family, as the longest-running British soap opera, had provided one throat-catching crisis from 1955–57, the arrested romance of Princess Margaret and Group Captain Peter Townsend, the entanglement of two stereotypes, the princess and the Battle of Britain hero. Not surprisingly the Group Captain's hasty wartime marriage had crashed like thousands of others and his divorced wife was still living. The traumatic memory of Mrs Simpson and the very idea of divorce seemed to throw the Palace advisers into a flat spin, although there was hardly any danger of Princess Margaret becoming queen. The situation bristled with ironies. The Church of England, which officially forbade divorce but in practice often condoned it, was itself founded on a royal divorce. The prime minister, Sir Anthony Eden, who finally advised the princess that to obtain a civil marriage to Townsend she would have to renounce her royal functions and income, was himself divorced and remarried. So were three of his ministers. As for the nation at large, there was no real evidence that the divorce element interested people half as much as the romance itself, when it was leaked from the foreign newspapers. Nevertheless, Townsend was packed off to Brussels while the Princess waited to become twenty-five and thereby free of provisions of the royal marriages act, instituted by George III to control the more wayward impulses of George IV. They waited in vain. The end of the affair was a statement from the Princess that she had decided not to marry him 'mindful of the church's teaching and conscious of my duty to the Commonwealth . . .'

It did not sound like the expression of the spontaneous feeling of a girl in her twenties – and in fact it proved later to be the wording suggested by her Group Captain himself. It was not a popular act of self-denial. If true love had been thought to endanger the Church and the Commonwealth in the romance-conscious 1950s, so much the worse for them. To many people, including Townsend, it was further proof of the unattractive stuffiness and outdatedness of the Establishment mentality: an old family friend had been dismissed as good enough to serve but not good enough to marry. In his memoir of the episode long afterwards, *Time and Chance*, Townsend wrote of how the Queen's private secretary, Sir Alan Lascelles, told him 'You must be either mad or bad'. He was not told by the Press secretary, Commander Colville, that the

*Early days of the romance – the Princess and the Equerry
thrown together on a Royal tour before the clouds gathered*

secret romance was being openly discussed in the rest of the world's
press. If only he had known, 'I would have got out fast.' He also pointed
out: 'I had been with the Royal Family for nine years. Now I was being
booted out of England . . . I had offended the Establishment by falling in
love with the Queen's sister for whose heart, let alone hand, I was by
Establishment rules quite ineligible. Now I was getting my deserts . . .
I had felt a bit of a misfit in that society: now I felt like a throw-out from
it.' He went off tight-lipped, but understandably bitter, on a 60,000-
mile drive round the world – to forget, in the John Buchan tradition.
The princess gained some popularity as a non-conformist royal who
preferred the company of commoners, especially comedians like Peter
Sellers, to her sister's court. As the decade ended she proved her un-
conventionality by marrying a photographer. How suitable a suitor the
Group Captain may have seemed in retrospect after that marriage ended
in divorce, one can only wonder.

The genuine regard for the monarch which was manifested at the death of George VI, who had worked so hard at sharing the wartime privations of his people – the five inches of bathwater, the spam on the gold plate – and which reached its apotheosis in the jamboree of the Coronation and the talk of a 'new Elizabethan age', had turned into sickly and excessive idolatry by the middle Fifties. It was a time of constant royal tours at home and abroad. It was possible to read in the *Daily Mail*: 'It will be strange to hear the Queen speaking from Australia on Christmas Day and to know that, this time, it is we who are on the other side of the world'; or in the *News Chronicle*'s report on a royal tour: 'Into this eager void came – the world's principal human being, Her Majesty The Queen'. 'After the Queen left,' reported the *Birmingham Mail*, 'Other workpeople rushed to shake hands with those who had been presented to Her Majesty. They called it sharing the royal handshake.' In this climate it was not difficult to make bestsellers of the memoirs of the long-serving royal governess known as 'Crawfie', who served up reminiscences of nursery trivia about little Princess 'Lillibet' in nauseating profusion. *Woman's Own* ran a weekly column signed by her on the royal appearances of the season in her usual oozing vein. Unfortunately it had to be written and printed in advance and when the Trooping the Colour and Royal Ascot were cancelled at short notice because of a strike in 1955, the magazine's production was not stopped in time. Crawfie's reflections that 'the bearing and dignity' of the Queen at the cancelled ceremony 'caused admiration among the spectators' did not add to her credibility any more than the fact that she was the only person to have seen the Queen at Ascot. 'Crawfie Comes A Cropper!' cried the headlines with satisfaction.

But the idolatry went on. So in 1957 it came as a profound shock to see the Queen and the customs of the Windsor family put in the pillory. Lord Altrincham, writing in his own sober monthly, *The National and English Review*, complained of the narrowness of the Queen's 'woefully inadequate training ('Crawfie', the London season, the racecourse, the grouse moor, Canasta . . .)'. He described her entourage as 'people of the tweedy sort, a tight little enclave of British ladies and gentlemen'. Finally he voiced a general feeling that 'her style of speaking is frankly a pain in the neck' and the utterances put in her mouth conveyed the personality of 'a priggish schoolgirl, captain of the hockey team, a prefect and a recent candidate for confirmation.'

This was restrained stuff compared with John Osborne's outburst in an anthology called *Declaration* two months later. He referred to 'that fabulous family we love so well – the Amazing Windsors!' – and to a 'trough of Queen worship . . . the National Swill'. Then he hit his stride with a memorable metaphor: 'My objection to the royalty symbol is that it is dead: it is the gold filling in a mouthful of decay.' It was hard to tell which image was more insulting – the gold filling or the surrounding decay. And with a few more pitying phrases about the royal round of gracious boredom, Osborne signed off: 'it distresses me that there should be so many empty lives in Britain to sustain this fatuous industry.' Now, many people felt, they knew at last what the young men in the headlines were angry about; they were outraged by the Palace. Before the ink was dry on this revolutionary declaration, the *Saturday Evening Post* came out in October to coincide with the Queen's visit to the United States with an article which asked its ten million readers: 'Does England Really Need A Queen?' It was by Malcolm Muggeridge, editor until that year of *Punch*, which had been the Establishment's own licensed jester until he got hold of it. He had doubts about the security of the English throne and then let fall the hint that it was the upper classes who criticized the monarchy most: 'It is duchesses, not shop assistants, who find the Queen dowdy, frumpish and banal.' Those who actually mixed with royalty socially, he added, refer to them in 'contemptuously facetious tones.' One began to wonder if the Queen poured the milk in first. Or was Mr Muggeridge (not a frequent visitor to the Palace) thinking of café society's comic nicknames for the Queen and her husband – 'Brenda and Brian'?

Taken together these criticisms, some of them reasonable enough, were more than traditional patriots could bear. Not all of them by any means were retired colonels writing disgusted letters to the papers from Cheltenham or Tunbridge Wells. After his obscure article had been republished all over the world, Lord Altrincham (who later renounced his title and became plain John Grigg) received a letter which showed that hearts just as brave and fair beat in back streets as in Berkeley Square:

> Altrincham, if we ever see you in the street, we'll do you in. We ain't no law-abiding boys and we don't hold with this police stuff but you go too flamin' far when you critisise our Queen who does more good than you if you lived to be 500. She's a grand lady and you bloody well know it.
>   Yours,
>   Eight (loyal to the Queen) Teddy Boys

Mayfair and *Debrett* produced some royal champions too. The Duke of Argyll said Altrincham should be hung, drawn and quartered, a punishment in abeyance since the reign of Charles I, while Lord Strathmore said he would shoot him if he had a gun, a curious omission from an English peer's equipment. The Archbishop of Canterbury condemned the article with all the authority of his bell, book and candle, although, being in America at the time, he had to admit he had not read it. Finally an elderly official of the League of Empire Loyalists struck Lord Altrincham in the face and was fined at Bow Street court, ironically in the circumstances, for a breach of the Queen's peace. However he had the satisfaction of hearing the magistrate suppose that 95 per cent of his fellow subjects were disgusted by Lord Altrincham's attack.

The Empire Loyalists also turned their attention to Malcolm Muggeridge. His barn doors were daubed with yellow painted slogans and a torrent of obscene letters and telephone calls descended. He and his wife were warned not to trespass on land neighbouring their Sussex retreat, where they had always gone for walks. Schoolboys burned him in effigy near the Queen's home at Sandringham, and a Berkshire vicar offered to black his eye in a doughty challenge issued in his parish magazine. The Establishment itself acted far more effectively. On the orders of the Director-General of the BBC, Mr Muggeridge was dropped from his fortnightly television appearances on 'Panorama' and plans to broadcast a university debate were cancelled because he was speaking at it. Close on this, the *Sunday Dispatch* which billed him as 'the most provocative writer in Britain' fired him for displaying the very talent for provocation they had been boasting of.

What the Americans thought of all this is hard to say, since many of them were busy cheering the Queen at the time. She was staying at Williamsburg when she sent for the offending issue of the *Saturday Evening Post* at breakfast time and delayed her day's timetable while she read it. Mr Muggeridge meantime was flown to New York to defend his views on the Mike Wallace television programme. He said that in person she was 'a most charming woman' but unfortunately the Queen never heard the compliment. The station in Washington, where she was staying, took no chances of giving offence and blacked Mr Muggeridge out.

Such reactions now have a somewhat ludicrous ring. Only twenty years later they were inconceivable. One has only to compare the mild stir which met the announcement of Princess Margaret's separation from her husband with the uproar over the Group Captain whom she did not marry. The difference is partly a result of the popular press having recovered somewhat from the bout of royalty fever it suffered in the Fifties, when pageantry and ceremonial seemed to be the consolation prizes for Britain's loss of real power. But even then there were signs that they had overestimated public enthusiasm for royal idolatry. Lord Altrincham claimed that the letters he received were three to one in favour of what he had written. The *Daily Mirror*'s correspondents were four to one in his favour. The notably royalist *Daily Mail* conducted a nationwide poll and discovered that 55 per cent agreed with his criticisms of the court, while 35 per cent agreed with him absolutely. This was enough to give the Palace, the newspapers and the magistrate at Bow Street pause for reflection.

By the next year it looked as though criticisms of the court, at least, had been taken note of. It was announced that that season's debutantes would be the last to be presented at court presentation parties, a break with a tradition that began in 1786. Debs were still news. The daily gossip columns, the glossy magazines and the loyal 'Jennifer' of 'Jennifer's Diary' were full of their doings and their photographs by Barry Swaebe, Tony Armstrong-Jones or Baron. Two of the most photographed debs were Frances Sweeny, who became Duchess of Rutland, and Henrietta Tiarks, who reached the staging post of Marchioness of Tavistock, *en route* to the dukedom of Bedford. 'The deb era has gone;' she wrote recently, 'I'm glad I did it but I would not want to relive one solitary second of it.' Socially ambitious parents continued to spend money on their daughters' debuts like water – though not like Henry Ford whose coming-out party for his daughter, Charlotte, in 1959 cost $250,000 and required flying two million magnolia leaves from Mississippi to transform the Detroit Country Club into a French château. Heiresses were at a premium and, as always, some of them gained a highly-publicized status as symbols of romance by running away for love. Isobel Patiño, the South American mining heiress, eloped to Gretna Green with Mr Jimmy Goldsmith in 1953 and Tessa Kennedy ran away to the West Indies with Dominic Elwes in 1958. The gossip columnists rubbed their hands and twittered like grasshoppers.

The London season survived the loss of that symbolic curtsy to the throne and the House of Lords survived the creation of the first life peers to join its deliberations, both in the same summer of 1958, but neither was to be quite the same again. The new political barons and baronesses were a safely Establishment collection, put forward by the Prime Minister and the Leader of the Opposition, but inevitably the temporary baronies would gradually outweigh the hereditary ones. Not, however, in the Fifties. Harold Macmillan dearly loved a lord, was related to a great many of them through his marriage to the daughter of a

'The Deb of the Decade' – Henrietta Tiarks, later Marchioness of Tavistock, in the classical pose of a Dorothy Wilding portrait

Duke of Devonshire and, like an eighteenth-century Whig, found places in his government for one duke (his nephew), a marquess (his wife's cousin) and four earls, mostly Scottish shooting pals. He found room for a son-in-law as a minister, a son's brother-in-law as ambassador to Washington and another cousin as governor of the Bank of England. During the Churchill-Eden-Macmillan administrations of the Fifties over 130 peers were created (not to mention seventy-four hereditary baronets) in the last burst of patronage before the meritocrats invaded the precincts of the aristocrats. There would be virtually no more new hereditary titles to replace the existing stock. Significantly Macmillan refused anything for himself on retirement, unlike Eden who took the usual earldom. Churchill only accepted the Garter, while turning down what was probably the last dukedom ever to be offered by a British sovereign, on his retirement in 1955.

In other ways the Establishment relinquished its exclusive hold on certain areas of power. The 'tight little enclave of British ladies and gentlemen' were a good deal less prominent in the entourage of Prince Philip and the upbringing of Prince Charles. In another ten years 'The Amazing Windsors' would be showing their own, specially made, home movies as a TV spectacular, managing to avoid giving people a pain in the neck. Meanwhile the Establishment employed one of its tested survival techniques: it attempted to embrace its critics. There is no danger these days of mistaking for Outsiders either Kingsley Amis or John Braine, while John Osborne is a National Theatre playwright (he was already able to enjoy the services of Sir Laurence Olivier in his second play, *The Entertainer*, in his Royal Court days, though that might have been described as Establishment slumming). It has to be admitted with regret that the mid-Fifties renaissance both in fiction and on the stage fizzled out rather swiftly. Few of the original talents hailed as a new dawn developed into major or enduring writers. The most enduring new playwright of the decade, Harold Pinter, was not an Angry Young Man nor part of the Royal Court coterie. He could look back only on a one-week production of *The Birthday Party* which failed ignominiously, having been rejected by every critic save one, Sir Harold Hobson.

Was it a breakthrough that came to nothing? Kenneth Tynan, its chief midwife, thinks not:

> It performed the essential task of liberating the articulate lower-class writer, the early off-spring of the Butler Education Act. It also educated the grammar school audience. Without them there wouldn't have been an audience for Stoppard and others today. Before the Royal Court saw it, Osborne's play had gone round and been rejected by every West End management, which wouldn't happen to such a play now.

As for the anger – that evaporated in the affluence that increasingly blurred the class barriers which had provoked it. When the young recognized anger again it was in the mid-Sixties in the United States and they had something more urgent to be angry about.

CHAPTER NINE

The Taste of the Time

Nothing accelerates change like the ending of a war. World War II arrested developments in the arts, fashion and taste for nearly ten years, counting the subsequent period of austerity and shortages, until 1950 in Europe and almost as long in the United States. The most significant visual revolution of the Forties had been Dior's dramatic New Look which outdated every woman's wardrobe overnight in 1947. Other couturiers and the ready-to-wear manufacturers were still catching up and exploiting Dior's lead in 1950 and the Look dominated fashion until 1955, so basic was the desire to look extravagantly feminine once again. Architecture and design also had their New Look, in Britain at any rate. It too was an extravagant reassertion of the desire for colour and frills born with the Festival of Britain in 1951 and maintained in the brief hey-day of 'Festival Style' which followed it.

There was an outburst of blocks of council flats whose end-walls, balconies and front doors hectically asserted themselves in primary colours. In smart and trend-conscious areas, like Kensington and Hampstead, front doors with one accord turned bright yellow, like fields of buttercups. Interiors, after a long period of anaemia in pastel shades, became feverish with 'contemporary' wallpaper, patterned with jazzy calligraphy on brightly-hued backgrounds. One wall of the room, usually the fireplace wall, would be made to 'stand out' – one might have said 'leap out' – by being papered with an even brighter and more gaudy paper than the others. Underfoot in millions of living rooms lay the earliest bestseller among wall-to-wall carpets. It was called 'Skaters' Trails' and was the very essence of 'contemporary' style – a hectic pattern of thin curved lines scraped on a ground of grey or burnt red. More than 2000 miles of it were run off the looms at Kidderminster. Amid this sat 'contemporary' furniture with spindly, splayed legs, moulded and laminated 'free-flow' chairbacks, coffee-table tops which flared upwards at either end. They might have been designed to fly. Instead they alighted in flocks in airport and suburban lounges alike.

It would not be fair to blame the more frantic aberrations of popular taste on the intentional gaiety of the Festival of Britain, but its co-

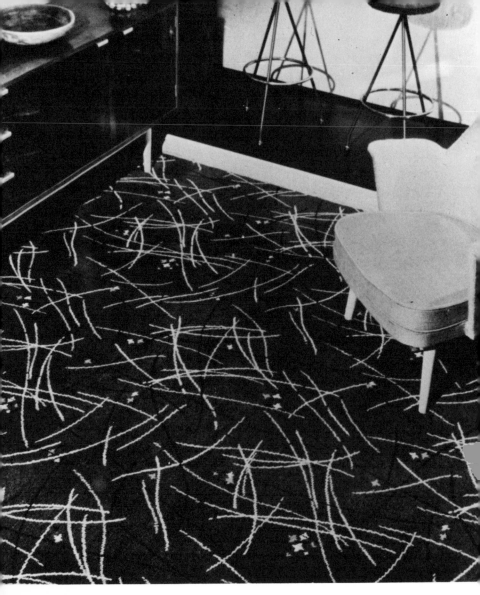

The very essence of 'Contemporary' style – 'Skaters' Trails' carpet design

ordinating architect, Sir Hugh Casson, remembers the psychological state of deprivation which triggered them off:

> After ten years of austerity and drabness people wanted the sensation of plenty. Everything for so long had been strictly utility – it was a time of 'any colour so long as it's brown'. The result was that people went on a binge of far too many colours and textures and changes of surface from brick to timber to stucco to glass. It was like going into a sweet-shop after being on a starvation diet. A lot of the architecture and design was frivolous and fussy and the Festival itself gave things a strong shove along that road. The spindle legs on everything were a reaction against the chunky blockhouse proportions of wartime and also the

result of regulations forbidding the use of pieces of wood more than so thick. All this produced a design style of multi-coloured millinery – and in due course that led to a counter reaction into Brutalism, the army boots style of shuttered concrete.

Jonathan Miller, a medical student in the early Fifties, recalls:

The Festival left behind two legacies, an enthusiasm for Victoriana and the idea of café life, which had not existed until then. This led from coffee bars to Soup Kitchens, with seventeenth-century engravings mounted on white Formica as table mats, wooden-handled steak knives, and rough peasant things like pepper mills, garlic crushers and ratatouille. Hence the enthusiasm to get back to stripped pine as decoration to go with the coffee in the earthenware or glass cups. It was a kind of primitivism, a rejection of the machine environment.

Decoration in itself was clean contrary to the rather earnest ethos of the age of post-war planning. The Modern Movement, as it had been preached by the pre-war pioneers – mostly refugees from Hitler's Europe – was an almost religious faith in purity and functionalism. It traced back to the Bauhaus, with its horror of applied decoration, and to Le Corbusier's famous slogan – 'The House – A Machine For Living In.' Brutalism developed from these tenets into the dogma of all self-respecting modernists. Applied to painting its principles produced Abstract Expressionism. Representation was banished, like original sin, from the canvas, just as decoration had been banned from building façades. In the words of Sir John Betjeman: 'Decoration was wicked and collected dust.' The form of a building was determined by its function and its materials: the subject-matter of a painting was its own constituents – the slab of pure colour or the traces left by the wielding of the loaded brush, signifying nothing beyond its own existence. The painting no longer had a subject: it was an object, an artefact, an event bearing witness to the actions that produced it . . . an action painting.

These developments coincided with a momentous shifting of the axis of the *avant-garde* from Europe to America. The capital of Bohemia was no longer Paris, it had moved to New York. The seeds of the 'New York School' had been sown by Hitler. The German designers, artists and architects of the Bauhaus, Josef Albers, Hans Hofmann, Walter Gropius, Mies van der Rohe, and the French-domiciled modernists and surrealists, Leger, Chagall, Max Ernst, André Breton, Yves Tanguy, Piet Mondrian, settled and taught in America. The 'New York

'Jack the Dripper' – Jackson Pollock at work

School' of painting and the architecture of American cities grew up under their influence. One of its principal midwives was the heiress and patron of painters, Peggy Guggenheim, and her museum of 'The Art Of This Century'. By 1950 the most talked-of innovator in modern painting was not Picasso, preoccupied with exploiting his mannerisms in portraits of young women, nor Matisse who, in arthritic old age, was making exquisite arrangements of coloured paper cut-outs, but an American backwoodsman from Wyoming called Jackson Pollock. Despite his reputation for wildness, he was no primitive. He had deliberately suppressed his artistic training to create a new visual language. His own description of his methods could hardly be more explicit:

> My painting is not done on the easel. I prefer to put it up on a wall or
> better still spread it out on the floor. When the canvas is on the floor,
> I feel as if I am part of the painting. I can walk around it and work from

all sides, literally be in the painting . . . I have eliminated the usual tools of the painter. I prefer sticks, a trowel, ordinary spoons or just to let the liquid colour drip or spatter . . . When I am painting, I have no knowledge of what I am doing. Only after a moment of returning consciousness do I become aware of what I have been about.

He added on another occasion: 'It is only when I lose contact with the painting, the result is a mess.' To many the methods described here were ludicrous and the result was always a mess.

Here were all the ingredients to begin a cult. What could be more Romantic – Byronic – than this torero of a painter hurling himself upon the canvas with anything that came to hand, fighting a hand-to-hand combat with his material in a trance of furious creativity? He was also undeniably original. Who before him had thought of punching holes in cans of ordinary household enamel and claiming that the resulting spillage, which mirrored the movement of his arms and body, was therefore art? Did he not set the half-finished canvas against the wall to contemplate for as much as a fortnight and then return to it for further feverish bouts until satisfied? It was like a love affair of the most tempestuous kind. Pollock became an alcoholic and perished in a car crash in 1956. He could hardly be directly imitated. But his principles were.

Willem de Kooning hurled himself at the canvas to obtain much the same sort of 'gesture painting' as Pollock except that his thick, turbulent brushwork used as a recognizable motif the grotesquely distorted, staring, bare-toothed image of a woman. Robert Motherwell, Franz Kline and Clifford Still painted mostly in black and white, using black masses or calligraphic brush-strokes against empty white space. Mark Rothko experimented with self-denial of another kind. He filled the canvas with two or three large, soft-edged rectangular blocks of even colour setting up tensions between them like a musical chord, or discord – 'Black In Deep Red' or 'Mauve Intersection'. Other 'colour field painters', such as Barnett Newman and Ad Reinhardt, attempted even greater simplification in monochrome. A typical Newman would be an unrelieved red broken only by one or two fastidiously placed thin, vertical lines in another colour. Reinhardt used only red or blue or gradations of black.

All this was grist to the mill of art criticism. Here was something to theorize about and the theorists became almost more important than the painters. Clement Greenberg and Harold Rosenberg were the undisputed high priests of the New York School. Greenberg, the champion of Pollock, wrote of the 'integrity of the picture plane', though that concept was as old as Cézanne. Rosenberg (champion of de Kooning) coined the label 'action painting' and talked of the canvas as 'an arena in which to act'. These were heady, cerebral spells they were casting even if the results seemed to give little actual visual pleasure to many people outside the intellectuals of the galleries.

Britain, which knew little of what was going on in New York until the Sixties, produced its abstract painters too. There was the carved and painted solid geometry of Ben Nicholson, the English pioneer. There was the dramatic conversion of Victor Pasmore, one of the most sensitive of colourists, from figurative painting to uncompromising abstract-constructivism. William Scott reduced his subjects to the barest of linear forms, like diagrams of widely spaced out saucepans and frying pans. Gradually the abstract painters began to outnumber the representational as it began to dawn on the art world that abstract painting not only looked easier to do but was actually quite easy to understand: it was a matter of receiving pure subjective sensation without bothering your head about what it could mean.

Not every artist took the abstract path. In England figurative painting still had its champions. Graham Sutherland was at his peak as a portrait painter. Having laid Somerset Maugham bare on the dissecting table, he added to his pathologist's gallery Helena Rubinstein, Lord Beaverbrook and Churchill, a portrait presented on his retirement from the House of Commons. Churchill described it with a rasp as 'a remarkable work of modern art' and it was never seen again. Twenty years later, after Lady Churchill's death, it was acknowledged that it had been destroyed on her order. At the other end of the scale were the deliberately coarse and unsubtle 'social realists', the best-known of whom was John Bratby, who gained an immediate notoriety from his choice of 'inartistic' subject matter. Almost as if sending up the fine, bourgeois interiors and table-settings of Bonnard and Matisse, he made compositions of squalid breakfast tables piled with garish packets of cornflakes or beer mugs, with his painter wife, Jean, as a nude figure. All of these were rendered in immensely thick and grubby-looking paint squeezed from the tube like toothpaste. This domestic detritus had the same shock value as the social realism of the novels and plays of the time. It literally justified the label 'kitchen sink' school, which was concentrated at the Beaux Arts Gallery. This showed, amongst others, Jack Smith and Frank Auerbach and the sculptors Elizabeth Frink and Eduardo Paolozzi (whose constructions were made of carefully cast machine parts).

One of Graham Sutherland's sketches for the contentious Churchill portrait

Far more disquieting portraits emerged from the tortured vision of Francis Bacon, often hailed as the outstandingly original talent of his generation. He continued to paint in the European illustrative manner but applied his virtuoso technique to unnerving material. Fascinated by the human figure in motion, which he studied with the aid of high-speed photographs, he often distorted a meticulously rendered head or body with a wipe of the brush (or even the sweater) into a blurred and ambiguous image like a photograph whose subject has moved too fast for the camera. In one way he resembled the 'gesture' painters across the Atlantic in opening himself to spontaneous influences. 'In my case all painting is an accident,' he said and also: 'If only people were free enough to let everything in, something extraordinary might come of it.' What came of it in his canvases of the Fifties and after was a sense of barely-suppressed violence, of inner demons. Soberly-suited men with smudged heads sit screaming; naked figures couple chaotically on beds. An atmosphere of sheer horror haunts these figures, especially those whose heads are outlined by a thin painted frame which appears to envelope them. Bacon's obsession with open mouths, crying out, came from a film still of a screaming nurse with blood running down her face, from Eisenstein's *The Battleship Potemkin*. 'I did hope one day to make the best painting of the human cry,' he admitted once. He married this obsession with another when copying a photograph of Velazquez's portrait of Pope Innocent x, which he believes one of the greatest portraits ever made. It is a study of total isolation. It was the first of a whole series of studies of screaming Popes (including the then current incumbent, Pius xii) that he made during the Fifties, giving off an atmosphere of horror, menace, hysteria, which memorably caught some nameless dread of the time. The rich collected him with awe. By contrast everybody who knew nothing about art but knew what they liked, liked the 'modern old master' Pietro Annigoni of Florence, whose fortunes were founded on his portrait of the Queen looking romantic and dashing in her Garter cloak, the way her subjects would have liked her always to look.

But beyond doubt, it was abstraction that made the running in the visual arts, no less in sculpture than in painting. Barbara Hepworth who had earlier discovered the abstract qualities of natural forms in wood and bronze continued to work as a law to herself. Henry Moore continued to explore highly schematic natural forms in stone and bronze. The younger generation of artists, like Reg Butler, Lynn Chadwick and Kenneth Armitage turned much more to man-made forms for inspiration until their works were welded more and more like pieces of machinery, piping, tubing, boiler casing, chains and pulleys and winding gear. An arrangement of metal plates entitled 'The Unknown Political Prisoner' caused an outcry of incomprehension when it won a £4525 prize for Reg Butler in 1953. Someone dubbed it 'the geometry of fear' but when it was exhibited a fellow artist and competitor smashed it.

Like abstract painting, post-war architecture exhibited a parallel concern with scale and rigorous simplification of forms – indeed with forms and textures and materials for their own sake. Like painting, it was fascinated by its own elements. Le Corbusier, the presiding genius of the Modern Movement, had bleakly defined architecture as 'the

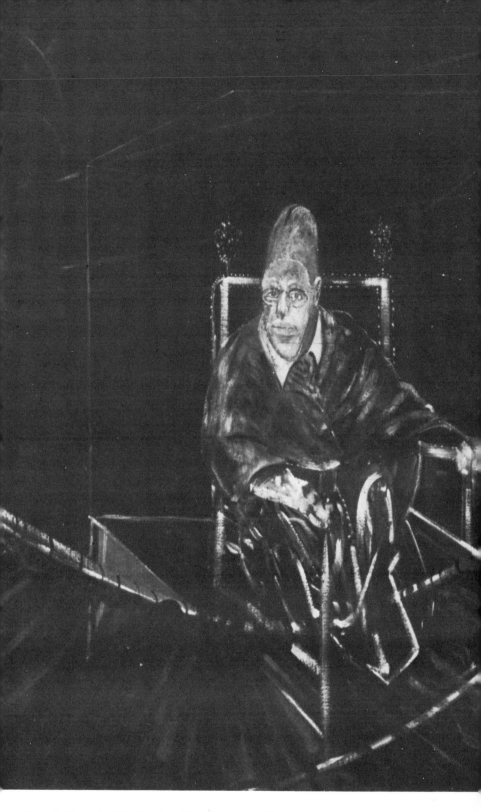

Francis Bacon's 'Study after Pope Innocent X', 1953

One of the missed opportunities of Fifties architecture: the Shell building, behind the Royal Festival Hall, photographed by Kenneth Scowen

cunning, correct and magnificent play of volumes brought together in light' – a definition that would have fitted many abstract paintings and sculptures of the time. Architecture, in the lofty Corbusian view, was a form of abstract art carried out in ferro-concrete on a massive scale. Big was beautiful. The first block on the post-war landscape that owed its conception to Corbusier was the United Nations complex on New York's East River, completed in 1950. At the time the Secretariat building went up, the New York skyline was still dominated by hints of romantic fancy. The moguls of big business in the Twenties and Thirties had built their skyscrapers to out-do one another in height and distinctiveness: their tips rose like castles in the air, some of them sculpted like pyramids, stalagmites, or minarets with knobs and needles and spires on top. Then came the United Nations – as flat-topped and straight-edged as an up-ended cigar box. The sides were of sheer glass. Thanks to its symbolism it became one of the sights of the modern world and its influence on architecture was immense. Suddenly slabs were in. So were flat roofs, however expensive and prone to leak. So was glass curtain-walling, arranged in grid patterns endlessly repeated. By the end of the decade such slabs were being sewn like teeth in the skyline of most of the world's great cities, doing more to destroy their individual character than war had done. All slabs look more or less alike, as do all tombstones. The UN itself was the product of a committee of ten architects of different nationalities, with control kept in American hands – the firm hands of Wallace K. Harrison, architect of the Rockefeller Center. Corbusier, whose original sketches are supposed to have settled the main lines of the tall Secretariat and the low fan-shaped Assembly Hall at its foot, attacked Harrison for 'stealing' his design. The committee broke up in rancour and the building has been generally dismissed as 'a great idea gone wrong'.

The rash of prestige office blocks like architectural filing cabinets that were launched by the example of the UN reflected the new role of the architect as the servant not of individual patrons but of insurance companies, banks and local authorities. Gone was the individualism of the early skyscrapers. To a cost accountant's mind, all those pinnacles and turrets were unlettable space. The architect's function was to produce as much rent as the site could support and the building regulations would allow. Flat roofs and geometrical shapes, giving large numbers of identical floors and units of accommodation were the logical and utterly boring solution. In city after city the human scale previous generations of architects had laboured to maintain was lost. Man was dwarfed and made to feel puny by the concrete poured over his head. Wren's churches pointing heavenward for so long over the City of London sank beneath the monolithic temples of Mammon. The Festival of Britain and its brief vision of a future of colourful and eccentric shapes was cleared away to make room for the headquarters of Shell. This complex, containing the population of a small town, does not appear in the architectural reference books for the very good reason that it has never been admired by the critics who write them. But its psychological repercussions on London were far greater than the design by the late Sir Howard Robertson warranted. After Barry's Houses of Parliament, it occupied the finest river frontage on the Thames – and squandered it on a mausoleum for multi-national-organization man expressing the aesthetics of the ant-hill. Had Wordsworth been crossing Westminster Bridge in the early morning in the late Fifties he would have begun his sonnet: 'Earth hath not anything to show more square'. This Portland-stone-clad palace of bureaucracy is, with bitter irony, placed between two examples of the styles it fell between. On one side the pseudo-classicism of the Greater London Council building, pillars, frieze, couchant lions and all, achieves at least a measure of pomp and ceremony. On the other the light-handed Modernism of the Royal Festival Hall is the only permanent legacy and architectural success of the Festival. Neither is a great building. But neither commits the sin of ill-proportioned dullness on what is potentially one of the most exciting sites in the world. Soon other companies hurried to emulate Shell's example of bullying the townscape to assert their prestige. In the later Fifties Castrol House, Bowater House and Thorn House profoundly altered the low street-scapes and intimacy of Marylebone, Knightsbridge and London theatreland respectively. In New York the UN building was swiftly joined by many more office towers of curtain walling. Two, happily, surpassed it: Lever House (1951–2) by Gordon Bunshaft and the Seagram Building (1955–8) by Corbusier's rival high priest of the Modern Movement, the Bauhaus's Mies van der Rohe, with his pupil Philip Johnson. Standing almost opposite each other, both were smooth and dazzling in their handling of glazed towers. The Seagram Building was the more refined, rising in narrower bands of darker copper-tinted glass. But it was the plainer Lever House that was imitated all over America.

Corbusier's next block had a hypnotic effect on architects, urging a whole generation of them towards bigger and bigger high-rise flats. It was the Unité d'Habitation at Marseilles, the biggest building he ever built, one immense rectangular block, 420 feet long and 185 feet high. It was a machine for a community of 1600 to live in – not a block of flats but a small suburb. Had he had his way, there would have been a cluster of ten or twenty such blocks, each in a twelve-acre park. The block contains over three hundred mostly duplex apartments, two floors of shops with a club, restaurant, clinic, creche and a 'hotel' of spare rooms for guests. These were arranged along 'interior streets', while on the roof he placed a playground, paddling pool and running track around the perimeter with a gymnasium and solarium. The most remarked feature of the Unité is that it is raised on stilts two storeys high to make the entire site feel like one large space flowing under and through the building. The concrete legs holding it up, which he called 'piloti', are as massive as a forest of giant trees. The greatest influence the legs had on the future of architecture was their surface texture. Corbusier decided to reveal the 'true nature' of poured concrete by leaving the pattern of the shuttering planks into which it was poured clearly visible on their flanks. The knots and grain and pattern of the planks became the surface decoration. Purists were delighted with this new example of the Brutalist dogma of truth to materials.

Brutalism also meant 'purism' which, like Puritanism, was full of 'don'ts'. A famous English example was the school at Hunstanton designed by Peter and Alison Smithson which was so pure that they proclaimed its structure by exposing the steel framework, painting its girders black and filling the spaces in between with glass. Since the metal frame was doing the work of holding up the building, it must be seen to be doing so, even if this meant exposing not only the frame but the building's occupants more than they might have wished – in the washrooms for example. To cover the frame with unnecessary walls of brick or concrete would have been 'dishonest' – a favourite term of architectural abuse at the time. Hence the gasps of admiration at the honesty of Corbusier's shuttering marks – even though the texture of wood looks very much more natural on wood that it does on unyielding rough grey concrete. Corbusier went on to leave this signature on the capitol buildings of Chandigarh in the Punjab and, twenty years later, it is almost obligatory that concrete should be left rough, not smooth, even on concert halls and art galleries and the National Theatre.

The Unité gave a cachet of approbation to high-rise residential building. Before World War II Corbusier had replanned Paris in strategically-placed tower blocks. Now it became the 'correct' solution to urban rehousing: the right place for the surplus population was up in the sky out of people's way. It was believed that this would save land and money – a proposition now gravely doubted. The blocks were built by prefabrication on the continental system. The London County Council, as it then was, became the high-rise pioneer in Britain with its Alton Estate at Roehampton (1952–6) where 100-foot high, eleven-storey blocks were mixed with maisonette blocks raised on legs like Corbusier's Unité and ordinary houses. All this was tactfully landscaped into a fine natural setting of steep wooded slopes. The tower blocks housed 120 people to the acre without destroying the impression of living in parkland on the edge of the village of Roehampton. The magnificence of the site helped to convince architects that here they glimpsed the promised land. Here was a vertical garden city, freeing the ground for pleasure as Corbusier had promised. Transferred to an urban setting, where the ground was bare and dusty and windswept and supported little except rubbish and graffiti, it did not look like a promised land after all.

But architects were highly idealistic in Britain during that period, which saw the completion of 200,000, and then 300,000 houses a year, the starting of fourteen New Towns and the building of over three thousand new schools. The most admired were the Hertfordshire schools – cheap, prefabricated, simple and modest but friendly. In the passionate spirit of the time, architects believed they were creating a new social order. Sir Hugh Casson, one of the team who worked under Philip Shepheard, on the New Town of Stevenage, recalls that spirit:

> The war and the restrictions on building had frustrated architects for ten years. Young architects in their thirties had had the chance to build nothing but huts and hangars. Half of them went into the public service for local authorities with the idealistic belief that planning and organization could solve any social problem. The philosophy of the Services still persisted. You could give people orders without being dictatorial and they could obey them without being servile. We were just emerging from the brick and tile era of the early New Towns. They were criticized by the intelligentsia as being greedy of land, 'cosy' and Welwyn Garden City all over again – although in fact that is the architecture most people in England like best. But the high-rise cluster was part of the ethos of the time. The social problems of living up there, such as neurosis and vandalism, were ignored. Corbusier must take a good deal of the blame. He was a brilliant propagandist – and a bully. His logic dictated that you must build towers to free the land under and round them – but who's going to look after it?

It would be absurd to claim that every new building was a disaster or wrecked its environment. But the successes were the exceptions. Two generally acknowledged masterpieces are the razor-edged, subtly tapered Pirelli Tower in Milan (by Nervi and Ponti, 1959) and the last testament to Frank Lloyd Wright's wayward genius, the Guggenheim Museum in New York, of the same year. By the end of the Fifties the Modern Movement had evolved shapes and individual buildings which were worthy successors to previous styles – and yet the general run of 'modern architecture' was heartily disliked by most people. But the real damage was not done until the property boom of the Sixties. By the late Fifties there were ominous portents. Jack Cotton, the developer, who had sponsored the world's largest office block in New York, announced a plan to build a tower, alongside Piccadilly Circus, of such barbarous vulgarity that even the slow-reacting British public cried 'enough!' Unfortunately that did not stop his plans, announced in 1959, to re-develop the centre of his home city of Birmingham. By the time such schemes were under way it was too late to save countless quiet, well-mannered towns from the blight of poured concrete and cheap curtain walling. High-rise flats continued to rise long after the architects themselves had lost faith in their supposed virtues.

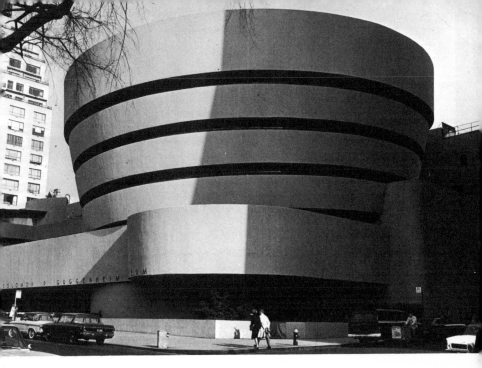

Frank Lloyd Wright's Guggenheim Museum in New York

Since taste in architecture, painting, sculpture and domestic design was so homogeneously inclined towards the simple, functional and elemental, it is curious that fashion itself remained determinedly 'out of synch' with the visual arts for the first half of the Fifties. The Paris dictators of Haute Couture were trying to re-create the pre-war world they had ruled so capriciously and the wild success of the New Look misled them into thinking that the clock could indeed be put back. For several years dress manufacturers slavishly obeyed the 'line' that was ritually unveiled each season before the moneyed audience assembled on the gilt chairs of the perfume-drenched salons of Dior and Fath, Balmain and Balenciaga. Their clothes were guarded like secret treasure – they could be sketched but not photographed until their millionaire clients had had their new season's wardrobe delivered. A change in hemlines made headlines. The 'Princess' line, the 'tulip' line, the H line, the A line, the Trapeze line succeeded one another like car models, their styling changed to make last year's wardrobe obsolete. All of them were conspicuously impractical for a working woman. There were no clothes to run for a bus in. There were pencil skirts and stand-out collars, there were tight, tight waists (achieved with 'waspie' girdles) or flared skirts that stood out like tents, buttressed by layers of under-skirts in the new crackle nylon that not only crackled but stood up on its own. Coco Chanel, who had retired more than twenty years earlier, re-opened in 1954 with the suit she had been making in the Twenties

The 'Trapeze Line' – one of the features of Yves St Laurent's 1958 season

and scored an immediate hit because of its convenience and freedom. Dior's last collection, in 1957, introduced his first concession to comfort, the waistless 'Sack'.

Socially, this was a very conservative era. Girls still dressed to look like their mothers and their mothers dressed as though the pre-war world had not changed. Still *de rigueur* on smart occasions were hats, with tied veils and floating 'follow-me' ribbons, long gloves, tight-waisted black suits, tall walking stick umbrellas and long cigarette holders. Beneath the seamless stockings of sheer nylon were shoes with stiletto heels, invented by the Paris bootmaker, Jordan, in 1951 and unveiled at Dior the next year. They ruined parquet, dance floors and airport lounges, all in the name of style. The effect was that girls in their twenties looked forty. It also emphasized the gulf between the classes – the fashionable woman or her debutante daughter with their long gloves and matching accessories could not possibly be confused with the working woman or the girl secretary, who could not buy French clothes and whose hair was tightly crimped in a Home Perm.

This fossilizing of a social hierarchy that had passed could not possibly last long. When Dior died in 1957, there was already a widespread feeling that Paris was losing its grip on the rest of the world. When his twenty-three-year-old dauphin, Yves St Laurent, presented the next Dior collection featuring the Trapeze line that owed so much to his master, headlines declared thankfully 'St Laurent has saved France!' It was an illusion. When, the following year, he raised the skirt to above the knee there was widespread revolt. 'British women will not stand for this nonsense,' declared a woman M.P., ignoring the fact that they had been standing for nonsense just as arbitrary for more than a century. But the young were not made of the same stuff as their parents had been. The teenage revolution was beginning and their eyes were on America, not Paris where rich women played follow-my-leader according to out-dated conventions. The mannequins who acted as clothes horses to the dictators also maintained a haughty aloofness until they, too, joined the ranks of the customers, like Jacques Fath's Bettina, as the property of Aly Khan, Balmain's Bronwen Pugh, as Lady Astor, *Vogue*'s Fiona Campbell-Walter, as the Baroness Thyssen, and Edda Hepburn van Heemstra, as the doe-eyed, Givenchy-dressed Audrey Hepburn. She inspired so many imitations that Sir Cecil Beaton remarked: 'The woods are full of emaciated young ladies with rat-nibbled hair and moon-pale faces.' England and the London couturiers bowed to the fabulous, aloof Barbara Goalen. She embodied the rule of the British upper classes: never be seen without pearls or with a smile. And then in 1956 they all began to look somewhat irrelevant. Brigitte Bardot, previously the demure bourgeoise who had modelled for *Elle*, was thrust into the world with her hair tumbled like an unmade bed, her make-up missing along with most of her clothes and a look that suggested she did not shave under the arms. Immediately every other young girl felt over-dressed – and most men decided that they rather liked their girls to look rumpled, like a cushion that could be booted about a bit. It was the near-death of the millinery and accessory trade. You could not look rumpled in a hat, still less a veil. You could not boot a girl who was wearing long gloves.

How were the young, growing up in Sloppy Joe sweaters and pedal-pushers or full-length trousers, to change gear into the ready-to-wear copies of Paris lines? A Welsh art student called Mary Quant asked herself this question and remembers how she answered it: 'To me adult appearance was very unattractive, alarming and terrifying, stilted, confined and ugly. It was something I knew I didn't want to grow into. I saw no reason why childhood should not last for ever. I wanted everyone to retain the grace of a child, so I created clothes that allowed people to run, to jump, to leap, to retain this precious freedom.' At first she designed purely for herself, then for a few friends from art school. Everyone demanded more and soon it was worth opening a shop. 'Bazaar' opened its doors in the King's Road as 1955 was ending, financed by her husband, Alexander Plunket Greene and his partner, Archie McNair, to the tune of only £8000. By the end of the Fifties their turnover was approaching £250,000 and they were poised to sell, through the J. C. Penney group of stores, all over the United States.

Mary Quant's early designs had all the naive flatness and simplicity of childhood – they were, typically, pinafore dresses in grey flannel with cutaway armholes and pleats. The flat-chestedness was significant as a gesture of protest. 'I didn't want to grow up to have candy-floss hair, stiletto heels, girdles and great boobs.' There were many other girls who also felt discriminated against because of their lack of great boobs. British chic was born with a flat chest and a jokey touch of childlike impudence. 'Bazaar' became the social centre for the Chelsea girl, member of the Chelsea Set – the new version of the Bright Young Things. Their habitat was the King's Road, then still a quietish street with proper grocers' shops and artists' pubs. Among them there now blossomed small, 'peasanty' restaurants with hard benches and knotty pine walls, huge pepper mills and handwritten menus mostly offering

The moon-pale face that inspired so many imitations – Audrey Hepburn in 1958

chilli con carne in some form. Next door you were likely to find a bright little boutique where the dresses hung on help-yourself rails and nobody called anybody 'madam'.

Those were the days before swinging London became a self-defeating cliché. The Chelsea Set, whose affairs dominated the gossip columns and who liked to rub shoulders with the working class playwrights at the Royal Court Theatre in Sloane Square at the end of the street, formed a new café society and some of them, like Miss Quant and her friends, a ginger group working on society like yeast. The same was true of the Greenwich Villagers of New York, which found its identity in 1955 with its local paper, *The Village Voice*. Its first number declared it would serve 'the most unique and interesting community in America, a vital creative centre, an exciting place to live'. The basis of the community's existence was the availability of cheap housing – cold-water flats ($16 a month) with a bath in the kitchen and a toilet in the hall, and lofts among the factories. It was an outpost of action painters, Beat poets, and experimental theatre troupes, which patronized off-beat fashion and off-Broadway theatre. 'The readers of the *Voice* felt they were members of a secret army of resistance in McCarthy's America,' said Dan Wolf, who founded it, with help from Norman Mailer, his columnist.

Socially the significance of the fashion revolution was that it was the first that came from below. After Quant's breakthrough, the old began to copy the young and the rich to copy their social inferiors for the first time in fashion history. Janey Ironside who, as professor of fashion at the Royal College of Art from the mid-Fifties, was responsible for training many of the next generation of designers, remembers their attitudes: 'The students didn't like Couture or what it stood for. They were nearly

The first view of Pop Art – Richard Hamilton's 'Just what is it that makes today's homes so different, so appealing?', 1956

all working-class and had never known the life they saw pictured in *Vogue*. What they wanted to convey in the clothes they invented was freedom and a short life. They would buy four or five dresses at a time and not worry about fine sewing. It was the first time fashion travelled upwards, from low to high. Mary Quant made clothes for anybody. As a result you could no longer tell who was who. You couldn't tell the secretary from the deb because the debs were copying the secretaries.'

The desire for a chic, cheap and independent life-style led to the widespread popularity of the bubble car and the Vespa motor scooter, which were often navigated in those days by young men in bowler hats as well as by girls in the Quant uniform. It was this reaction against the inflated self-importance of American car styling and its British counterparts that led to the other major design revolution of the Fifties, the Mini. Sir Alec Issigonis, design chief of the British Motor Corporation, became obsessed with compactness in 1957, when petrol rationing, following the Suez crisis, led to a spate of bubble cars: 'Basically I decided that it was going to be a box, not more than ten feet long.' Out of that decision to save road space followed the necessity to put the engine in sideways and to cut out all styling which added length to the car. The Mini which emerged after two years' work in 1959 was an example of humane functionalism, expressing its designer's faith: 'What matters most in designing a car is the pleasure it gives you to drive it. That really means the sense of control that you get from it which stimulates you to drive well. If a car doesn't inspire you it's not a good car.'

Like fashion, photography was being revolutionized by the penetration of the working class into what had been a gentlemanly enclave. Cecil Beaton, Norman Parkinson, John French, had dominated the field with soft-focus portraiture and fashion pictures with romantic backgrounds and flattering retouching. Now came the harsh unblinking stare of Richard Avedon and the tricky, unexpected juxtapositions of Anthony Armstrong-Jones (who was self-made 'working-class' with a studio in London dockland). The cherry blossom and gauzes were blown away for good. Mass media images became suddenly more exciting and this led artists to reappraise them as material for pictures.

The word 'Pop' was coined by the critic Lawrence Alloway at a meeting at the Institute of Contemporary Arts in London to describe this fascination with the signs and images of popular magazines, newspapers, film posters, advertisements, strip cartoons and so forth. Richard Hamilton, who was present, became the leading innovator of Pop Art in England, contemporary with Jasper Johns and Robert Rauschenberg in the U.S. In 1956 he rocked the audience at the Whitechapel Art Gallery's 'This Is Tomorrow' exhibition with a collage entirely composed of images from the mass media. It bore the first of his many long and teasing titles for pictures: 'Just What Is It That Makes Today's Homes So Different, So Appealing?' Peter Blake, another pioneer of Pop Art, concentrated on the dreams people put on their walls. 'The Girlie Door', for example, is exactly that – a collection of pin-up photographs arranged on a solid-handled door. Abstract art had been irrelevant to reality. Now reality was brought back into art in its raw state. Rauschenberg would stick a fork in a picture to create a sort of visual happening, while Johns turned his entire canvas into a careful reproduction of an archery target or the American flag. 'Painting relates both to art and to life,' said Rauschenberg, 'I try to act in the gap between the two.' Soup cans and Brillo boxes were only just around the corner.

CHAPTER TEN

Television Opens its Doors

In 1950 you would have taken it for a tall, rather ungainly cocktail cabinet. It stood in the corner with a pair of double doors veneered in walnut or mahogany, which were kept closed like eyelids. The little grey screen inside was not much more than a letter box giving onto the outside world, nine or ten inches across – fourteen inches was a large one – but it made people feel uncomfortable to have it staring blankly into the sitting room like an intruder pressed against a window pane. So they shut the doors with which it had been modestly provided, like the skirting on Victorian chair legs. It was called *the* television, as in 'Have you got the television?' and, in Britain in 1950, a mere 350,000 householders could say they had. Even in 1952, when most of the country could receive it, there were only two million sets grouped around the main cities.

The hours of viewing, like the hours of public drinking, were restricted in the interests of temperance: BBC transmitters opened at 3 p.m. on weekdays and 5 p.m. on Sundays. They closed down religiously from 6 p.m. to 7 p.m. to make sure the children were put to bed at a proper hour. They closed for the night at 10.30 p.m. or, on special occasions, 10.45 p.m. Even in between there were frequent 'interludes' when the screen was occupied with soothing images – a windmill turning, horse ploughs ploughing, waves breaking eternally on the rocks, a potter's wheel revolving hypnotically, calmingly or maddeningly, according to the temperament of the viewer. For quite long periods the viewing day was devoted to absolutely nothing happening either in restful silence or to restful Mozart.

The programmes themselves were also of a blandness that is hard to recapture. There was about them a strong flavour of evening classes run by a well-endowed Workers' Educational Institute: cookery lessons from the TV chef, the goatee-bearded Philip Harben; gardening hints from the TV gardener, the venerable Fred Streeter; 'Music for You' – nothing too demandingly classical – conducted in a black tie and introduced with an ingratiating few words by Eric Robinson; and, for

Gilbert Harding, 'the Dr Johnson of the Fifties' – in WHAT'S MY LINE?

nursery tea, the dancing, or rather jerking, puppets, Muffin The Mule, Andy Pandy and the Flowerpot Men. Variety agents and managements viewed television as a sinister way of using up a lifetime's material in an evening, and forbade their clients to appear on it. Live entertainment consisted mainly of stultifyingly dull continental cabaret artists, Slav acrobats, Czech jugglers, dancers in clogs, boots and lederhosen without the command of English to risk a joke even if they knew one.

The main BBC concession to fun was the party guessing game which was popular and cheap to stage (the BBC spent only £3 million a year on programmes in those days). In this vacuum the American *What's My Line?* seemed in 1951 like a Socratic dialogue among panel games and captured an audience of a million, a staggering figure. The panel, as in the United States, was supposed to balance beauty, brains and 'personality'. 'Panellist' became a profession especially suited to well-mannered ladies with a sense of fun and a repertoire of hairstyles and earrings, like Lady Barnett, Lady Boyle and Barbara Kelly. The 'Personality' that the game threw up in Britain was a former law student, former policeman, former schoolmaster, former broadcaster on farming programmes, named Gilbert Harding, who was destined to become Britain's first totally television-bred star. His natural schoolmasterly crotchetiness, bow-tie, florid moustache and fruity saloon-bar voice endeared him to the public who waited each week for him to insult some hapless contestant's mangling of the English language or coyness about being a sagger-maker's bottom-knocker or whatever obscure trade had befallen him. They were seldom disappointed. To his surprise and ultimately to his disgust, he was hailed for his brusque impatience as almost an intellectual oracle, a national institution, in constant demand to deliver opinions, write magazine columns or make public appearances as if he were a latter-day Dr Johnson. 'Who receives the kind of attention that used to be given to Shaw, Wells, Chesterton and Belloc?' asked J. B. Priestley testily, 'The answer is Mr Gilbert Harding.' Harding referred to himself as a 'telephoney'. At least he was an honest one. He was the earliest discoverer of the law of telecelebrity: that familiarity through the screen breeds not contempt, but a sense of ownership by the audience – 'every pimple and pustule belongs to them,' he once said with loathing. His resentment showed and, in the charm school of television, he resembled the performing bear of the new Elizabethan fairground, baited weekly inside the box in the corner.

With this output it was little wonder that the status of television remained socially low, something best kept behind doors, a trivial pastime for intellectual and often social inferiors. Snobs made a point of not having a set and bigger snobs added that they kept one for their servants. In the eyes of the BBC itself television was a trifling offshoot of the serious medium of radio. Its programmes were printed as a four-page afterthought at the back of the *Radio Times*. The story was told of a BBC mandarin meeting a producer after a long interval in the corridors of Broadcasting House. 'I thought you were dead,' he said. 'Ah, gone to television? Well, it's the same thing.'

Against this background it is not quite so surprising that the request to televise the Coronation from inside Westminster Abbey met with a flat 'No' from the Palace. The committee headed by the Earl Marshal, the Duke of Norfolk, and the Archbishop of Canterbury feared disruption of the ceremony. Above all, there was no precedent for such people as these electricians, these tradesmen, to be present at a solemn crowning. It took months of energetic persuasion to change the minds of the Duke and Archbishop. A demonstration was given of how well the gear could be concealed, and the smallest cameraman who could be found was sunk in the floor of the Abbey choir, shooting between the orchestra's legs. High up in the triforium above the altar was concealed, in so far as possible, the massive figure of Richard Dimbleby, the BBC's specialist in royal occasions, an honorary member of the Establishment, who knew the liturgy proper to these solemnities better than anyone. He entered his sound-proof glass box at 5.30 a.m., together with his stack of carefully prepared, cross-indexed cards which enabled him to expatiate on every move and personage of the ritual. So steeped was he in the romance of heritage and history, ceremony and panoply that his sepulchral voice appeared almost to be conducting it all himself. Thanks to his faultless performance for an audience of twenty million this was the day when television came of age in Britain. After all, it had a better view than even the most exalted participant.

By now the lines were being drawn for the battle to bring commercial television to Britain. A high-powered pressure group was formed with Lord Woolton as their chief spokesman in the Cabinet. Norman Collins, the BBC's head of television, who had resigned complaining that the BBC high-ups were hostile to the new medium, was its chief spokesman in the country. The defenders of the BBC monopoly were a curious blend of Establishment and anti-Establishment figures, rather like the later lobby against the Common Market. They comprised the Labour Party, which prophesied a 'national disaster', university vice-chancellors, who wrote to *The Times*, the Archbishop of York and many lesser clergy, Lords Hailsham and Halifax in Westminster, Lord Beaverbrook in Fleet Street and, in the House of Lords, Lord Reith, the founder of the BBC in the 1920s, uttering sibylline warnings of the doom to come. 'Somebody introduced Christianity into England,' he began ominously, 'And somebody introduced smallpox, bubonic plague and the Black Death. Somebody is now minded to introduce sponsored broadcasting.' Reith, who himself introduced the world's first television service in 1936, considered most of it irredeemably trivial and beneath consideration. The Reithian principle, patronizing, paternalistic and pig-headed, was that the BBC was a cultural priesthood, diffusing such culture through the community as it thought good for it. As soon as the public was presented with the choice between being patronized and being exploited they voted with both hands for being exploited.

The strongest card the anti-commercial lobby could play was to point to what had already happened to television in America. Horror stories were retailed of how the film of the Coronation was interrupted there by J. Fred Muggs, the *Today* programme's tame and trousered chimpanzee. The programmes had been described as a device to keep the commercials from bumping loudly together. The gold rush in exploiting television was becoming a stampede. The hundred stations of 1950 had turned into five hundred by 1957. The three million viewing homes had multiplied to 32 million by 1955 and reached 46 million (90 per cent of saturation) by 1960. Nothing in entertainment had ever caught on so fast. And, of course, the advertisers' expenditure rocketed up and up to a billion dollars a year . . . despite the interesting discovery made by the Toledo water commissioner in 1954 that the peak demands for water coincided precisely with the commercial breaks. They were a signal to the viewers to fill kettles and flush cisterns as one man. It was the advertisers, through sponsorship, who also had the last word on the content of the programmes and their requirement was clear: do nothing to disturb the prejudices of the audience.

I Love Lucy, the top-rated programme of 1952–7, filled their specifications perfectly: lulled by the sound of studio audience laughter (augmented from the can when need be) the viewer was in receptive mood for the equal unreality of the advertisements. Lovably dotty, redheaded Lucille Ball, with the timing of a trouper, actually had her baby in January, 1953, on the very day on which the screen Lucy gave birth. The coverage for this ecstatic event for her fifty million viewers was almost as big as for Eisenhower's inauguration the same month. In real life Miss Ball was very far from dotty. She and her husband, Desi Arnaz, formed a company called Desilu to produce many of the very series that competed with their own. They ended up by buying a major Hollywood studio.

In the early days of television lovability counted for a great deal more than acting ability. Most Hollywood movie stars ignored the 'boob tube' unless it was to submit graciously to a little late-night flattery on late-night chat shows conducted by Jack Paar or Steve Allen. The actual live shows, with all their dangers of technical disaster, were left to second-rate entertainers who had less to lose. A vaudeville hack like Milton Berle became 'Mr Television' (or Uncle Milty) to the millions on the strength of a many a borrowed joke. Phil Silvers lovably evaded regulations as Sergeant Bilko. Gracie Allen volubly silenced her partner, George Burns. And chubby, cuddly, schmaltzy Liberace was the most determined of all to be loved. From 1950 onwards he, his pianos, his candlesticks and his white tail suit began to spread a roseate glow over TV. In no way deterred by considerations of taste, he made his costumes

A scene from I LOVE LUCY: *Lucille Ball, dotty on screen,*
if not off, with her brilliant stooge (seated), Vivian Vance

ever more glittering until, quite logically, they resembled a bullfighter's
suit of lights. The bull he played, of course, was not the piano but the
audience. 'I talked to viewers as if they were my friends,' he said. 'I
showed them my pets. I talked about my mother and my sister and my
brother. My family became everyone's family, sort of.' When his
saccharine charms were treated with contempt by the critics he coined
the phrase that became the refuge of every corny performer afterwards:
'I cried all the way to the bank' – taking care that the tears did not fuse
the lights in his cowboy shirt.

Yet amid much mediocrity there was a brief flowering of television
drama, put on in weekly playhouses-of-the-air by such sponsors as
Philco-Goodyear, Kraft, U.S. Steel or Revlon, which made reputations
for such players as Paul Newman, Rod Steiger, Joanne Woodward and
Kim Stanley and were a showcase for new playwrights like Gore Vidal
and Paddy Chayevsky. It was lucky for these productions that film was
too expensive and videotape was not yet perfected. The drama had to be
live, economical and indoor drama, shot at close range using the human
face for its stage. Small-scale excellence often resulted, along with truth
to life. 'I tried to write dialogue as if it had been wire-tapped,' Chayevsky

wrote of his celebrated play *Marty*, the shy love story of a plump little Bronx butcher and a plain girl, which later won four Oscars as a film. 'Most of my friends are not so lucky,' he wrote, explaining television's limitations. 'The fifty-three minutes of drama that go between the commercials are considered as essentially part of the sales talk. The agency is most concerned with neither offending nor disturbing possible customers, a policy that stringently limits the scope of television drama.' Gore Vidal, who wrote nearly twenty television plays in the mid-Fifties, was untypically optimistic. 'With patience and ingenuity there is nothing the imaginative writer cannot say to the innocent millions. Most television plays are bad but, considering that television uses up hundreds of new plays a year, they can be excused their failures if their intentions are honourable . . . All things considered I suspect that the Golden Age for the dramatist is at hand.' Sadly he was wrong. American television was on the point of abandoning drama for quiz shows, which were cheaper to mount and attracted bigger audiences. By the mid-Fifties all major television had moved to California where play directors were directed to cast them with Hollywood 'personalities', irrespective of their acting ability. Telefilms which were about to pour forth in the genres of cowboy and cop operas, were a much safer investment. Even in those, care had to be exercised not to offend the sponsor. In *Man Against Crime*, for example, nobody was allowed to *cough*. It was sponsored by Camel.

The most cautionary tale of all about sponsored television was the story of Edward R. Murrow. His half-hour news show, *See It Now*, which began in 1951, gave Americans the unfamiliar sensation of being addressed with cigarette-smoke-wreathed integrity on subjects like atomic fall-out and civil rights and war, from Korea to Suez. It screened humble victims of injustice and the banned atom scientist of genius, J. Robert Oppenheimer, in his laboratory at Princeton. One of the humbler victims, U.S. Air Force Lieutenant Radulovich, who had been suspended on security grounds, was reinstated on the programme five weeks later by the Air Force secretary. The programme had discovered that the security risk involved was the fact that his father read a pro-Tito newspaper in Serbian. The following year, 1954, came the famous McCarthy exposure programmes, a compilation of all the most damning McCarthy footage available. It was capped by Murrow's comment: 'The terror is right here in this room.' But despite the fame and the twenty awards it won in 1954, *See It Now* was dropped by its sponsor, the Aluminum Company of America, the following year in favour of a big-money quiz show. It moved out of prime, or peak, viewing time into the cultural ghetto of Sunday afternoon and turned into an occasional documentary show. 'See It Now And Then' was the snide reaction of the industry. In 1958 CBS dropped its expensive and trouble-prone protégé altogether. John Crosby wrote in the *New York Herald-Tribune*: 'That CBS cannot afford it but *can* afford "Beat The Clock" is shocking.' Murrow soon left television, a frustrated and despairing man. The system had proved unable to use its most admired serious broadcaster.

Wisely, Britain rejected the American system of sponsorship in favour of regional programme companies which sold advertising time under the eye of a Nanny, the Independent Television Authority, charged with carrying out the provisions of the 1954 Television Act requiring good taste and political balance. On paper, at least, it looked very like the BBC board of governors all over again. Oddly enough, one of the first people to offer to serve under the new chairman, Sir Kenneth Clark, 'in any capacity', was Lord Reith, an offer which Clark very wisely declined as another shot in Reith's war with the BBC. It fell to the politician least interested in television, Sir Winston Churchill, who called it 'the peep-show', to cast the die in favour of competition. Norman Collins substituted the face-saving word, 'Independent', for the dirty one, 'Commercial', and British ITV was launched on 22 September 1955. In fact there were only just enough groups with the capital and the nerve to set up the four main companies and that nerve was to be severely tested in the next eighteen months, during which they lost £11 million. The service opened to an audience of only 190,000 homes and the rate at which people converted their sets was leisurely. Among the jittery investors, one of the largest, Lord Rothermere and his Associated Newspapers group, got out in 1957 just before the tide turned. When it turned the profits began to rain on the just and the unjust like oil from a gusher. By the end of the decade they were positively indecent. In two more years Associated Rediffusion, the London weekday station, now without Lord Rothermere, was making £7 million. The Canadian buccaneer, Roy Thomson, coined one of the sayings of the decade when he said that a television licence was 'a licence to print money'. Yet in 1957, when he tried to raise £400,000 to start Scottish Television, he could wring the promise of only £80,000 out of all the canny Scots he approached, from heads of clans downwards to the Scottish Co-op. In his memoirs *After I Was Sixty* he commented: 'Many excuses were offered . . . It is ironic now to think of the money those men, some of them shrewd in business, could have made.' The smallest contribution was a sporting tenner from Sir Compton Mackenzie, who had not had a winner like *Whisky Galore* lately. It was a good bet. By the time the company went public its value had multiplied by twenty-two. During the first eight years, by Thomson's own account, his share of the profits was £13 million and enabled him to buy the largest newspaper chain in Britain from Lord Kemsley. Founder shareholders made fortunes as giddily as in the days of the South Sea Bubble.

What had been done to deserve such riches? The first issue of *TV Times* claimed in an editorial: 'Viewers will no longer have to accept what is deemed best for them. The new independent television programme planners aim at giving viewers what viewers want – at the time viewers want it.' This, of course, soon meant nothing but reliable Admass programming at peak time, between 7 p.m. and 10.30 p.m. when the advertising rates were also at their peak, then about £2000 a minute. Early attempts to put on classical music or Shakespeare were massively turned off. Not surprisingly, *I Love Lucy* and *Dragnet* made their bow in the first week, together with giveaway quiz shows like *Double Your Money*, *Take Your Pick* and *Opportunity Knocks*. Imported Westerns, imported cops-and-gangsters series like *Dragnet*, imported hospital dramas like *Dr Kildare* (though there was home-grown competition from *Emergency Ward 10*), imported children's programmes (Hopalong Cassidy and Will Rogers) – only a 14 per cent quota limit prevented 90 per cent of Britain's 'independent' television entertainment being American in the early days. *Sunday Night At The London Palladium* and *The Adventures of Robin Hood* were rare British exceptions. The quiz programmes *had* to be British. With their modest prizes of kitchen furniture, a refrigerator or, at most, £100 in cash, they looked homespun beside the American $64,000 *Question* and its rivals, on which a Cadillac was a consolation prize for *losing*. However they did not suffer the same obliterating fate when the quiz-rigging scandal hit the United States. What help could a British quiz contestant be given with the question: 'Who wrote Mendelssohn's *Spring Song*?' – which won a woman five years' supply of nylon stockings.

The British proved docile viewing fodder. The advent of the first commercial had been looked forward to as suspiciously as if it had been a touch of rabies, though in the event the voice urging them that Gibbs SR toothpaste was tingling fresh did not result in a siege of chemists' shops by televiewers foaming at the mouth. But large numbers of the audience liked the commercials. They even listened politely to such startling statements as 'Omo improves even on *perfect* whiteness.' Within three or four years, ITV's share of the audience was not 50 per cent but 70, and sometimes 72 or 73 per cent. Mr. Sidney Bernstein, head of Granada Television admitted: 'Television is a very unusual business. You don't necessarily make more money in television if you provide a better product.' On another occasion he commented: 'The BBC can be just as bad as ITV.'

The effect of competition on the BBC had indeed been traumatic. To retain little more than a quarter of the viewers who could choose was shaming – even though the BBC's own audience research department, using different methods of counting, made its share nearer a third of the audience. A third was bad enough. In 1955 the Director-General, Sir Ian Jacob, had addressed a message to the staff, looking forward to the rivalry ahead: 'Standards might be lowered to maintain big audiences. This must be avoided at all costs.' Now it was driven to play the commercial game, putting on Western for Western, *Wells Fargo* for *Wyatt Earp*, and to counter cops with cops – though P.C. George Dixon of Dock Green and his comforting 'Evening all' was hardly the dramatic equivalent of *Dragnet's* tight-lipped sergeant and his 'My name's Friday, I'm a cop.'

But the BBC's most signal defeat came where it should have been strongest, the field of news and current affairs. Independent Television News knocked spots off the BBC's news presentation. BBC news readers were still unnamed (they were not even shown in vision until 1955) and looked as though they had been handed their bulletins by some respectful flunkey a moment before. ITN called their men 'newscasters' and claimed that they 'worked on' the news stories themselves, though there cannot have been time for much of this. In practice it meant that Christopher Chataway, Robin Day and Ludovic Kennedy were supposed to look interested and concerned. The BBC convention was to read the news like a company chairman with a large loss to report.

Competition undoubtedly raised the standard of television in two other departments – drama and current affairs. Drama was immensely stimulated by ITV's *Armchair Theatre*, especially under the Canadian, Sydney Newman from CBC, who brought in new writers and plays about factory life and the kitchen sink – which had soon become a term of abuse, as it had in the post-Osborne theatre. A week before ITV went on the air the BBC introduced a new *Panorama*, a world news survey fronted by the weighty Dimbleby. Soon opposition stars, Chataway and Day, had been lured to be its reporters. The silent interval from 6 p.m. to 7 p.m., known as the 'Toddler's Truce', ended in 1957 and was filled by *Tonight*, a nightly magazine blending film report and studio interview with a light touch and a taste for the bizarre and eccentric story. Its personality, still mourned and never replaced, was due to its producer, Donald Baverstock, and a small team of hard-hitting, irreverent and somewhat cocky reporters, fronted by the genial Cliff Michelmore whose task was to look mildly amused or bemused by what these abrasive fellows had discovered. It was a cunning ploy to give the audience the feeling it had a representative in the studio. The programme was a sort of televisual equivalent of the magazine *Picture Post*, which expired in the year *Tonight* began and supplied several of the programme's roving reporters, Kenneth Allsop, Trevor Philpot, Fyfe Robertson and Alan Whicker. After another year came *Monitor*, the first magazine programme to popularize the arts, and the most success-ful. Under the avuncular, some thought pompous, Huw Wheldon it introduced the art-film made for television, giving their first chances to directors John Boorman, John Schlesinger and Ken Russell, whose film miniatures of Elgar, Debussy and Delius avoided the excesses that he later inflicted on the wide screen. In 1959 came *Face To Face*, the interview-in-depth first practised by the silky, tenacious John Freeman who politely refused to accept evasions, while the camera looked un-blinkingly over his shoulder at the face of the subject. The people who submitted to the ordeal memorably included Bertrand Russell, Carl Gustav Jung, Dame Edith Sitwell, Augustus John, Evelyn Waugh and Lord Reith himself – 'I left the BBC and regretted it profoundly,' said that tormented man, 'I have not been happy and I have not been suc-cessful.' But the best-remembered interview was in 1960 with Gilbert Harding. Two creatures of the medium came face to face and there was a touch of cannibalism about the outcome. Harding was brought to tears as much by his own honesty as by Freeman's persistence: 'The thing that is really lacking is a sense of purpose, you know. There's not much point in asking people whether they're coal-heavers from Wigan or chimney sweepers from Stoke-on-Trent . . . My bad manners and bad temper are quite indefensible . . . I'm almost unfit to live with. I'm pro-foundly lonely . . . I should be very glad to be dead.' It was a confession that many people thought should not have been extracted (though Harding was not among them) but it made some of the most riveting television of the time. When, two months later, Harding dropped dead almost on the steps of Broadcasting House, he was mourned as a national figure, which, despite his protests, he was. He had been partly responsible for erasing the image of the BBC as 'Auntie' to the nation.

This change was about to be confirmed by the newly arriving

Director-General, Hugh Carleton Greene, brother of the novelist Graham Greene, and the first BBC-bred chief to get the job in preference to the customary retired general or diplomat. His first act was to declare that the BBC must recover half of the audience, which in due course it did. But there was no disputing that the working-class audience, which provided ITV's massive surplus in the ratings, had clearly identified the commercial channel as 'Us' and the BBC as 'Them'. This presented the BBC with a financial and political dilemma in which either way it lost the argument. If the large majority of the audience chose the commercial channel, why should they pay a licence fee to finance BBC television programmes which they did not want? Alternatively, if the BBC won back some of the big audiences by concentrating on light entertainment in peak hours (as it had begun to do), then it was charging a licence fee for the sort of programmes that commercial television provided free. There was no answer to this that would ward off hostile critics in Parliament. Some people claimed (unjustifiably on the whole) that more choice of television had ended up by being a choice of more of the same thing.

It was in the Fifties that television turned whole populations into voyeurs. Watching it became the chief leisure activity of civilized man in most parts of the world and has been ever since. By 1959, 60 per cent of British adults were tuned in every evening for periods estimated to average five hours a day in winter, three and a half hours in summer. Americans were estimated to devote an average of five to six hours daily to it. The sheer quantity of viewing led to predictions that it would have transcendent effects on society, transforming the audience either into paragons of informed opinion or alternatively into manipulated zombies who would be easy meat for brainwashing by any message that came out of the tube from Big Brother. Such studies as there have been of television's impact show that both the hopes and the fears were much exaggerated. The only effects of television that are not highly disputable and inconclusive are those which it had on its rival media. The immediate victim was radio – 'steam radio', as it was then christened, patronizingly or affectionately. Television licences in Britain overtook licences for radio only for the first time in 1957. By a stroke of irony, it was just when BBC sound radio was enjoying a late flowering as an original medium that its audience melted away, seduced by the box. Such varied radio performers as the Queen, Tony Hancock and Wilfred Pickles were regularly commanding twenty million listeners. Long-running serials – a form soon to be exploited more effectively and just as vapidly on TV – were at their peak. *Mrs Dale's Diary*, broadcast twice daily, offering the predictable reassurance of middle-class suburbia, contrasted with the countryfolk of *The Archers*, whose crops were saved from late blight, and whose calves were born attended by twelve million listeners who had just got home from work, most of them without brushing through any long grass or cow parsley. When Grace Archer died in a blazing barn on the night that ITV began transmission, the newspapers had no doubts about which event was of widest public interest. The headlines plumped for Grace and there were dark mutterings of BBC sabotage in commercial television boardrooms.

But radio in the Fifties was far more than an anodyne for addicts or aural wallpaper. Radio drama was often found running level with the avant-garde of the theatre. The BBC commissioned and broadcast Samuel Beckett's first radio play in 1957. *All That Fall* was the first work to break his silence since *Waiting For Godot* had baffled or intrigued audiences in Paris in 1953 and in London in 1955, where the uproar and controversy it caused also brought to notice its director, Peter Hall, only just down from Cambridge. There was a further Beckett radio play, *Embers*, and it was natural for a new, unorthodox playwright, Harold Pinter, to submit his work to radio before he won his entrée to the stage. It was radio that turned the barrister-novelist John Mortimer into a playwright by encouraging and putting out his masterly one-acter, *The Dock Brief*, whose stage and film versions never bettered the radio performance. And what is probably the most famous radio play, *Under Milk Wood*, was dragged out of Dylan Thomas over ten years of nagging by the BBC producer, Douglas Cleverdon. Thomas completed it just before he sailed to New York and his death in the Chelsea Hotel in 1953. His last, typical act in London was to lose the manuscript on a pub crawl in Soho, whence Cleverdon recovered it after he had left. The name of the little port situated under Milk Wood and inspired by Thomas's own home, Laugharne, was changed by the BBC from Llareggub (which Thomas chose because of its meaning spelt backwards) to Llaregyb but in all other respects it rose to the occasion when it gave it the first of countless broadcasts in 1954. The sonorous opening lines, entrusted to Richard Burton as narrator, have echoed ever since with the resonance of an enduring work of art:

> It is spring, moonless night in the small town, starless and bible-black, the cobblestreets silent and the hunched, courters'-and-rabbits' wood limping invisible down to the sloeblack, slow, black, crowblack, fishingboat-bobbing sea . . .

It was on radio that situation comedy, later to be the staple fodder of

Dylan Thomas: UNDER MILK WOOD *took ten years to be delivered*

television, had been invented. The first glimmers came from a whimsical pair of writers, Denis Norden and Frank Muir, who introduced a sketch which got extended from week to week in their early Fifties show *Take It From Here*: the saga of a coarse, ignorant, moronic working-class family called the Glums. The father, played by Jimmy Edwards, was all booze and bluster. The imbecile son and his wistful fiancée, Ron and Eth (Dick Bentley and June Whitfield) were the epitome of a slow, wet, unpassionate courtship, always to be found on the sofa in the front room exchanging depressing, chaste and unconvincing visions of a married bliss to come. True situation comedy only began, however, where it was no longer thought necessary to interrupt the half-hour with musical interludes or other diversions from the main theme. This was the achievement of Ray Galton and Alan Simpson who wrote *Hancock's Half-Hour* for radio from 1954 and transferred it to television without noticeable change two years later. This was gagless comedy of character, namely the lugubrious, indignant, bored, hopeful, out-of-work but aspiring character of Anthony Aloysius St John Hancock, of Railway Cuttings, East Cheam. He did not have to tell jokes – indeed he had none to tell. He simply had to be his pretentious, put-upon, puffed-up self, a man of cultural pretensions who would snort: 'Ingmar Bergman? Half of them round here have never heard of her.' He savoured words which he did not understand, examining his 'bicuspids' or referring to his rascally friend played by Sid James as a 'poltroon'. After a panegyric delivered into the shaving mirror in favour of traditional methods ('You can't beat the cold steel and badger') he would apply an after-shave lotion and jump: 'Fancy paying good money for stuff that hurts you!' He was at his best in soliloquy, ruminating alone or trying to pass the tedious hours of Sunday afternoon by pretending to read a good book. 'The character I play isn't a character I put on and off like a coat,' he said in one of his rare moments of self-analysis on *Face To Face*, 'It is a part of me and a part of everyone else I see. You take the weaknesses of your own character and exploit them. You show yourself up.' So loved was he that there was a sense of national dismay when he abandoned this character, and its enjoyable weaknesses, committing professional, and later actual, suicide.

The rogue elephant of radio comedy was *The Goon Show* which was given a very doubtful go-ahead in 1951 under the title of *Crazy People*. The Goons insisted they were not crazy people, they were Goons, and the show soon attained the status of a sort of national park for beloved British evolutionary freaks. It is always referred to as a breakthrough in English humour but it owed much to the surrealist tradition of Edward Lear, inherited most aptly in our time by J. B. Morton ('Beachcomber') who was still at the height of his powers. Spike Milligan, the Goon's principal begetter and scriptwriter, acknowledged such influences (and there was more than a touch of the Marx Brothers as well) but the breakthrough was the use of the freedom of radio to leap through time and space in pursuit of a purely verbal joke or non-sequitur. The plots, so-called, existed to provoke anarchy, and centred on such exploits as the ascent of Everest from the inside, or the discovery of the last London tram, still waiting for its official send-off ceremony after two years in the Kingsway tunnel. A typical script begins with the announcement, 'Tales Of Men's Shirts – A Story of Down Under', followed by the instruc-

Tony Hancock: 'The character I play isn't a character I put on and off like a coat. It is a part of me and a part of everyone else I see'

The Goons – Peter Sellers, Harry Secombe and Spike Milligan
The wonder is that they were ever put on by the BBC

tions: SOUND EFFECTS – Series of shirt-tail explosions and shouts of rage. Inventive sound effects were the speciality of the show. There is a celebrated story of Milligan ordering an egg custard from the BBC canteen, pouring it into his sock, hitting the wall with the sock and then shaking his head sadly. The sound effect of someone being hit over the head with a sockful of wet custard had to be made by other methods. Like Milligan, the remainder of the cast, Peter Sellers, Harry Secombe and, originally, Michael Bentine, were all ex-Service ex-entertainers well used to the seedier side of variety. They invented Goon humour to amuse themselves in the pub which they frequented between engagements. The mystery is why it caught on so fanatically. Partly it was an appeal to a deep-seated English love of anarchy that slumbers beneath the placid surface. Partly it appealed to a National Service conscript generation because it mocked the officer type. The characters included bullying and suave lunatics such as Major Bloodnok or Hercules Grytpype-Thynne, who were scored off by downtrodden idiots like Bluebottle and Eccles, who corresponded roughly to a knowing, squeaky-voiced Boy Scout and a human Goofy. Generations of schoolboys and students seized gleefully on these voices as a verbal equivalent of nose-thumbing of a deliberately infantile kind aimed at one's superiors. Imitations, repetitive and unwearying, could be heard in every technical workshop or Oxbridge common room until it seemed that some people spoke no other language than Goonish. Part of the wonder of *The Goon Show* was that it was put out by the BBC, albeit very unwillingly. The producer, Peter Eton, counted thirty attempts by BBC mandarins to stop the show, redoubled after every outrage such as the imitation of the Queen inaugurating an attack on the pigeons in Trafalgar Square. Spike Milligan finally gave up his struggle to 'shake the BBC out of its apathy' at the end of 1959. No television equivalent was ever successful, though the influence of *The Goon Show* lives on and is probably partly responsible for inspiring *Monty Python's Flying Circus*. Sadly, the golden age of radio comedy finished then.

After radio, television's most spectacular victim was the film industry. In the end its influence may well prove health-giving. By eating up the rubbish that used to clutter cinema screens, television may do the film industry a favour. But in the Fifties Hollywood lost its nerve. Its bloated post-war audiences melted away like Spring snow. The figures are particularly clear in telling the story in Britain, whose movie-hungry populace in 1950 still brought 1400 million admissions. Commercial television began in late 1955. During 1956–60 cinema attendances were halved, dropping to only 500 million admissions in 1960. The lesson was the same on both sides of the Atlantic: people would no longer go out to see second- or third-rate films when they could see exactly the same sort of thing for nothing at home.

Hollywood's instinctive reaction was to counter-attack the small screen with a bigger and bigger one. 'Wider still and wider let thy bounds be set,' might have been the studios' refrain in the early Fifties as Cinerama (1952), Three-D Movies (1952), Cinemascope (1953), Vistavision (1954) and Todd-AO (1956) were successively unveiled with much fairground barking and ballyhoo. The wonders of wide-screen, new colour processes and stereophonic sound were real enough but the processes had serious limitations, especially in cost. Three-D required special Polaroid glasses, which the public soon tired of putting on, even if they promised you the sensation of 'a lion in your lap'. A nearly three-dimensional effect was produced without glasses by Cinerama's three projectors trained on a huge curved screen. Fine for a travelogue like *This Is Cinerama*. The problem, as with Paramount's VistaVision (*White Christmas*), was what more to fill it with. Suitable subject matter for covering those acres meaningfully was hard to find. How was Mike Todd to follow *Around The World In Eighty Days*, which required guest appearances by every non-contract star he could collect, to be waved at by David Niven as he hurried past? *How To Marry A Millionaire* required two other lovelies, Lauren Bacall and Betty Grable, to fill the vacant spaces on either side of Marilyn Monroe. The biggest novelty business was done by Cinemascope's first picture, *The Robe*, which earned a phenomenal $20 million worldwide. But none of these wonders stemmed the desertion of the movies in general. The four hundred pictures a year that Hollywood was turning out on the eve of the Fifties had shrunk to three hundred by 1954 and ruin looked an uncomfortable possibility. In 1955 Hollywood capitulated and joined the enemy it could not beat. Jack Warner, who had decreed that no TV set should ever be seen in any of his pictures, now turned Warner Brothers' energies to producing telefilms like *Cheyenne*. Soon the studios were humming again as MGM, Fox and the rest joined the rush with *Maverick*, *Gunsmoke*, *Wyatt Earp*, *Wells Fargo*, *Wagon Train* . . . More than thirty westerns, out of a hundred television series, were in production by 1958. It was an economical way of using up left-over footage from the days of the real Westerns – cattle stampedes and Indian charges that bit the dust of the cutting room floor. An inside joke about cheap-budget telefilms at the time was: 'If you can see more than two characters at once, it's stock footage.' Further profitability was promised when the British came into the market, followed by other European networks. The huge non-English-speaking audience was waiting only for a dubbed sound-track and that was no great task when the dialogue came from terse cowboys and cops. Soon almost the entire western world enjoyed a Hollywood diet of mini-Westerns on the screen in the sitting room or over the public bar. It was a gain in convenience over the Gary Cooper article they had previously gone out to the cinema to enjoy but it was scarcely a gain in the quality of the experience. But then the coming of television was generally associated with a lowering in the quality of life. The invention of the 'TV Dinner' with its plastic tray, in 1954, only confirmed that for many people domestic life was now being lived glued to a seat watching inferior entertainment in a kind of darkened airliner.

What *would* they go out to see? Hollywood in the Fifties was not the place to ask for brave or innovative solutions. The UnAmerican Activities Committee hearings, the Black Lists, the talents that had moved out, the mental climate of McCarthyism produced a pussyfooting timidity and conformism that discouraged thought or enterprise. Social criticism was dangerous. Any hint that America was not already the best of all possible worlds had to be excised. And as the founding moguls died out, their places were taken by bankers and accountants who aimed for profits, not controversy or creativity. So Hollywood turned to its most reliable genre, the musical, to keep it out of trouble: *Annie Get Your Gun, Singin' In The Rain, South Pacific, The King And I, Seven Brides For Seven Brothers, Gigi* . . . Some, like *Oklahoma!*, were smudged carbons of brilliant stage events; some, like Cole Porter's *High Society*, were brilliant originals. But all of them were an escape from reality.

Another irreproachable genre was the Biblical epic, whose sincerity was attested by the amount of money spent on it. While Fox Cinemascoped *The Robe*, Cecil B. De Mille parted the Red Sea in Panavision for Paramount's *The Ten Commandments*. Biggest and most fraught of the epics was *Ben-Hur*, MGM's re-make of a silent movie whose script now took the successive talents of S. N. Behrman, Maxwell Anderson, Gore Vidal and Christopher Fry to fail to make interesting. Sheer size and spectacle left it staggering under eleven Oscars. Funniest of the epics was the earliest, *Quo Vadis*, of which Peter Ustinov remarked very charitably that the nonsense he was made to speak as Nero was very much like the nonsense Nero probably did speak. Nero did not, however, have the advantage of being directed by Mervyn Le Roy, who waved his cigar at the spectacle of burning Rome and said to Ustinov, to help his performance, 'Don't forget, you're responsible for all this.'

When Hollywood was not persecuting early Christians – or early Jews – on a gargantuan scale, it still found time for really big Westerns that made those on the box look like the puny things they were – *High Noon, Shane* and *The Big Country*. The moviegoing faithful would also turn out for certain big stars. They did for Brando, Dean and Monroe. They lined up to see Bogart, already suffering from cancer, when he movingly played the lonely, paranoid and disastrous Captain Queeg of *The Caine Mutiny*. They lined up for Judy Garland's comeback in the tear-streaked greasepaint of *A Star Is Born*. They could be intrigued by the over-ripe childish sensuality of Carroll Baker sucking her thumb in Tennessee Williams' *Baby Doll*, a sight that launched a frothing tide of shortie nighties. But despite such exceptions, Hollywood's Fifties, certainly when compared with the Forties, were non-vintage years.

The only vintage ingredient in the British film industry at the time was Alec Guinness, who revealed himself as a versatile character actor of genius. He followed up his nine polished cameos in *Kind Hearts And Coronets* with a set of early Fifties performances of shy, whimsical anti-heroes, notably the tramp-painter in Joyce Cary's *The Horse's Mouth*, of which he also wrote the screenplay. He then surprised everyone by transforming his usual mixture of benevolence and guile into the fanatical and constipated prisoner-of-war colonel in *The Bridge On The River Kwai*, a film whose wartime heroics attracted much nostalgia in 1957 after the debacle of Suez. War was still Britain's favourite theme but fond, backward-looking films about anything old and English and eccentric were the self-indulgent recipe for success – whether it was an old jalopy, as in *Genevieve*, an old lady as in *The Lady-Killers* or Margaret Rutherford in any form. While Lindsay Anderson and Karel Reisz were flexing their talents in short, shoe-string documentaries, the only British director to break new ground was Jack Clayton, whose *Room At The Top* pushed back the narrow boundaries of British 'good taste' and blew away the cosiness of British comedy by exhibiting some far from lovable characters on the make, notably Laurence Harvey's Joe Lampton.

But it was in Europe and, of all places, Japan that the *avant-garde* found new directions for the cinema: Fellini and *La Strada*, Resnais and *Hiroshima, Mon Amour*, Kurosawa with *Rashomon* and *The Seven Samurai* and Truffaut who launched the French 'New Wave' with *Les Quatre Cent Coups* as the decade ended. These did more to change the art of film than Hollywood's entire output. Above all this was the decade on which Ingmar Bergman stamped his signature with *The Seventh Seal*, *Wild Strawberries* and *Smiles Of A Summer Night*. His anguished earnestness and bleak Nordic mood poetry made him the patron saint of the art houses and their audiences. A more approachable poet of the human comedy emerged in Jacques Tati, the Russian-French writer-director-performer. His Monsieur Hulot was introduced in 1952, first observing the French bourgeoisie taking their seaside pleasures solemnly in *M. Hulot's Holiday*, a little masterpiece of comic observation, then in *Mon Oncle*, where he is baffled by progress as exemplified in a hygienically modern, gadget-ridden house. No film-maker has found as much comedy in the discomfiture of man by the machines he misguidedly invents to improve life.

Television profoundly affected radio and the cinema but the effect it would have on reading was completely miscalculated. It was thought too obvious to need proof that people would give up the printed word for the picture. When proof was sought of this proposition, it could not be found. Britain, with the most voracious newspaper-readers in the world, began the Fifties buying just under six hundred newspapers per thousand of population and ended it buying very slightly more. Some of the mammoth post-war circulations were shrinking – the *News Of The World*, for example, came down from eight million to 6·7 million. Against this the sale of 'quality' Sunday papers showed quiet but steady gains, as did the serious weeklies and monthlies. The most serious sales loss was in evening newspapers, whose readers could not both read and watch. The most directly hit were general interest picture magazines. Three weeklies which started the decade with circulations of over a million collapsed and died in 1957 – *Picture Post*, *Illustrated* and *Everybody's*. In the United States, *Colliers* folded in 1956, the harbinger of things to come. *The Saturday Evening Post*, *Look* and even *Life* were to follow it in due course, strongly suggesting that the big news-picture magazine is a dinosaur headed for extinction. The reason for the casualties was not so much the competition for readers' time as the competition for advertising. By 1959 British commercial television advertising revenue exceeded that of all the Fleet Street papers put together. Few papers had yet folded but several were moribund economically, including three Sundays and the *News Chronicle*. A glance at book publishing shows that it was not true that television diminished people's appetite for reading. Book turnover doubled in the Fifties.

Television, the one-eyed monster, has been blamed for just about every social evil and for encouraging every kind of physical deformity except flat feet. Most frequently it has been blamed for delinquency and violence among the young. Surely, the argument ran, the electronic babysitter to which the child is exposed for between three and five hours a day must be as powerful an influence on the growing mind as school or even home? Since so much of what is shown involves crime, shooting and sudden death and since juvenile crimes of violence have risen sharply all over the world, it is obvious that screen violence and real violence are cause and effect. People were already wondering this in the Fifties. Like all simplistic arguments it has an obvious appeal though there is nothing to prove it. Crime, which existed long before television, must be the result of complex factors. It is unlikely that a completely new one, television violence, has suddenly taken over as its prime cause. It is equally possible to argue that television's fictions of cops and robbers, cowboys and Indians, goodies and baddies have been the staple diet of adolescent fiction, books, comics and cartoon films for years and, instead of stimulating actual violence, provide an outlet for violent impulses in fantasy form.

The whole discussion is bedevilled by the *non sequitur* that if millions are invested in commercials to affect people's buying behaviour, then all forms of television affect all forms of behaviour. No evidence has been found to support this, any more than the early beliefs that television was ruining people's eyesight, posture and giving children 'TV neck'.

The belief that TV was killing conversation is not any longer taken seriously. The wonder is that it ever was. 'It didn't destroy conversation for us,' said an East End mother memorably when interviewed by the BBC, 'It *was* the conversation. I don't know what we talked about before'. To her and millions like her the screen was a flickering fireside around which the family could share the one occupation they had in common.

Perhaps the biggest disappointment about television was its puny role in politics. In the Fifties, with the prospect of direct personal impact on the electorate of statesmen and parties seeking office, there were visions of television, the modern equivalent of the public mass meeting, bringing us nearer to true democracy than at any time since the Athenians listened to Pericles in their forum. In Britain a Party Political Broadcast was a signal for 80 per cent of the electorate to switch over – until it was put on both channels so there could be no escape. The first general election covered on both channels, in 1959, was followed up afterwards by two sociologists. Joseph Trenanan and Denis McQuail. They reported that the political broadcasts viewed by their sample had made no difference whatever to the way they voted. The viewers were either too apathetic or too prejudiced to be influenced.

To begin with, politicians were reluctant to appear on television. The cameras were excluded from the hall when Eisenhower announced he would run for president in 1952. Ike was never at ease on camera and Churchill hardly bothered to appear. Gradually the pendulum swung the opposite way. At the time of Suez, Eden tried to commandeer the BBC airwaves in order to justify his actions to the public on grounds of national emergency. It was only the spirited resistance of the acting Director-General which insisted that the Opposition case was also put. Six months later Colonel Nasser used an interview by Robin Day to appeal directly to the British people for the restoration of friendly relations. In the same year Khrushchev amazed CBS by accepting its invitation to appear on the programme *Face The Nation* – he used it to appeal to the American people to accept 'peaceful competition'. In 1959 he and Richard Nixon wagged their fingers at each other with well-simulated indignation in the so-called 'kitchen debate' for the benefit of the colour cameras at the American exhibit in Moscow. Later that year, Khrushchev seized his chance on his US visit to turn it into a television spectacular and road show combined. Joking, clowning, arguing, boasting and raging by turns, followed everywhere by four hundred reporters and cameramen, he put on a virtuoso display of how to use the medium. By then even the tardy British politicians were becoming extremely touchy about whether they were getting their fair share of television time. Question Time in the House of Commons began to be outshone by the questioning of ministers on television. The parties set up studios to groom their stars to act naturally and conceal the fact that their impromptu address was in fact being read off the autocue. Mr Macmillan was the first to use this device from 10 Downing Street, in 1957.

It was widely held that television would infallibly expose the insincere politician. Grace Wyndham-Goldie, the BBC's head of talks, wrote in *Facing The Nation*: 'Resolute words made little impression if the man who used them appeared irresolute. Generous sentiments could be denied visually by a cold eye.' It was said that no politician could gain supreme power in future if he or she did not go over well on the box – there would be no more untelegenic prime ministers like Chamberlain, or presidents, like Coolidge. If true, will this make much difference? Most ambitious politicians are natural actors, as well able to simulate sincerity on the screen as on the platform. Nixon supposedly did badly in his gladiatorial debates with Kennedy in 1960 because of his five o'clock shadow and sweaty look but that should not erase the memory of his 'Checkers' speech on television before the 1952 election – one of the oustanding examples of throwing dust in the eyes of the public. Instead of directly answering the charges about the 'secret fund' of $18,000 contributed by Californian millionaires for his use as a Senator, he went into his act as a poor but honest self-made politician whose wife did not have a mink coat but a 'respectable Republican cloth coat' and who refused to look a gift-dog in the mouth – the black and white cocker spaniel which his six-year-old daughter had named Checkers. 'And you know, the kids love that dog,' he said, now on the home stretch, 'and I did just want to say this right now, that regardless of what they say about it, we're going to keep it.' No matter that the problem was not the dog, sent by an admirer, but the money to which who knows what strings were attached. This was a highly effective use of television, sweat or no sweat. Republican headquarters immediately received 300,000 messages of support for Nixon and a reluctant Eisenhower had no choice but to keep him on as his running mate. On Nixon's next appearance before the cameras, at the airport where he met Eisenhower, he managed to cry. So much for the lie-detecting camera. 'Sincerity is the thing that comes through on television.' Who said that? Why, it was Richard M. Nixon.

Gore Vidal believes that the Checkers speech demonstrated that in future American elections the influence of television would be crucial – 'It proved that the country could be entirely swayed by a television appearance. In 1960 it was television alone that made John Kennedy into a viable candidate. He was thought to be too young, a Roman Catholic and a playboy, and he looked like a silly kid against this wiser, older statesman Nixon with all his experience as vice-president. But as soon as they had watched the debate, people said 'That Kennedy doesn't look so young to me' – and that was the end of Nixon. TV had created its first president.'

'When the future of the medium comes to be written,' said Wilson Dizard, 'it may be said that Big Brother met his match in Lucille Ball – and lost.' Far too much was claimed for it, especially in the Fifties when the world was in thrall to its novelty. It turned human life into a spectator sport to a greater degree than had ever been dreamed possible. Dramatic public events, wars, assassinations, Olympic Games and title fights, world cups and space probes were communicated instantly from end to end of McLuhan's electronic village. But as a spur to action it was a disappointment to Utopians and doom-prophets alike. 'I believe television is just a mirror,' says Peter Black, leading television critic of the period and author of *The Mirror In The Corner*, 'It was seen in its early days as a window on the world but its habit-forming tendency makes it a soporific rather than a stimulant. Rather than change people's minds, it reinforces their prejudices. It reflects life. It doesn't change it.'

Why was the impact of television so overestimated? Because it is easy to assume the audience is paying attention when it is not. Children and old people do tend to pay concentrated attention and their lives have been, on the whole, enriched by it. But for much of the audience the television in the background is a dripping tap, often blocked out mentally while the 'viewers' are knitting, gossiping, playing cards or have left the room. The programme planners soon realized that it took more effort to turn the set off than to let it go on dripping. 'The screen has a strongly hypnotic effect and viewers find themselves just sitting on, programme after programme,' pointed out a research booklet for programme planners. By sandwiching a weak programme between two stronger ones they could easily increase its viewing figure. J. B. Priestley, in a late-Fifties essay on Televiewing, translated this discovery into terms of personal behaviour. 'After half an hour of *The Future Of Our Fisheries* or *Africa At The Crossroads*, the programme personalities stare accusingly at me and ask what I propose to do about it. As a viewer, I don't propose to do anything about it. I listen dreamily to the end music, light another pipe and float into the next programme.' People are still doing exactly that. Perhaps they always will.

CHAPTER ELEVEN

Retrospect and Prospect

If there is a common theme to the developments charted in the preceding chapters, it is the psychological unification of the planet and of its dominant species, man. It was slow; it was reluctant; but it was there. Very dimly men began to see themselves as one species instead of as a competitive hierarchy of races. The environment began to look all too finite, something that demanded to be conserved rather than exploited to the utmost. Psychologically, the beginnings of space travel in 1957 had the effect of dramatizing the oneness of the earth which a living creature could now leave. Meanwhile on its surface the implications of atomic weapons began to proclaim the ineluctable truth: that a Cold War was the only kind of global war the globe could ever again support. At the same time mass affluence, beyond the dreams of all previous generations, starkly highlighted the contrast between the Haves and the Have-Nots in a new way: there were so many more Haves that the others could not much longer be expected to put up with being left out. The Third World of Asia and Africa, which had least, was hastily being given freedom from colonial status before it simply rose and took it. Among the affluent countries the new Meritocracies, vastly outnumbering the old Establishment oligarchies, were demanding their equal share of society's privileges. The next sub-group to insist on recognition was the hitherto dumb but now deafening teenage generation. Then the first stirrings of discontent could be detected among a much larger and more powerful sub-group – women – preparing to throw off the yoke of exploitation by men.

The most thoroughly exploited and cynically ignored underdogs of all – the Negroes – were the sub-group which made the least headway, because they met with the most obstinate opposition. The Fifties was the decade of black awakening but it was an awakening brought about by defeat, by the beating against closed doors. Discrimination, which had been taken for granted in the hundred years since the end of slavery, was not going to yield for a long time, and in these early years the aggression was all on the side of the whites. This itself was a sign of an insecurity and funk unknown in earlier times. Early in the Fifties there were quixotic attempts to prove by example from the top that black and white could live together in harmony and love. Peggy Cripps, daughter of Sir Stafford, married a Ghanaian lawyer, Joe Appiah, and Seretse Khama, an hereditary chief of Bechuanaland, took his wife Ruth back from England along with his Oxford education. But both couples met with extreme initial distrust and scepticism among their own people.

South Africa declared apartheid to be the official policy of the Union in 1952. In the southern United States undeclared apartheid was every bit as much the natural and unquestioned way of life. It was not confined to the Deep South. Cicero, Illinois, provided a dramatic object lesson in 1951 when a black war veteran and university graduate, Harvey Clark Jnr, rented an apartment in a white area costing $60 a month and was physically prevented from moving into it by the local police chief. When he finally moved in under the protection of a court injunction to prevent the city from 'shooting, beating or otherwise harassing' him, a mob of four thousand gathered outside. They smashed his windows, hurled bricks and lighted torches through them, ripped out fittings and threw his furniture from the windows, watched by police who did nothing to stop them. After three days of rioting Governor Adlai Stevenson sent in the state militia to clear the mob with fixed bayonets. The apartment owner was subsequently indicted for causing depreciation in the selling price of the property. And this was not the Deep South but the enlightened North. Race riots and organized bombing and arson directed against black families were as common in Chicago as in Dallas. The South virulently supported the Ku Klux Klan and created White Citizen's Councils. Even children could be lynched. The best known victim of 'Southern Justice' was a fourteen-year-old boy called Emmett Till in 1955. Throughout the u.s., blacks earned about half the average wage of whites and were largely debarred from skilled or professional jobs. They lived in segregated city ghetto slums, had a lower expectation of life, a far higher infant mortality rate and, more often than not, no indoor sanitation. In the South they were effectively without the vote as well. Only about a quarter of those eligible actually registered to vote, because of intimidation.

It was in this implacably hostile atmosphere, on 1 December 1955, that a seamstress of forty, Mrs Rosa Parks, refused to give up her seat near the front of the bus home from work to a white passenger, when

Mrs Rosa Parks sat nearer the front of the bus than a white passenger

ordered to do so by the driver in Montgomery, Alabama. This simple, tiny act of defiance by a tired woman sparked off the first act of mass defiance by the black community. The next day, and for a year afterwards, none of Montgomery's fifty thousand blacks would use the city buses. They walked to work, inspired by a twenty-six-year-old minister and apostle of non-violent non-co-operation, Martin Luther King; after a year they won their point. King, like Gandhi, had become a symbol to an entire nation, both execrated and admired. He was invited to India by Nehru and his phone was tapped by the FBI, a double accolade. In the year of the bus boycott at Montgomery, the Supreme Court under Chief Justice Warren had ruled that segregated school districts in seventeen southern states should be desegregated 'with all deliberate speed' as separate education was 'inherently unequal'. In the South this provoked the passing of state laws blocking integration. In September 1957, Governor Orval Faubus of Arkansas called out the National Guard to protect the Central High School at Little Rock from nine black children who were descending on it for the purpose of obtaining education.

Racists flocked to the city and white mobs attacked black children who appeared anywhere near the school, as well as reporters and bystanders. President Eisenhower, who was on a golfing holiday, continued with his game. After conspicuous delay he finally federalized the National Guard and sent in airborne troops to enforce the court order. Nevertheless, at the end of the decade, six years after the Supreme Court's original ruling on the subject, only 765 Southern school districts had been desegregated, leaving nearly six thousand which were not. Only 0.1 per cent of black pupils went to school with whites – Governor Faubus closed Little Rock High School rather than sully it with mixed classes. Throughout the South, lunch counters, theatres, toilets and drinking fountains were still segregated, and the first sit-in, at a Woolworth lunch counter in North Carolina, was to take place in February 1960. The sign in an Alabama bus station – 'Remember: More Americans Have More' – had an ironic ring. The blacks were still America's 'invisible people'.

In Britain their numbers were comparatively tiny but they were very visible indeed. West Indian immigration began in the early Fifties and reached an annual inflow of 25,000 in 1956. By 1960 there were just about half a million residents (one per cent of the population) from what was tactfully called the 'New Commonwealth', which meant non-white. So few could have been spread out and 'lost' – after all, the Irish outnumbered them – but they were soon the target of discrimination. As in America, they were confined to overcrowded, rack-rented housing, and the only jobs generally open to them were in hospitals, the Post Office, the railways and the buses for which many of them had been specially recruited in a time of labour shortage. There were still few, if any, shop assistants and no policemen. But, for a time, optimism prevailed. Officially no colour bar existed since colour was not officially recognized. West Indian resentment seemed to be outweighed by gratitude for their luck in getting away from the unemployment at home, however cold the British climate or the British welcome. Samuel Selvon from Trinidad was the first West Indian novelist to take the immigrants as his subject. He saw the scene through the eyes of one of his Damon Runyan-like characters in 1956 in a book called *The Lonely Londoners*:

> This was a time when any corner you turn, is ten to one you bound to
> bounce up a spade. In fact, the boys all over London, it ain't have a
> place where you wouldn't find them, and big discussion going on in
> Parliament, though the old Brit'n too diplomatic to do anything drastic
> like stop them coming to the Mother Country . . . It have a kind of

communal feeling with the working-class and the spades because when you poor, things does level out, it don't have much up and down.

But it was the working class, in the form of Teddy Boys looking for trouble, which provoked Britain's first colour riots in Notting Hill in 1958. For nights afterwards it was unsafe for blacks to walk the streets. The media reacted with sorrowful amazement that racial hostility had been exposed as a fact of British life. The sentences on the trouble-makers were exemplary, and put a stop to race riots for a while.

By then it was clear that peaceful integration was not going to occur naturally in either the African or the American South and Britain's hopes of it were appreciably fainter. In Africa, where Ghana led a large number of former British and French colonies to independence, it became obvious that before long they would be numerous enough as members of the United Nations to rival, if not out-vote, their former European masters. Black Power, both of the diplomatic and the protest variety, belonged to the Sixties. But in the Fifties young American blacks were already beginning to question the efficacy of Martin Luther King's non-violent methods of winning civil rights with Christian patience. James Baldwin, once a boy preacher in Harlem, published his first collection of essays on the black experience, called *Notes Of A Native Son* after the powerful Negro protest novel, *Native Son*, written by Richard Wright in the Thirties. What did it mean to be a Negro to this gifted and highly articulate young novelist in the Fifties? In 1951 he wrote: 'There is, I should think, no Negro living in America who has not felt, briefly or for long periods, simple, naked and unanswerable hatred: who has not wanted to smash any white face he may encounter in a day, to violate their women, to break the bodies of all white people and bring them low, as low as the dust into which he himself has been trampled.' Those who read these portents must have wondered how long it would be before the hatred could not be restrained.

It was significant that the chief focus of the struggle was a black pastor, marked down for martyrdom, who demanded civil rights in the name of Christianity, and a black ex-preacher turned away from Christian loyalties by racial bitterness. Few other Christian voices of influence were raised on the subject of the rights of blacks, though there were courageous bishops who spoke out in South Africa. In America religion had become a form of holy patriotism directed against the Communist anti-Christ rather than at evils in its own midst. 'In God We Trust' was symbolically added to the coinage, which can have been

ABOVE *The most loved Pope for centuries: Pope John XXIII*
OPPOSITE *God's super-salesman, Billy Graham*

little comfort to the blacks who tried to earn enough of it to live. But
church membership in the U.S. reached a record 110 million in 1958, the
year the new Pope, John XXIII, was elected. Few people then expected
this nice old man to be more than a short-lived, peaceable caretaker.
Up till then the best-known and best-publicized Christian leader of his
time was undoubtedly a Baptist evangelist in his thirties, Billy Graham,
who appealed to his audiences of millions to come forward for a personal encounter with Christ: 'I'm going to ask every one of you tonight
to say, "Billy, I will give myself to Christ. I want to be born again".'

He would assure them there would be a minimum of embarrassment or inconvenience – 'I'm not going to ask you to say anything'.
The new disciple would go back to 'your situation' and be 'courteous,
gracious, kind and loving your neighbour'. There was no need to give
up all worldly ambition or possessions as had been suggested two
thousand years earlier. No medieval crusade to smite the infidel was
organized with half as much attention to detail as Billy Graham's
crusade to smite the mass audience of one city after another. He never
moved in without extensive advance preparations and assurance of support and finance. There were committees, posters, bumper stickers
and a small army of counsellors and church workers organized to receive
the respondents and follow up their 'decisions for Christ' with the help

of 'decision' card indexes and the direct mailing of 'I.R. Packs' – 'Instructions in Righteousness'.

Graham himself was a new kind of prophet in a grey silk, rather than flannel, suit. His hawklike good looks and blond hair, waving as he pounded a Bible in his hand, were as much part of the technique as the miniature microphone pinned to him and the atmosphere of mass emotion. 'I am selling the greatest product in the world,' he declared revealingly (he was formerly a Fuller Brush salesman), 'why shouldn't it be promoted as well as soap?' His methods certainly packed them in. In England and Scotland in 1953 two million people came to hear him, partly no doubt to see the show and wonder at all things American, including its highly sophisticated marketing of religious zeal. His New York crusade filled Madison Square Garden in 1957. Estimates of its effectiveness were doubtful – *Time* considered his effect on New York City was 'negligible in concrete terms' despite the numbers coming forward to make 'decisions'. Since church membership was already so high it was not surprising that sixty per cent of them were already churchgoers and therefore not so much converts as 'retreads', as Murray Kempton described it. Of Billy Graham he wrote: 'He has somehow sterilized the old shouting faith and made it polite, tamed and fit for broken people.'

In this respect he was very like the other inspirational religious figure of the Fifties, the Reverend Norman Vincent Peale, whose book, *The Power Of Positive Thinking* (1952), appeared in the bestseller lists year after year. It went unerringly to work on the reader's inferiority complex. 'Always picture success no matter how badly things seem to be

going at the moment.' Positive thinking turned out to mean unbounded belief in yourself with a bit of backing from the Almighty. This Dale Carnegie of the spiritual life promised: 'You will become a more popular, esteemed, well-liked individual.' Well-liked! 'Was he well-liked?' It was the cry of Willy Loman in *Death Of A Salesman*. The anecdotes in the book usually seemed to concern businessmen worried about their ability to pull off a deal until Norman Vincent Peale had referred them to such helpful texts as 'If ye have faith . . . nothing shall be impossible to you' – Matthew 17:20. The author frankly ascribed the two million copies sold in hardback alone to his faith in God as a partner in all his activities. 'When the manuscript was ready for the publisher, Mrs Peale and I prayed . . . When the first of these two million copies came from the press it was again a spiritual moment.'

There was a stronger force than religion working for psychological unity in the human race – science, especially the technical advances that were revolutionizing human mobility and communications. Sputnik Shock began in 1957. The first Sputnik, launched on 4 October, was a metal sphere only 23 inches in diameter which orbited the earth in the time it took to watch a feature film, ninety-three minutes. A month later, Sputnik II carried the Eskimo dog, Laika, who was the first creature to live and die orbiting the earth. Later dogs were recovered from space in good condition – perhaps aided by the Canine Defence League's protest on Laika's behalf to the Soviet Embassy. By 1959 three Russian Luniks had circled the sun, landed on the moon and photographed the moon's farther side, never before seen by human eyes. Stung by their comparative failure to launch satellites, the American National Aeronautical and Space Agency launched the space race, the costliest race to a dead end in history. Two teams of astronauts were training hectically in the U.S. and the U.S.S.R. to be the first in space and then on the moon. Space took over the glamour of exploring at the very time when the earth's own challenges had been more or less exhausted. After Everest had been conquered by Hillary and Tenzing in 1953, the Antarctic was scrutinized by teams of scientists from seven countries. The South Pole was reached overland by Hillary in 1958, only after the U.S. expedition had flown straight there and turned it into a comparatively hospitable stopover.

The immediate side effect of the fascination with space was the sudden

OPPOSITE *Everest conquered – the Union Jack shredded by the wind Hillary's photograph of Tenzing at the moment of triumph, 1953* boom in the UFO-spotting industry, which took off on a big scale in the ten years preceding the take-off of the Sputniks themselves. Many of the books which flooded the market such as *Flying Saucers Have Landed* or *Inside Flying Saucers* gained a superficial credibility from the semi-official reports on unidentified objects observed on airport radar screens or by pilots. The U.S. Air Force investigated them under the name of Project Blue Book. Captain Edward Ruppelt in his *Report On Un-identified Flying Objects* concluded that whatever it was people had seen performing incredible manœuvres at amazing speeds, including the ability to appear and disappear like ghosts, must be paraphysical, not natural phenomena. Very few saucer sightings tallied with others – though they had a funny habit of occurring in batches, especially on Wednesdays, which was puzzling. CIA officials and scientists were called in and rejected any suggestion of visitors from other planets, plumping for misinterpreted natural phenomena like weather balloons. The Air Force was told to stop discussing them, which only added to suspicion that there was some secret to hide. In Britain too, the R.A.F. refused to reveal the findings of its investigations. This was an encouragement to the barmier controversy about whether saucer crews had been sighted, an idea of strong appeal to wishful thinkers of all kinds. Many people, of no great reliability, claimed to have seen the Ufonauts, who sometimes glided as if on wheels rather than legs and communicated by direct telepathy. Lord Dowding, who had directed the fighters of the Battle of Britain, lectured on his belief that UFO occupants were immortals who could make themselves invisible on earth and walk among us unnoticed – a belief that took no risks of disproof. Common to all enthusiasts of saucer theories was the desire to believe that here was evidence of a superior intelligence at work in the universe, a role that used to be filled quite capably by God. Carl Gustav Jung wrote a short book explaining that Flying Saucers were a projection of man's unconscious mind, ex-pressing its yearning for a wholeness the universe now seemed to lack.

Science fiction, like saucer fantasy, poured forth in prodigious quan-tities in the Fifties. The cruder bug-eyed monsters of the early pulp magazines had now been displaced by writers of literary distinction, such as Ray Bradbury (*Fahrenheit 451*) and the early Kurt Vonnegut (*Player Piano*) and in Britain John Wyndham (*The Kraken Wakes* and *The Day Of The Triffids*) and the prolific Arthur C. Clarke.

Kurt Vonnegut's first novel, *Player Piano* (1952), pictured a world in which everything could be done with computers and automation and people were superfluous. It was an anti-Utopia in which human beings found themselves forced into the Reconstruction and Reclamation Corps, known bitterly as the 'Reeks and Wrecks', while the technocrats themselves were victims of computerised bureaucracy. Appearing at a time when so much hope was pinned on the automatised future it caused a sensation. Vonnegut denies his work is science fiction:

> I am not qualified to write that but economists were interested in my book. They said that people would not be put out of work by automation. They would move into service industries. Now we have had a good depression in the U.S. and only about two-thirds of the work-force in Detroit was hired back again at the end of it, I tend to think I will slowly be proved right – that unemployment will remain high or grow steadily. Not that that is necessarily a bad thing for the people concerned: the object of life is not to work your ass off in an automobile factory.

It was as if the advance of real science had produced a compensating urge for the magical and irrational. Applied science and technology leaped forward in the Fifties, promising cheap and plentiful energy from atomic power stations such as Calder Hall (opened in 1956) and the Dounreay fast breeder reactor (operational in 1958). Nuclear-powered ships made their bow in 1958: the Russian ice-breaker *Lenin* was launched and the American submarine *Nautilus* passed under the North Pole ice-cap, while 1959 saw the launching of the first nuclear-powered merchant ship *Savannah*. In practice there was no rush to sail the seas under atomic power, apart from the submarines, and nuclear power stations proved not only immensely costly but full of the hazards of radiation leaks and nuclear waste disposal.

Of far more immediate impact was the coming of jet passenger travel, pioneered by the De Havilland Comet which began the first scheduled jet service between London and Johannesburg in 1952. Its success was phenomenal and orders for the plane were pouring in when in 1954, after a series of explosions in the air, later traced to metal fatigue, the aircraft was grounded and withdrawn. The British aircraft industry saw its five-year lead whittled away by the French Caravelle, based on the Comet design, and the Russian TU 104. But redesigned Comets made their come-back in 1958 to inaugurate the first Transatlantic jet airline service – just beating the Boeing 707s of Pan American. This was the first year in which more people crossed the Atlantic by plane than by ship. Within a very short time the jet had taken over from the luxury liner as the smartest way to travel. The airlines competed in pampering their passengers with free drinks and *eau de cologne*, with free make-up and scent in the toilets, with sweets, face fresheners and magazines. Even the food was good – Pan Am boasted that Maxims of Paris catered for their customers. Hostesses were paragons of beauty, efficiency and pluck, the geishas of the air, and every good-looking teenage girl dreamed of being one. What if the noise of jet engines drove people frantic round the perimeter of international airports? Their peace was expendable in the cause of high mobility, not yet downgraded by charter flying to the level of bus travel.

The luxury ocean liners, which were silent except for their mournful, haunting sirens, finally lost the battle for survival except as freaks or cruise hotels, because of the time factor. The last Blue Riband of the Atlantic was won in 1952. The *United States* broke all records by crossing in under four days – but what was four days compared to the Comet's ten and a half hours? The *France* announced that instead of attempting speed records it would rely on the services of its chef. But no temptation to lotus eating could prevent the sad procession of these graceful swans to the breakers' yards. Thither also travelled on their last journey the less graceful London trams in 1952, while the last steam locomotive was built in 1958 for the fast-declining network of British Railways. It was no accident that that was also the year when the first parking meter was unveiled. The flight from public to private transport was just beginning to defeat its object by choking the cities which the motorways were beginning to connect – the first stretch of the M1, from London to Birmingham, was opened in 1959. The most original innovation in transport, Sir Christopher Cockerell's air-cushioned Hovercraft, made its first Channel crossing in the same year – destined, of course, to carry cars.

The speeding of transport was accompanied by the shrinking of the world by new communications. Television, promising to reduce the world to an electronic village, went into colour experimentally in 1953; the Eurovision network was established in 1954. Transatlantic telephone service began in 1956. Stereophonic recording was pioneered in 1958, adding to the booming sales of Long Playing records which began to be produced in quantity only in 1950, the year also when the tape recorder began to be developed. Never before had so many had the chance to know so much about each other so quickly.

The Fifties were a peak period of scientific advance and yet, in the field of pure knowledge, almost every advance made the universe and man himself seem more mysterious than before. Cosmology was turned upside down by British radio-astronomy. The radio telescope at Jodrell

Bank, whose steerable 250-foot dish was the only means of anybody tracking the Sputniks, was finished partly on faith and by school-children collecting money until Lord Nuffield stepped in to save the situation. At Cambridge, Martin Ryle operated a different type of radio telescope with moveable ground aerials. Both could pick up signals from almost inconceivably distant sources in the universe and it seemed as though astronomy was on the verge of settling the question of its origin. The signals that were picked up had taken perhaps 10^9 (ten thousand million) years to arrive and were perhaps almost as old as creation itself. Some very remote galaxies, rushing away from ours with greater and greater speed, were nevertheless emitting puzzlingly strong radio signals: later they were to be named Quasars, quasi-stellar objects – a new mystery of the universe. The debate on the origin of the universe, by evolution from a 'big bang' or by continuous creation in a 'steady state' remained as inconclusive as ever at the time. The steady state theory was to lose credibility later as radio astronomy proved the universe to be more thickly populated in its outer reaches.

While knowledge expanded at such a breakneck rate, it was still assumed that man was progressing inevitably and triumphantly towards omniscience. And yet, and yet . . . With every advance the horizon retreated step by step. The benevolence of progress also became increasingly doubtful. It must have seemed much more self-evident to the late Victorians, or even the late Georgians of 1945–50, than it did by the late Fifties. Progress did not look so benevolent when the first studies of atmospheric pollution in the wake of the first H-bomb tests were published in 1952. Progress did not look so inevitable after the first serious studies of world population in relation to world resources were made by PEP in 1955. Every technical ladder climbed seemed to involve a corresponding slither down a snake, whether it was the danger of accidental nuclear war or nuclear leakage of radioactive material, pollution of the cities by indiscriminate internal combustion or pollution of the countryside by insecticides and indestructible plastic. The price of mass mobility was pollution of the world's beauty spots by too many sightseers. The final Fifties forecasts were already reading: Famine – through overpopulation – or the Pill. But the Pill, even if widely disseminated, promised to reduce the fertility of the most advanced, responsible and resourceful populations who would be outnumbered by the others – the principle of the survival of the least fit.

Thus, anxiously, helplessly but still hopefully, the world staggered out of the decade in which its maturity can be said to have truly begun.

Chronology

1950

Alger Hiss jailed for perjury in concealing Communist Party membership (January)

Senator McCarthy alleges the State Department employs over 200 Communists (February)

Klaus Fuchs sentenced at Old Bailey for betraying atomic secrets to the U.S.S.R. (March)

U.S.S.R. announces its possession of an atomic bomb (March)

Petrol rationing ends in Britain (May)

North Korean forces invade South Korea and capture Seoul (June)

UN Forces land in South Korea (September), cross 38th parallel and capture Pyongyang (October)

Chinese forces cross the 38th parallel

ARCHITECTURE	United Nations Building (Wallace Harrison)
LITERATURE	Anthony Powell: *A Dance to the Music of Time* begins
	Thor Heyerdahl: *The Kon-Tiki Expedition*
	Arthur Koestler: *The God that Failed*
	Death of George Orwell, Bernard Shaw
THEATRE	T. S. Eliot: *The Cocktail Party*
	Irving Berlin: *Call Me Madam*
	Carlo Menotti: *The Consul*
	Jean Anouilh: *The Rehearsal* (Paris)
FILM	*Sunset Boulevard* (director, Billy Wilder)
SPORT	Uruguay win the World Cup

1951

General MacArthur dismissed as Far East commander (April)

Festival of Britain (May)

Premier Mossadeq nationalises Iranian oil industry (May)

Burgess and Maclean defect to U.S.S.R. (June)

State of war with Germany officially ended (July)

Korean armistice talks broken off (August)

Conservatives return to power under Churchill (October)

Korean armistice talks renewed (October)

ARCHITECTURE   Royal Festival Hall (R. Matthew and J. L. Martin)
Basil Spence wins competition to design Coventry Cathedral

LITERATURE   J. D. Salinger: *The Catcher in the Rye*
J. B. Priestley: *Festival at Farbridge*
C. P. Snow: *The Masters*
N. Monsarrat: *The Cruel Sea*

MUSIC   Benjamin Britten: *Billy Budd*
Igor Stravinsky: *The Rake's Progress*

THEATRE   Rodgers and Hammerstein: *South Pacific*

FILM   *A Streetcar Named Desire* (director, E. Kazan)
The African Queen (director, John Huston)

RADIO   *The Archers* serial begins

1952

Death of George VI (February)
Identity Cards abolished in Britain (March)
European Defence Community (May) and Coal and Steel Community (July) inaugurated
Army coup in Egypt exiles King Farouk (July)
Death of Eva Peron (July)
British atom bomb test, Monte Bello islands (October)
State of emergency in Kenya due to Mau Mau (October)
Gen. Eisenhower elected U.S. President (November)
U.S. thermo-nuclear explosion, Eniwetok Atoll

ARCHITECTURE   Unité d'Habitation, Marseilles (Le Corbusier), completed

LITERATURE   Ernest Hemingway: *The Old Man And The Sea*
Evelyn Waugh: *Men At Arms*
Angus Wilson: *Hemlock and After*

THEATRE   Agatha Christie: *The Mousetrap*
Terence Rattigan: *The Deep Blue Sea*

FILM   *Limelight* (C. Chaplin)
Cinerama

MUSIC   Pierre Boulez: *Structures*
Vaughan Williams: *Symphonia Antarctica*

SCIENCE   Contraceptive Pill first manufactured

TECHNOLOGY   De Havilland 110 jet fighter breaks sound barrier

1953

Death of Stalin (March) Malenkov succeeds him
Dag Hammarskjold elected U.N. Secretary-General (March)
Conquest of Everest by Hillary and Tenzing (June)
Coronation of Queen Elizabeth II (June)
Korean armistice signed (June)
Dr Mossadeq arrested in royalist *coup d'etat*, Iran (August)
Russian H-Bomb exploded in Siberia (August)
Nikita Khrushchev becomes First Secretary of Communist Party,
    U.S.S.R. (September)
Lavrenti Beria, Stalin's secret police chief, executed (December)

ART	Henry Moore: King and Queen
	Reg Butler: Unknown Political Prisoner
LITERATURE	William Faulkner: *Requiem for a Nun*
	Ian Fleming: *Casino Royale* (James Bond's debut)
THEATRE	Arthur Miller: *The Crucible*
	Tennessee Williams: *Camino Real*
FILM	*From Here To Eternity* (F. Zinnemann)
	Cinemascope – *The Robe* (H. Koster)
MUSIC	D. Shostakovich: Tenth Symphony
	Benjamin Britten: *Spring Symphony*
SCIENCE	Crick and Watson discover structure of DNA molecule
SPORT	England win the Ashes

1954

U.S. H-Bomb tested at Bikini Atoll (March)
Dien Bien Phu falls to Viet Minh (May): French surrender
Billy Graham's crusades in London and New York (May–July)
J. Robert Oppenheimer found a 'security risk' (June)
Geneva conference splits Vietnam into North and South (July)
Food rationing ends in Britain (July)
Algerian nationalists revolt against France (November)
U.S. Senate 'condemns' Senator McCarthy (December)

ART	Graham Sutherland: portrait of Churchill
	Death of Matisse

LITERATURE	Kingsley Amis: *Lucky Jim*
	John Betjeman: *A Few Late Chrysanthemums*
	William Golding: *Lord of the Flies*
	Francoise Sagan: *Bonjour Tristesse*
	J. R. R. Tolkien: *Lord of the Rings*
RADIO	Dylan Thomas: *Under Milk Wood*
THEATRE	Julian Slade: *Salad Days*
	Tennessee Williams: *Cat on a Hot Tin Roof*
	Sandy Wilson: *The Boy Friend*
FILM	*On the Waterfront* (E. Kazan)
	Rear Window (A. Hitchcock)
	The Caine Mutiny (H. Dmytryk)
SPORT	Roger Bannister runs first four-minute mile

1955

Bulganin and Khrushchev succeed Malenkov in U.S.S.R. (February)
Eden succeeds Churchill as Prime Minister (April)
Gaitskell succeeds Attlee as leader of Labour Party (December)
Execution of Ruth Ellis (July) hastens campaign to end capital punishment in Britain.
Lynching of 14-year-old boy in Mississippi (July)
Geneva Summit Conference on re-unification of Germany (July)
European Parliament holds first meeting at Strasbourg (July)
Juan Peron resigns as President of Argentina (September)
Commercial television introduced in Britain (September)
Montgomery, Alabama, bus boycott begins (December)

ART	Pietro Annigoni: Portrait of the Queen
	John Bratby: Still life with chip fryer
LITERATURE	Graham Greene: *The Quiet American*
	Vladimir Nabokov: *Lolita*
	The Diary Of Anne Frank
	Death of Thomas Mann
THEATRE	Samuel Beckett: *Waiting For Godot*
	Arthur Miller: *A View From The Bridge*
FILM	*Rebel Without A Cause* (N. Ray)
	Rock around the Clock (Bill Haley)
	Richard III (L. Olivier)

SCIENCE   Dr Jonas Salk makes an anti-polio vaccine
                     Death of Albert Einstein after signing Pugwash
                        Manifesto to renounce war
TECHNOLOGY   Wave of Flying Saucer sightings reported

1956

Dulles' 'Brink of war' speech (January)

Khrushchev denounces Stalin at 20th Congress of Communist Party
(February)

Bulganin and Khrushchev visit Britain (April)

Prince Rainier of Monaco marries Grace Kelly (May)

British troops leave Suez Canal bases (June)

President Nasser nationalises Suez Canal (July)

Insurrection in Hungary. Imre Nagy becomes minister-president
(October)

Israeli troops invade Sinai. Anglo-French ultimatum calls for cease fire
and withdrawal from Canal (October)

Russian tanks crush Budapest rising (November)

Anglo-French forces invade Egypt (November)

President Eisenhower re-elected (November)

Anglo-French forces evacuate Suez Canal (December)

ARCHITECTURE   London County Council Roehampton Estates
LITERATURE   W. S. Churchill: *History of the English-Speaking
                   Peoples*
                Colin Wilson: *The Outsider*
                W. H. Whyte: *The Organisation Man*
                Death of Walter de la Mare
THEATRE   John Osborne: *Look Back In Anger*
                Brendan Behan: *The Quare Fellow*
                Lerner and Loewe: *My Fair Lady* (New York)
FILM   *Baby Doll* (E. Kazan/Tennessee Williams)
                The King And I (W. Lang)
                Around The World In Eighty Days (M. Todd)
TECHNOLOGY   Calder Hall, first nuclear power station, opened
                Trans-Atlantic telephone service begins
                Air speed record of 1132 m.p.h. established by
                   Fairey Delta fighter
SCIENCE   Neutrino particle discovered

1957

Anthony Eden resigns as Prime Minister (January). Harold Macmillan
  succeeds him
Ghana becomes independent (March)
Treaty of Rome signed, setting up Common Market (March)
British H-Bomb tested at Christmas Island (May)
Malay Federation becomes independent (August)
Wolfenden Report on homosexual offences (September)
Integration riots at Little Rock, Arkansas (September)
Queen Elizabeth visits U.S.A. and addresses United Nations (October)
Russians launch Sputniks I (October) and II (November) and first
  Inter-Continental Ballistic Missile
U.S. attempt to launch earth satellite fails (December)

ART	Jacob Epstein: Christ In Majesty (Llandaff Cathedral)
ARCHITECTURE	Brasilia begun (Lucio Costa)
LITERATURE	John Braine: *Room at the Top*
	Jack Kerouac: *On the Road*
	Iris Murdoch: *The Sandcastle*
	Doris Lessing: *The Habit of Loving*
	C. Northcote Parkinson: *Parkinson's Law*
	J. B. Priestley: *Thoughts in the Wilderness*
MUSIC	William Walton: Cello Concerto
	Igor Stravinsky: Agon
	Deaths of Sibelius, Gigli, Toscanini
THEATRE	John Osborne: *The Entertainer*
	Robert Bolt: *Flowering Cherry*
SCIENCE	Radio telescopes at Jodrell Bank and Cambridge completed
TECHNOLOGY	Appeals to ban nuclear tests by the Pope, Dr Schweitzer, Nehru and the British Labour Party

1958

The Common Market comes into force (January)
Campaign for Nuclear Disarmament launched (February), holds first
  Aldermaston March (April)
Khrushchev becomes chairman of Council of Ministers (March)

After Algerian insurrection, De Gaulle becomes Prime Minister of
France (June)

Imre Nagy executed in Hungary (June)

U.S. forces land in Lebanon, British in Jordan (July)

Communist Chinese begin bombarding offshore islands of Quemoy and
Matsu (August)

Notting Hill race riots in London (August)

Pope John XXIII elected (November)

ART	Henry Moore: Reclining figure for UNESCO Building
ARCHITECTURE	Seagram Building (Mies Van Der Rohe and P. Johnson)
	Pirelli Tower, Milan (Nervi and Ponti)
LITERATURE	Boris Pasternak: *Dr Zhivago*
	J. K. Galbraith: *The Affluent Society*
	Graham Greene: *Our Man in Havana*
THEATRE	Leonard Bernstein: *West Side Story*
	Harold Pinter: *The Birthday Party*
MUSIC	D. Shostakovich: Symphony No 11
	Death of Vaughan Williams after completing his Ninth Symphony
FILM	*Mon Oncle* (Jacques Tati)
SCIENCE	Discovery of Van Allen radiation belt by first U.S. Explorer satellites
TECHNOLOGY	U.S. submarine *Nautilus* passes beneath North Pole
	British expedition reaches South Pole overland under Fuchs and Hillary
	Stereo recording begins
SPORT	Manchester United lose seven players in Munich air crash
	Brazil wins World Cup

1959

Fidel Castro takes power in Cuba (January)
De Gaulle proclaimed President of Fifth Republic (January)
Alaska becomes 49th State of Union (January)
Prime Minister Macmillan visits Moscow (February)
Mao Tse-Tung succeeded as Chairman by Liu Shoa-Chi (April)
Death of John Foster Dulles (May)
Singapore becomes independent (June)
China invades N.E. frontier of India (August)
Hawaii becomes 50th State of Union (August)
Conservatives increase majority in House of Commons (October)
Archbishop Makarios becomes President of independent Cyprus
  (December)

ART	World record of £275,000 paid for Rubens' 'Adoration of The Magi' at Sotheby's
	Deaths of Epstein and Stanley Spencer
ARCHITECTURE	Guggenheim Museum (Frank Lloyd Wright)
LITERATURE	Saul Bellow: *Henderson the Rain King*
	Norman Mailer: *Advertisements for Myself*
THEATRE	Jean Anouilh: *Becket*
	Eugene Ionesco: *Rhinoceros*
	Arnold Wesker: *Roots*
FILM	*Gigi* (V. Minelli)
	Room At The Top (J. Clayton)
TECHNOLOGY	Russia launches Luniks, which photograph far side of the Moon, and the ice-breaker *Lenin* (nuclear-powered)
	New air-speed record, 1520 m.p.h. by U.S.A.F. pilot
	Hovercraft makes maiden cross-channel voyage
	First section of M1 Motorway opened in Britain

Index